Real Footballers' Wives

Real Footballers' Wives

The First Ladies of Everton

BECKY TALLENTIRE

MAINSTREAM
PUBLISHING
EDINBURGH AND LONDON

First published in Great Britain in 2004 by
MAINSTREAM PUBLISHING COMPANY
(EDINBURGH) LTD
7 Albany Street
Edinburgh EH1 3UG

ISBN 1 84018 879 0

Front cover photograph (from left): Lesley Ball, Gwen Wright, Celia Morrissey,
Ann West, Rosemary Hurst, Sue Barnett, Pat Labone, Jeanette Brown,
Nancy Young and Pat Wilson en route to Wembley for the
FA Cup final versus West Bromwich Albion, 18 May 1968

A catalogue record for this book is available
from the British Library

Typeset in Garamond and Opti-Design Medium
Printed and bound in Great Britain by
Creative Print and Design Wales

This book is dedicated to my mum, Maureen Booth,
the finest woman I know.
How lucky I am.

In memory of Lesley Ball,
much missed by all who knew her.

Acknowledgements

Special thanks to:

Mark Tallentire, my brother, proofreader, stats man, cheerleader and harshest critic. I knew I was on to something when I saw you smile.

Mikola Williams, my online PA, for cheering me on from the Cologne HQ. Coincidence? Not really.

George Booth, my little brother, for endlessly chauffeuring me to interviews, and flat-sitting and feeding the cats in my absence.

Phill Doran, for your unwavering support and guidance. You're a truly gifted man and it's my pleasure to know you.

Mum, George, Claire and Stephen for running around after me – as ever.

Nancy Young, my inspiration.

Dominic McGough, for worrying about me.

My charming nieces, Georgia Robyn and Arabella Star, for helping me choose the photographs and keeping me constantly entertained. The world is a better place with you in it.

The families of the wives, who rallied round and supplied me with dates and minutiae that otherwise would have been lost forever – in particular, Margaret Trivett, daughter of my grande dame, Dolly Sagar. What an absolute pleasure it was.

As for me, well, I still can't believe my luck.

Contents

Introduction

Whenever I'm invited to attend an Everton Football Club function, I often end up sitting next to Nancy Young. It's a stroke of good fortune for us both; for me, because she's such great company and always makes me laugh, and for her, because she doesn't stand a chance of speaking to her husband for the entire evening, as he's swamped by Evertonians wanting to bask in his golden aura of greatness.

Despite the many hours by her side, chuckling into our serviettes, it was only during a routine phone call that I happened to ask how she'd met Alex all those years ago, and her answer took my breath away. That night I couldn't sleep.

I pondered why every little thing about Alex Young and his playing career was so carefully documented, yet nothing at all was known about his wife and children. I rang Nancy back the following morning with a list of questions and promised I would write it all down for her grandchildren, before her memory faded and her side of the story was lost forever.

I was enchanted by her replies but mystified as to why I didn't already know her story. It dawned on me that it had never been recorded because nobody had bothered to ask. Quite how the historians were foolish enough to overlook the real eyewitnesses, I'll never know, but I'm glad they did because their loss was, undoubtedly, my gain and my absolute pleasure.

The modest, unassuming women featured in this book dedicated their lives to their husbands' careers, continually shelving their own ambitions, security, support networks and families to sustain their partners' dream and to follow them wherever the rallying cry sounded. And don't for a minute be fooled by their dainty appearance; these girls were made of stern stuff. While the men headed off to Goodison Park in search of glory, they repaired the trail of chaos left in their wake – more often than not with a clapped-out car in the driveway and a baby under each arm.

In the time I've spent researching this book, I've learned an awful lot about the human spirit: how obstacles can be overcome, pain endured and broken hearts mended. These women are living proof that love conquers all and I truly believe it's because of their fortitude and determination that the foundations of our football club stand so firmly.

They've taught me a great deal about life and I'm immensely proud to have been entrusted with their stories. Each one is so poignant and unique yet they're all cut from the same cloth.

Ladies, your spirit and your strength of character are something to behold. I know your families are fiercely proud of you and they have every reason to be; you're the unsung heroes of Everton Football Club, decades ahead of your time, and to you my cap is forever doffed.

I Felt Like I Belonged There

Nancy Young

Alex Young, 'The Golden Vision', was signed from Hearts for £40,000 in November 1960 and was considered to be overpriced by the Scottish media. However, he quickly proved his worth and did so time and time again. He debuted the following month against Spurs and went on to play 268 games, scoring 87 goals. He wore the number 9 shirt and peaked in the 1962–63 season when he scored 22 of those goals and laid on many more, despite suffering from appalling blisters which were to trouble him throughout his career. Young left to become player–manager of Glentoran in Northern Ireland in August 1968 but soon returned to end his career at Stockport, where a long-standing knee problem became too much for him. Capped eight times for Scotland, Young now lives in Penicuik and runs a soft-furnishings business in nearby Edinburgh.

Born Nancy Smith, 12 April 1939,
Newtongrange, Midlothian, Scotland

When the pit horn went at 3.50 p.m., you could hear it all over the village and the women would get the dinner on the table knowing their men would be home in ten minutes. Back then, they didn't have showers at the pithead, so the miners would come home dirty and wash in a tin bath in front of the fire. They reminded me of black beetles swarming up the streets.

My dad was a mechanic at the Lady Victoria colliery and used to maintain the vehicles that delivered the coal. He occasionally worked underground but spent most of his life under a lorry covered in oil. He wore a beret and overalls all the time and when he was issued with a new set of working clothes, he used to make us laugh by parading up and down the living room like a catwalk model. I was the second of six children – five girls and one boy called George. Mum stayed at home and looked after us but before that she was in service and worked as a kitchen maid in a big posh house.

The pit closed in 1981, but the houses still stand proud on 1st, 2nd, 3rd, right up to 10th Street. We lived on 9th Street and Newtongrange primary school was right over the road. At playtime, I used to run home to have a wee go on the piano, although I could only play 'Chopsticks'. In fact, nobody in our family could play anything and I don't know why we had the piano. I used to love it and dreamed of having lessons, but there was never any spare money for such luxuries. Life was like that for pretty much everyone in Newtongrange.

Although I passed my exams to go to grammar school, my dad thought it would be pointless. He said I wouldn't stay in and study because I would want to go out to play all the time. Newbattle Junior secondary school was all right, but instead of learning languages or science, you got domestic science, dressmaking and lessons on how to iron. I didn't really excel in anything but I was quite good at sports because I was double-jointed.

You had your pick of jobs then, so I left school at 15 and went and worked in a grocer's shop for a few months and then Isa, my older sister, got me a job in her office at an insurance company. I didn't like writing in the ledgers or anything like that but the machines they used for invoices back then fascinated me. They were called punch keys and they punched data into a card that the tabulators would read. I used to sneak away to look at them at lunchtime when everybody was out, then one day one of the bosses asked what I was doing. I told him I liked the machines, so they moved me to the Hollerith department and that was where I stayed for the next four years.

There wasn't much for teenagers to do in Newtongrange, so every Wednesday and Saturday night my best friend Helen and I would go to the Bonnyrigg Regal dance hall. It was 1957, the Bill Haley era, and we would get dressed up in high heels and flared skirts with two or three petticoats underneath, but we'd take our flat shoes with us so we could jive the night away. One night, I managed to break her wrist with my enthusiastic jiving, and she still reminds me of it to this day.

Alex was from a nearby village called Loanhead. He worked down the mines as an engineer during the week and played for Hearts at the weekends. This particular night he turned up with a couple of other players – Dave Mackay and Tom McKenzie. They were all dressed the same, in maroon blazers and grey flannels, because they'd been at a club do and thought they would drop in at the local hop for an hour on the way home. Alex had been to Bonnyrigg before but it was the first time I'd noticed him. He caught my eye because he had lovely blond hair and was so good-looking. He was feeling especially brave that night because he'd had two halves of lager, and plucked up the courage to ask me to dance. When it was over, we made a date for the next week and I couldn't wait for it to come.

Trades Week was when all the local factories and mines closed down for annual holidays: the Edinburgh side used to have the first fortnight in July and the Glasgow side the second, and during that time, entire villages would be deserted. You'd see people at the beginning of Trades with their big suitcases bursting open on their way to Blackpool and Scarborough and, in the summer of 1957, Helen and I had booked to go to Butlins in Ayr. It was the first time we'd been away without our parents and we couldn't believe we'd been allowed to go. One evening, we were in the Butlins dance hall when Helen nudged me and looked over towards the door and there was Alex – he'd followed us up there in his car. 'Mr Wonderful' by Peggy Lee was top of the hit parade and it all seemed very appropriate.

Alex and I were together for about a year before we got engaged, then in 1959 he went off to join the army. For 12 months of his national service, he was based in Aldershot but he was still playing for Hearts, so he got to come home every weekend. They would fly him and Ron Yeats to Turnhouse airport near Edinburgh and I would drive his mother there in Alex's little black Volkswagen Beetle every Thursday night to collect them. This was before cassettes existed and he was the second person in Edinburgh to have a record player in his car, so off we'd go with Frank Sinatra crooning at full blast.

Big Ron was so huge; he would be hitting the roof with his head while his knees were tucked under his chin all the way to Mrs Young's house, where he would stay the night. There was no sleeping together in those days, so I would go home and on the Friday morning Alex would drop Ron off to go to Dundee United and he'd go to Hearts for training.

When we were courting, we'd sometimes go to the pictures. We never used to eat sweets; we would take cherries and different kinds of fruit and halfway through we would change seats because there would be a mound of pips and we didn't want anyone to know we'd left a mess. We never saw the beginning or the end of a film because we'd have to wait until the lights were down before we went in and leave before the end so nobody would pester him. In Liverpool, the fans were lovely – they were interested and genuinely liked him, and loved the game – but the Scottish supporters were different.

Mr and Mrs Young were so sweet. She was really fond of me and was just like my mother; she was so timid that if you spoke to her she would blush. She was of the generation that was brought up to respect people in authority and would practically doff her cap to policemen and doctors. Alex was the baby of the family, with two sisters and two brothers, but he's the only one left now.

I didn't know much about football, but by coincidence my older sister was already married to a bloke called Jackie Neilson. He played for St Mirren and sometimes Jackie and Alex played against each other. My dad wasn't football-minded at all and didn't follow anybody, but he did go to one or two games once I started courting.

I remember my mum being ill for a long time but it never crossed my mind that she would die. Nobody ever mentioned the word 'cancer' and it was an awful shock when we lost her because we spent all our time reassuring each other that she'd get better. I was twenty and gave up work to take care of the house and my two younger sisters, Marian and Kate, who, at the time, were eight and four. I think it was a tremendous relief to my dad because he had no idea what he would do with them. I didn't feel as if I was making any sacrifices; I didn't really have any aspirations or ambitions, so it suited me to look after the family and I willingly volunteered my help. I looked after them for a year or two, until I married, then my other sister, Ellen, took over.

Eventually, Dad remarried. His new wife, Katie, had been in his class at school and was also widowed. She was wonderful and we all called her mum and loved her dearly – she brought the girls up with her own daughter, Carine, and we became one big happy family again.

When I heard Everton wanted to sign Alex, I was thrilled to bits because I had an uncle and aunt who lived in Wakefield, and I would stay with them during the summer holidays when I was a kid. I always said I would live in England when I grew up and got married. I loved it and really liked English people, so although I didn't know anything about Liverpool, it was all terribly exciting for me. Alex signed in November 1960 and moved into digs in Maghull with Mickey Lill and Jimmy Gabriel. He was still doing his national service but he was injured at the time so was getting treatment from Everton. He made his debut just before Christmas while I stayed in Newtongrange with my dad and sisters but I missed him terribly.

We waited until the summer of 1961 to marry because we couldn't have had a honeymoon otherwise. Alex was demobbed on the Friday night and we married the next day, in Newtongrange church. It wasn't a huge white wedding – it was supposed to be a wee, small occasion – but the local press got wind of it and they turned up, so we'd have been as well having a big wedding after all. I didn't mind the press being there but I was terribly shy in those days and blushed all the time. For our honeymoon, we flew from Edinburgh to London then caught a train to Bournemouth and stayed there for two weeks. It was the first time I'd flown and it was a great big adventure.

After the honeymoon, I moved straight down to England. Everton had found a house for us in Bullbridge Lane, Aintree, and we bought it for £3,000. It was a brand-new, three-bedroom semi and really big compared with what I was used to, but we had to stay in the Lord Nelson Hotel for six weeks because it wasn't quite ready to move into.

While Alex was in the army he was only allowed to earn £8 a week. It went up to £20 when his national service was over, but there was a ceiling on wages until 1962. As soon as it was lifted, he and Roy Vernon got a pay rise to £35. My dad was only earning £14 a week then and my father-in-law was a miner on about £8, so it was big money.

Roy's wife, Norma, became my best friend. She was absolutely beautiful, like a little blonde doll. We were together every day for the six weeks Alex and I stayed in the hotel and we became very close. Neither of us had a car to go anywhere so while Alex and Roy were training, I would be at her house helping her control her two boisterous boys, which was harder than any training session. I don't think any of the wives worked and we were often on our own while the men went off training, or for days in hotels to build team spirit. At times, it was quite an isolated life.

If I could get a lift, I'd go to the away games, usually with Pat Gabriel's dad, who would drive us there in his van, but I would go to all the home games without fail. Normally, I would travel with Alex to Goodison and sit in the car reading until it was time to go in because there was nowhere for the wives to wait. The other players had to report an hour before kick-off but he had to be there two hours early so they could try and do something to stop his feet from blistering.

His feet were the bane of his life and would have to be bound up with foam and bandages and plasters before he played to help ease his pain, but by the time he got home his socks would be stuck to his feet with blood. We'd have to soak them off and he would pop the blood blisters with a pin. It was so horrible. They used to allow tackling from behind back then and they would scrape down the back of his heels. He never had any toenails either – especially on his big toe – but I think that was just an occupational hazard because they've grown back now.

It was great to see him run onto the pitch, but I didn't understand the game at all and had no idea what was going on; I just used to watch him even when he wasn't on the ball. Alex didn't have any pre-match rituals and wasn't particularly superstitious, but he always wanted to be the second-last man out of the tunnel, and, when he was at Hearts, his mother would give him a drink of raw egg in sherry before a game because it made him feel great.

Apart from the match, the highlight of the week was going out on a Saturday night in Liverpool with teammates and their wives. We'd all go to the Royal Tiger Club and occasionally the Pink Parrot. The Tiger was our favourite and there was always a crowd milling around outside hoping to be let in. When an Everton player knocked on the door, a little peephole would open and we were whisked straight inside. If I'd been in Scotland, I'd have been going home at 10.30 p.m. instead of just starting the evening. I'd never been to a nightclub before – it was all terribly exciting and made up for the two years I'd spent staying in while Alex was in the army.

I fell pregnant early on in 1962. My mother was gone and I had nobody to turn to who could tell me what to do, so six weeks before I was due, I went to stay with Mr and Mrs Young because it would have been tragic if it had been a boy and he'd not been able to play for Scotland. There was nobody I could ask. I just did what I thought was right and spent the last six weeks of the pregnancy at their house. Mr Young went into the spare room and I shared a bed with Mrs Young in case something happened during the night.

You didn't speak about your emotions then – everybody does now – but then you just got on with it. When you're expecting, your hormones are changing but nobody explains it to you, so I was crying all the time because I missed Alex so much and I didn't understand what was wrong. We shouldn't have been separated like that – we know that now – but back then you just did as you were told. A fortnight before Jane was born, I couldn't bear to be away from him any longer so I went against all advice and travelled down to visit him for a few days. I was like a barrage balloon and I'm surprised I even fitted on to the train, but it made me feel so much better.

Jane was born in November 1962 at Simpsons Memorial hospital in Edinburgh. Everybody raved about what a great place it was but it was so regimented I'm surprised they didn't clap me in irons. You were tucked in at night and you hadn't to move the covers. Nobody was allowed to sit on the bed and you could only have one or two visitors at a time and only one of them was allowed to be male. It took Alex ten hours to get from Liverpool to visit us because 1962 was the year of the big freeze. He was only able to get away because all the games were cancelled as the pitches were frozen solid and I don't think there were any matches played for six weeks. I was in hospital for ten days but it seemed like a lifetime and I couldn't wait to get back home to Aintree.

When they'd finished training, the players had a lot of spare time on their hands. Alex used to love playing golf but his real passion was the races. He and Roy Vernon were always together at Manchester, Aintree or Haydock and when Roy left, Alex hooked up with Alan Ball. They would go to the races whenever they had the chance, and he and Bally even went halves on a racehorse called Daxal, but they didn't make any money out of it. One afternoon, after he told me they had extra training, I was changing Jane's nappy on the living-room floor when I glanced at the television and there he was with Bally, right in the middle of the screen at the Aintree racetrack.

I don't think I ever met anybody official from Everton. The wives weren't encouraged at all and were generally regarded as trouble. We were kept in the background as much as possible and, although we got a free ticket for the home games, it was in the stands like the rest of the crowd. Mr Catterick wasn't very keen on the wives being around – he thought we were a distraction.

After we won the League in 1963, the club took us all to

Torremolinos for a fortnight and it was absolutely wonderful. All we did was lounge around the pool sunbathing and eating nice food. That was all we could do – the hotel had just been built so it was in the middle of an undeveloped building site and there was nothing but rubble outside. Apart from Alex Parker's wife, Jean, breaking a leg when she fell into an empty fountain, and Norma's suitcase going missing for a day and a half, we had a great time. Jane was only about six months old and we left her with Mr and Mrs Young. They would often come down to Liverpool to stay with us and they loved it because they didn't get any holidays at all until we moved to England.

All the wives went down to Wembley by train for the 1966 Cup final against Sheffield Wednesday. We were booked into the Waldorf Hotel and it was really special because we didn't get away very much. There we were, all dressed up to the nines and dying for the lads to win and suddenly we were 2–0 down. It was just terrible; the most gut-wrenching feeling you could imagine and there's nothing you can do about it.

Eddie Cavanagh was a mad Evertonian – all the players knew him well because he spent a lot of time at Bellefield in their company – and when we drew level at 2–2 he couldn't contain himself and ran onto the pitch. When the policeman finally caught him, he wriggled out of his jacket like an eel, weaving and ducking and diving; it was hysterical. Nothing really surpassed that day; I think it was the proudest moment of my life when I saw Alex holding up the FA Cup.

We'd moved house to Aughton by that time and when Roy Vernon was transferred to Stoke City in 1965 Alex lost his dear friend and teammate and I lost Norma. I missed her terribly but, shortly afterwards, Alex was introduced to Mike Pender of The Searchers and he invited us to his house just up the road to meet his wife, May, and his family. May and I hit it off immediately and the four of us are still great friends to this day; our children all grew up together and we still see each other frequently. We still laugh about our first meeting. Mike confessed that he was all excited about 'The Golden Vision' coming to his house, and Alex and I were equally thrilled about being in the company of a pop star and the singer of the hit record 'Needles and Pins'.

During his last couple of years at Everton, Alex played number 7 – wide-right. Harry Catterick didn't pick him for the 1968 Cup final against West Bromwich and Jimmy Husband took his place. We both travelled down but we didn't get to find out the team until we were actually there in the hotel room. He was supposed to be sub but at the last minute he put Sandy Brown in instead and Alex was absolutely devastated.

Catterick didn't like Alex but I don't know what that was all about; he's so placid and there are not many who wouldn't be able to get along with him. The previous manager, Johnny Carey, had signed Alex and before Catterick even arrived at Goodison, he'd passed on a message via the journalist Les Edwards that he didn't like Alex or the way he played.

It seems very strange that he would pass judgment before he'd even met him, but that's the way it was and he really seemed to go out of his way to make Alex's life a misery. Alex used to say the vibes were not right and that was it. It was probably a struggle for Alex most of the time but it was the crowd that kept him there, I think. The fans adored him and he loved them back.

It was about this time that the film-makers approached Alex to see if they could make *The Golden Vision*, a BBC Play for Today. They came to the house and shot the parts where he was talking, and Jane made her TV debut too. It took days and days to shoot a few minutes of film – I had no idea it was so complicated. Jane was only about five at the time but she wasn't fazed by it at all and performed magnificently. We still have a copy of *The Golden Vision* and every few years we dust it down and watch it again.

There was no way I was going to have my next baby up in Scotland and go through all that nonsense again, so I booked myself into Park House, the nursing home run by nuns in Waterloo, when Alex Jnr was due. There were some complications and Alex had to consent to a Caesarean birth. I remember Alex arriving to visit us at about ten o'clock at night but not realising there was a night bell and a day bell. He was ringing and banging on the door for ages trying to get in but he was pressing the wrong bell. A stony-faced nun eventually opened the door but she let him know how strongly she disapproved of the noise he had made.

Alex didn't really sustain any serious injuries that I can remember but he did have a cartilage operation and it was a knee injury that finished his career in the end, but his blistered feet were legendary. You really had to see them to believe them and it was the same every week. If the ground was dry and hard, then he suffered even more. We got hundreds of letters from people with remedies, old wives' tales and tried-and-tested tonics, but nothing worked. Somebody even posted him a pair of boots, but it was hopeless. He almost got used to it.

Some nights he would re-live matches in his sleep. I could feel him starting the game, with the odd twitch now and again, and it would progress to full-blooded kicking of an imaginary ball – but, of course, it was the back of my legs. I remember one night, after a match, he stood up on the bed and was scrabbling around on the wall behind the headboard. The next morning, he said he was dreaming that he'd scored and got tangled up in the net trying to get the ball back.

There was nothing I really hated about being a footballer's wife. There were times when other women were after him but it didn't bother me too much. The only thing that got on my nerves was that we didn't have a lounge where we could wait after the match, like the Liverpool players' wives did. It was awkward because we were all sitting in cars – assuming you had a car, of course; those that didn't would be standing in the rain. It was nothing to do with the fans, it was to do with the club and they just didn't cater for us. The players were their livelihood but we were their wives and it showed such disrespect to us. We weren't treated very well at all. I don't think it would happen now.

One day, in the summer of 1968, Alex came home and told me Harry Catterick had sold him to Glentoran in Northern Ireland. I don't remember having much of a reaction because we all knew that was part of the deal. I didn't question things really; I just went along with it. He went over there to have a look then we packed up and all went with him. We didn't sell our house, we didn't even rent it out, we let a friend of a friend move in and look after it so it wasn't standing empty.

We left Glentoran after about two months because the Troubles were just starting and there was a very unnerving atmosphere in the town. He signed up with Stockport County, where we stayed for about ten months until his knee finally gave out and he hung up his boots for the last time.

He was two or three months without a job and we decided we'd go into the licensed trade. There was a pub called the Linton going in Peeblesshire and we chose it because it had a house attached where we could all live. We did that for two years but they were a long two years. We enjoyed it but it was hectic; it was a working men's pub that was out in the country so it wasn't horrible or anything, but you couldn't get it clean. I was scrubbing the floors all day then watching customers come in at night and grinding their cigarettes out on my clean linoleum. For the first six weeks, we didn't have one day off, from first thing in the morning till midnight, and we had to buy a sun lamp to give us a bit of colour because we looked like a couple of ghosts. It was one of the old-fashioned ones you would just sit in front of to give you a bit of a glow.

After that, we took one day off a week and got Alex's dad to run it for us while we went out for the afternoon. His mum looked after the kids and we'd come back again in the evening. It was the only break we ever got. We did it until I fell pregnant with Jason. It wasn't going to be a normal birth again and I had to go into hospital a month before he was due. Jason was also born by Caesarean on 1 March 1972 and when I came out of hospital the pub was sold and Alex had bought a pram and a house in Penicuik, near Edinburgh, where we still live.

We were both unemployed for six months and all our savings seemed to disappear. We'd been self-employed, so we couldn't go on the dole or anything like that. That was when Alex went into business with the husband of my best friend, Helen, and they opened up a soft-furnishings warehouse in Edinburgh called Richard Wylie Ltd. We still have the business and we all still work there to varying degrees.

Alex Jnr played football when he was younger and Jason still plays semi-professional now. Alex was quite good but Jason was better and signed for Hearts as a schoolboy; Celtic were after him, too. He was 15 when he was chosen to play for Scotland in an Under-16s tournament in St Malo, France, and he used to partner Duncan Ferguson up front. He suffered a horrific injury against East Germany when he broke a thigh bone and was never the same again. He lost a bit of pace and never went on to fulfil his potential. He's played First, Second and Third Division Scottish senior leagues but sadly not the Premier League, which is a shame because Alex says he had the ability to be a better player than himself and that he would have been a star.

I loved being a footballer's wife and there was nothing about it that irritated me. People would knock on the door occasionally to say hello or to ask for autographs and it never bothered us. He was always signing them when we were out but that was just part of the job. I don't know whether I'd like to be a footballer's wife now; I imagine they don't have much of a private life and I would hate that. The money would be nice because you could do a lot for your family but I wouldn't like to be in the limelight like they are these days.

There were some proud moments for me, and I loved it when we won the FA Cup in 1966, but the most amazing feeling was when I went onto the pitch at Goodison Park. The first time was when Alex was presented with a Millennium Giant award at half-time during a night match against Leicester and he took me with him. The place was packed. I felt a bit nervous while I was waiting in the tunnel but when they announced his name and we walked out, it was to the loudest roar I'd ever heard in my life and I felt like I belonged there. I told Alex I'd have been scoring goals all day with a crowd like that cheering me on.

The last time I went was for Alex's testimonial. Both teams formed a guard of honour and our whole family was there. Our granddaughters were the team mascots and our children were in the stands. It was absolutely amazing and made the hairs stand up on the back of my neck.

Whenever we go back to Liverpool, people always recognise Alex. Hardly anybody in Scotland does or, if they do, they don't let on. His status among Evertonians never fails to surprise me. It's been an awful long time now but people still adore him; it's just wonderful and I still love seeing his face light up.

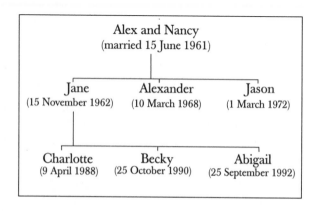

Alex and Nancy
(married 15 June 1961)

Jane	Alexander	Jason
(15 November 1962)	(10 March 1968)	(1 March 1972)

Charlotte	Becky	Abigail
(9 April 1988)	(25 October 1990)	(25 September 1992)

We Were Surrounded By Wonderful People

Maureen Harvey

Colin Harvey signed as an apprentice in October 1962 and made his debut against Internazionale at the San Siro in Milan in the European Cup 11 months later. He scored the winner in the 1966 FA Cup semi-final against Manchester United and went on to collect a winners' medal, while becoming an integral member of the celebrated midfield triumvirate with Howard Kendall and Alan Ball. He picked up a Championship winners' medal in the 1969–70 team and after 380 games for the club and 24 goals, joined Sheffield Wednesday for £70,000 in September 1974, where he played 45 games before injury forced him to retire. He returned to coach and then manage Everton. Capped only once for England, he retired from coaching in 2003 due to chronic hip problems.

Born Maureen Murray, 9 June 1949,
Prestatyn, North Wales

My parents were Irish but we were born and bred in Prestatyn, North Wales. Dad was very ill with tuberculosis when I was little and he couldn't work for three years but he made a full recovery and worked as a wages clerk and a bookkeeper until he retired at the grand old age of 79, but mum worked all the time. She'd trained as a nurse at Walton hospital during the war and her claim to fame was that she'd met General de Gaulle, who'd come over to visit the injured French troops. Mum would plan her shifts to fit in around us – I had a sister and two brothers – so she would take us to a little café in the morning and make sure we had our breakfast, then go and get the bus to the hospital. We'd get the bus home after school and she'd be back about an hour later. She was very good like that and we had a lovely, innocent childhood.

In 1966 I was studying for my A levels but getting a bit disillusioned with it towards the end of the first year. Proper jobs were few and far between in a place like Prestatyn and my sister Kathy had followed Mum's lead and also gone up to Liverpool to train as a nurse at Walton hospital. She'd moved out of the nurses' home and into a flat above a corner shop just off Rice Lane with a couple of other nurses. I went up to visit and they threw a party – it all seemed so grown up and exciting in the big city and I didn't want to go home. Kathy knew I was miserable at school and she said I could move in with them if Mum and Dad would allow me. I went home and asked them and they said if I could get work in Liverpool, then I could go; I couldn't believe my luck.

I went back to Kathy's and looked through the *Liverpool Echo* for a job. A few people had told me good money could be made at Littlewoods Pools, so I went along for an interview. They were based in Walton Hall Avenue and, since I was such a small-town girl, I thought an avenue would be a little, short, tree-lined cul-de-sac, so I set off walking down to Queens Drive and turned left. I walked and walked and walked for about three miles, I couldn't believe the distance and was starting to panic that I was completely lost, but I got there eventually.

They gave me a test and said they would take me on but thought I would be bored with the work and could do much better for myself. They suggested I keep an eye out for a job that would offer me a brighter future. Buoyed with confidence, I found a civil service job and started work as a clerical assistant in the Department of Health but probably on less money than I would have been on at Littlewoods.

World Cup fever had gripped the nation and I couldn't have arrived in Liverpool at a more exciting time. Brazil had played at Goodison Park and Everton had just signed Alan Ball. I remember the Brazil fans banging their drums and doing the samba down County Road.

We lived a ten-minute walk from Goodison and nearly everybody in the street was an Evertonian; they were such lovely people and they really looked after us. My sister went out with a lad from around the corner who was a rabid Blue — he used to sort out tickets for us, although he would go in a different part of the ground. He said the Gwladys Street End wasn't suitable for girls because it was too rough but we'd walk down to the ground with him and then take our places in the Paddock – we still had to stand but I think it was a bit calmer.

You could have a great time in Liverpool but nowhere could beat Rhyl in the summertime because it was full of lads from the cities, so I would go back home to see my mum and dad most weekends. I'd get on the train after I finished work on a Friday and come back on the Sunday evening ready to start the week again.

Rhyl was only three miles along the coast from home and that was where it was all happening. The trendiest place to go was a hotel on the promenade called the Palace; there was a downstairs cellar-type club and in the summer it would be full with kids from Liverpool and Manchester on their holidays. It was just before people started going abroad for their holidays and holiday romances were rife.

I was out with my dad and my brother Terence one Sunday lunchtime and they'd gone on ahead of me. A few lads from Liverpool were sitting around and they called me over and we started chatting. One of them walked me home and I met him for a coffee later that day. He told me there was a crowd of them staying in a friend's caravan in Talacre and they were down for a week or two. He offered to give me a lift down the following weekend, met me from work and dropped me at my mum and dad's. The next night, I was with my friends in the Palace and that same gang of lads were all in there again – this time Colin was with them. It was June 1967; three weeks after my eighteenth birthday. Colin would have been just short of 23 and already an established footballer. It was his grandma's caravan they were staying in.

We were all introduced to each other and stayed together for the evening as a crowd. Those lads were really funny and boisterous and great company, but what struck me about Colin was that he was just so normal and unassuming. We didn't make another date or anything, we just went our separate ways, but I saw him from time to time through the summer. Rhyl was his retreat and he made good use of his gran's caravan – it was part of his routine really, especially during the close season. I thought he was absolutely lovely and so handsome.

Like any girl with a crush, I knew Colin's car by sight – it was a silver-grey Jaguar and the registration number CBN 220B was etched into my mind. I fancied him like mad but never thought I'd have a chance of going out with him in a million years. Still, every time I saw a car that looked like his, I would do a double take, just in case. This one day, I was standing at the bus stop outside Walton church in Liverpool. I was on my way to meet my friend to go to the cinema and, sure enough, this time it was him. He looked over to the bus stop and waved then he stopped to give me a lift into town. I found out later that he was only going as far as Goodison Park, but he didn't let on. When I got to know him better, I used to kid him on about that Jag; he was such a quiet and modest sort of fella and yet he had such a flash car.

Colin and Tommy Wright were best mates; they were both local lads and always used to room together. Colin was Tommy's best man and they're still friends to this day. On our very first date, we went out with Tommy and his wife Gwen, and Andy and Margie Rankin. We met at a hotel in Liverpool then went on to a nightclub called the Beachcomber in Duke Street. It was the most popular club in town and they used to say you needed a letter from God to get in there – or to be an Everton player.

I started going out with Colin regularly from the November of 1967 and Saturday night was the absolute highlight of the week. Sometimes, we would meet in a lovely little hotel called the Shaftsbury at the bottom of Mount Pleasant. It's not there any more but it was quite an elegant hotel in those days and we would go into the lounge bar until about ten o'clock with whoever happened to come along. There might be four or five football couples there some nights. Other times, we'd go to a lovely cocktail bar just up behind the Empire. In places like that, you didn't get bothered at all, and I'm sure that's why the footballers went – there was nobody wanting to come up and discuss the match or anything. It was different if they were all out with the lads, but if it was with wives or girlfriends, they were nice places to go to and from there we'd move on to the Beachcomber.

The Beachcomber was on two levels and the third floor was a really nice little Chinese restaurant. I think they sometimes had live music but they mostly played Tamla Motown. It was owned by a lovely man called Jim Ireland, who was a big Evertonian and a great fella, and the chap who managed it was Len McMillan – he's still very well known today. Jim was a lovely man and a real gentleman – they called him Gentleman Jim.

We met during the era of the Beatles and the Beach Boys but it was the Motown sound that we loved the most. Colin would never dance – in fact, you wouldn't get him up to dance if his life depended on it because people would look at him and he's so shy. It always used to amaze me that they could run out onto a pitch in front of 60,000 people and play football where they scrutinise your every last move, yet I never met a footballer who would get up and dance. Colin said the size of the crowd at a game was irrelevant and it wouldn't have made any difference if there were a million people or none at all because his mind was so focused on the game.

I went to Wembley to watch the 1968 Cup final against West Bromwich but we weren't married then and so I had to make my own way. A neighbour took my mum, dad, Kathy and I in his car. Jeff Astle ruined that day for us all, God rest his soul.

When we won the League in 1969–70 there was a big dinner at the Prince of Wales in Southport. I have some great photos from that night. I don't know where I got them from but they're lovely.

Colin wasn't very superstitious but he always had a small glass of Harvey's Bristol Cream and a sandwich before he left for the game. It would just be the smallest liquor glass and it was the only time he would ever drink sherry. I think his mum used to roast the Sunday joint on the Saturday and cut off a couple of the slices to make him a hot sandwich at about twelve o'clock. People weren't educated about diet and nutrition back then, but it seemed to do the trick.

I was so tense and nervous at those games. I'm hopeless on football and for ages I couldn't understand why because I've been to so many games, then it dawned on me that I was only watching Colin and not taking in the whole spectacle. Even if he wasn't on the ball, I was watching him and praying that he didn't get injured.

In the close season of 1968, we had a touring holiday in southern Ireland. It was my 19th birthday and we had a lovely time exploring and looking around, then in August I was diagnosed with tuberculosis of the right lung. My whole world fell in around me.

I was in Fazakerley hospital for three months, but I was more worried about losing my boyfriend than losing my lung. I was in partial isolation and I had what they called an 'antibiotic umbrella', so once you were on all the right drugs they would allow visitors.

He didn't let me down. He was there every single day except when he was away with the team. Eventually, they let me go home but only if I promised to go and stay with my mum in Wales, where I could get the sea air and recuperate. I was there for another three months, so I was off work six months in all. Colin would come down and see me when he could and, if I was feeling well, I would sneak the odd weekend up in Liverpool with him.

My hen night was in Liverpool about a week before my wedding and a big gang of us landed on the doorstep of the Beachcomber. Everybody had to queue to get in there, even the members, because it was so popular, but Len McMillan gave us special treatment that night and we were straight in the door. I remember him saying: 'Maureen Murray and all her guests are in courtesy of Mr Ireland tonight.' I still bump into Len occasionally and it's always good to see him, he's a fabulous man too. They were both really good to us.

Our wedding day was a bit hectic. We'd arranged a white wedding in Prestatyn and had tried our best to keep it quiet but, coming from a small town, it was impossible. We married on a Wednesday in January 1970 and Harry Catterick gave Colin a couple of days off work.

Prestatyn is on a bit of a hill and we lived at the seaside end. The church was inland, so the drive there was right through the town and all the people had come out of their shops to wave to us and wish us well. It was only a small church and it took just our families almost to fill it but there were absolutely loads of people outside – mainly Evertonians who'd come to see Colin and to wish us luck. It was nerve-racking for me because I wasn't used to any attention but it all went fine and we had a great day.

We didn't go on honeymoon because it was the football season but we stayed in Rhyl for a week in our friend's holiday bungalow and Colin commuted to Liverpool for training; they only trained in the morning, so he could drive back again in the afternoon.

He'd already been away with the England squad and was hoping to get selected for the 1970 World Cup squad but had developed a problem with his eye. It wasn't as serious as the papers made out, but it was an inflammation of the optic nerve and he had blurred vision. He didn't have an operation but he went into St Paul's eye hospital for treatment and it healed itself in the end. It was an ongoing thing, though, and lasted for a few months; I think that dashed his chances of getting a call-up.

After we married, I had to learn to cook a Sunday roast – it was his favourite meal and he was used to having one every week. I hadn't the vaguest idea where to begin and I remember phoning his mum to ask how to cook mushy peas because I'd never cooked them before in my life. They were in a box and you had to soak them overnight in a net bag.

House-hunting took up a lot of our spare time and while we were looking, we'd rented a flat in Aigburth Park. One day when we were coming back from visiting Colin's family in Cheshire, we drove over the Runcorn Bridge and into Liverpool through Gateacre. We happened to see a little close with new houses being built so we went and had a look. They were half-finished and it was a nice, peaceful little road so we ended up putting a deposit down and that was our first home.

There wasn't a lot of spare money around and when we first got married I didn't even have a washing machine. The highest wage back then was £100 a week but workers at Ford's would earn about £50 or £60 a week, so although it was a bit more it wasn't a massive amount. Now, you move into the house and it's decorated from top to bottom and has all the mod cons, but then you built it up yourself.

My friends were Val Husband and Janet Royle. We all got married in the same year: Janet and Joe in June, and Val and Jimmy in September. Most of the players in those days used to live in Maghull, Lydiate and Aughton, but hardly any lived in south Liverpool. Jan and Joe moved straight out to Ormskirk but Val and Jimmy moved to Woolton, so they weren't far from us, and Val and I would spend a lot of time together. I didn't drive then, so she would pick me up every week and we'd go and do our grocery shopping. I didn't work at that time, but Joanna came along pretty quickly so I soon had my hands full.

Like a lot of the Everton babies, Joanna was born in Park House, Waterloo. It was July and pre-season training had just begun. I started with the pains late at night and Colin drove me in. The nuns told him to go home and get a good night's sleep, and to come back the next day after training because the baby wouldn't arrive until the following afternoon, but Joanna had other plans and was born at seven in the morning.

We didn't even have a phone, so we couldn't contact him, but we had an arrangement with a neighbour that we could ring them and they would pass on the message. He got the call and hotfooted it over so we had a couple of hours together with the baby before he went off to work. She was the absolute image of him when she was born and I couldn't stop looking at my miniature Colin Harvey.

Melanie was born two years and two days after Joanna – they were due on the same date but she was a bit late. Park House had stopped doing maternity by that time and had become a nursing home, so she was born in Oxford Street maternity hospital in Liverpool. Emma was born in Oxford Street, too, but not until 1980, so there was quite a gap. There are no boys in our family – we've got three daughters and one granddaughter and Colin's brother Brian has got a girl, too. It's funny how it works out.

I went to as many games as I could, certainly to every home game, but mainly Cup games away. We had a good friend called John Gallagher who would drive me all over the country. Colin's dad would go to the games, so it was his mum who took the babies and she would have them absolutely every weekend if need be. She was just wonderful like that.

Occasionally, Colin would go to the races but only when it was a day out with the club. He's not a racing or a betting man, so it might only be once a year to Chester and he would go along for the camaraderie. He really enjoyed playing and watching tennis, though, and would play for hours with his brother Brian during the close season. He was an absolute fitness fanatic and he couldn't wait for the season to start again.

I didn't have anything at all to do with the club; I liked it that way and was very happy to remain anonymous. Before we married, I would make my own way to the match. Most of the wives will tell you that we would sit in the car waiting until it was time to go in. The players had to report two hours before kick-off so, once we were married, I would try and get a lift in with somebody else so I wasn't sitting around on my own. We'd get into other people's cars and chat until it was time to go in. I remember when they first opened the players' lounge and they had a bit of a party. We thought it was wonderful, although Manchester United had had one for years.

The Shakespeare was a cabaret club just off London Road and it was a great night out. It used to be a theatre that dated back to Victorian times but by the '70s it had moved with the times and even had go-go girls dancing in cages. The resident compère was Pete Price, who was brilliant and so funny. They had big names appearing and I remember seeing Tommy Cooper there one night. The stars would stay in a hotel and appear for the whole week because the club was open every night and was really popular. We would all go as a group and occupy big tables near the stage, and Pete Price would be absolutely merciless, ribbing the players, but we all loved him and got on really well. In 1971, Georgie Fame and Alan Price came. We used to see Peter in the club between shows and we got talking. I told him that Georgie Fame was my absolute favourite, and didn't he just arrange for me to meet him? It was wonderful. Georgie was staying in the Adelphi and we went back there and sat in the lounge talking to him for hours. Colin was a big fan of his, too, and we had a wonderful evening.

We lived in Gateacre for four years until Colin was transferred to Sheffield Wednesday in 1974. Billy Bingham had come in as manager and I think he wanted to build his own team and maybe he thought those boys were past their best. Managers like to do things their own way and put their stamp on the club. Maybe they were a bit jaded and he felt he should gradually change the side. Alan Ball went off to Arsenal, Howard Kendall to Birmingham City and Colin to Sheffield Wednesday. The fans were furious and I remember there was an outcry about his transfer, but the players were powerless to say no back then. I heard that the Evertonians had unfurled a flag at the next game calling Colin 'The White Pele' and I was so proud and flattered.

The transfer came as a real shock – it was completely out of the blue and I was absolutely terrified because I'd only ever lived in North Wales and Liverpool, and to think of moving to another part of the country was so frightening. I needn't have worried, though, because when we got there everyone we met was lovely and, once again, we were surrounded by wonderful people.

Colin went ahead of me and stayed in a hotel while he was house-hunting. I stayed behind with the children to sell up the house and moved over in the October with the girls. He'd found us a place in an old pit village called Pilley, somewhere between Sheffield and Barnsley. There were three newly built houses between the local village pub and the farm where we got our milk in the mornings. It was right out in the countryside and we absolutely loved living there.

There was one aspect of being a footballer's wife that I hated and Colin would probably say it didn't even exist, but I hated when girls would be all over him. Men don't really understand when women are being like that but we do and it used to make me furious. I might go to the ladies' and when I came back they would be hanging off him. I would be seething inside but would keep cool and just say, 'You haven't introduced me to your friend.' My sister used to laugh at me because I would get jealous so easily but, until it happens to you, you don't know what it's like. I could have scratched a few eyes out over the years, I can assure you of that.

Everton is entwined in our lives. Colin has done literally every job from apprentice, cleaning Brian Labone and Alex Young's boots, to manager. I can't name a job he hasn't done, apart from scouting. Howard Kendall's days as manager were magnificent and Colin was very much involved with that side. It was a great time to be a Blue but, from then on, it's been pretty much downhill. When Colin took over as manager, they were doing really well and never went below eighth in the League but he never reached those same heights as in the mid-'80s.

We lead a very quiet life and always have done, but I went to a function in the Adelphi in 2003 and there were 600 fans in the room. They introduced the Old Boys one by one as they came in and I couldn't get over the noise; it was just incredible. It was amazing to hear them, especially as it's been so long since he played, and it just totally overwhelmed me.

I was never especially ambitious; all I ever really wanted to do was settle down and be a good wife and mother. Colin was a good provider and I was happy with that. I loved having the children at home and spending time with them. It was different then – women didn't go out to work because there was nobody to look after the kids. Footballers' wives are different now. I can't imagine any of our generation modelling underwear or doing anything outrageous; the men would have been mortified for a start because their wives were drawing attention to themselves.

The *Daily Mirror* wrote an article about the old Leeds manager, Don Revie, and they mentioned his wife; they said that 'unlike most footballers' wives, Mrs Revie is an educated lady'. I took umbrage at this and wrote to the *Daily Mirror*. I told Colin I'd written and he didn't say anything. The *Mirror* printed my letter, which I didn't really want them to do, but then they sent a reporter round to speak to me and take a photograph. That was the only time I ever drew attention to myself and I didn't really mean it to go that far.

It was when we were at Sheffield that Colin was diagnosed with an arthritic hip and it came as a terrible shock to us all. He's had three hip replacements so far. His left hip was replaced about 20 years ago and that's still working well. Then he had his right hip replaced in 1995 in Wrightington, but had to have that replaced again in 2001, and it was in a pretty bad way. One of the reasons is because he trains too much. He's addicted to training even now he's retired; the doctor has said he can still go on the static bike in the gym and you can bet your life he's there now. His fitness was a challenge and he wanted to still be the fittest at the club even though the players were 30 years younger than him.

I think I fell for Colin when I first met him, and when he asked me out, I just couldn't believe it was happening. I can still remember that feeling of excitement waiting to hear from him and my heart beating too fast whenever the phone rang. We've had a great life; we live in Ormskirk now and we've got three successful children and a beautiful granddaughter, Bethany. I don't know if there will ever be any boys in our family to carry on the footballing tradition and maybe that's the way destiny says it should be. Football has given us a great life and, given the chance, I'd do it all over again and wouldn't change a single minute.

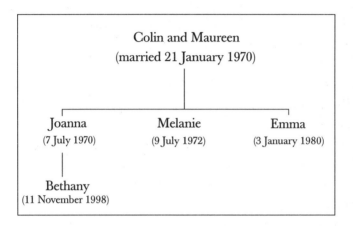

Even After All These Years

Pat Labone

A one-club man who joined Everton in July 1957, and retired 530 games and 15 seasons later with 2 goals and 2 bookings to his name, Brian Labone was later described by Harry Catterick as the 'Last of The Corinthians'. In 1962, the central defender became the first Everton player to be capped by England since the war and captained the club for much of his career before retiring in 1971. He won 26 England caps and still works for the club in a promotional capacity.

Born Patricia Lynam, 9 September 1942, Dublin, Republic of Ireland

I used to just love dancing. Sometimes when I hear those old songs, it takes me right back and my feet start tapping. I love all kinds of music: from light classical to the very old songs of my father's era and everything in between. My father was a musical man who liked Flanagan & Allen and I know all the words to all those old songs. I always say that when I'm in my coffin, just put the music on and I'll come out and have one last dance.

I think it runs in my blood; my grandmother and her sister were in the theatre and, by the time I was nine, I was already going to the Brendan Smith Academy of Acting in Dublin. I had two much older brothers from my father's first marriage and the eldest one, Denis, had the most beautiful singing voice – he was known throughout Ireland as the Irish Boy Wonder. When I was a little girl he'd be performing in shows and he taught me some of the songs. I remember one time I was in the audience and he got me up on the stage. The strange thing was that off-stage I wouldn't say boo to a goose – I was so shy I would hide behind my mum's skirt – but when I got on the stage, it was totally different and I just knew that was what I wanted to do.

I was born in the Rotunda hospital in Dublin to an English mother. My sister Linda is 11 years younger than me but the strange thing is that my mum was in the same ward and the same bed when she had both of us. My father was a bookmaker – the Lynams, my father's family, were very well known among the racing fraternity in Ireland. He thought the bookmaking business was going downhill and mum wanted to go back to England where the work situation was better, so we upped sticks and sailed over to Liverpool.

My father had an aunt who didn't live far from Anfield so we lodged with her until we sorted ourselves out and then we moved to a house in Spencer Street off West Derby Road. I don't think it's there any more. My father worked as a hydraulic inspector and my mum stayed at home with my baby brother Charles.

You do learn to conquer shyness over the years but I was stricken with it back then. I'd been schooled in a Catholic convent and had only ever been in the company of girls and nuns, so when I went to my new school where it was mixed, it was quite literally a shock to my system and I had terrible difficulty coping with it. I'd never come into contact with boys before; they were alien creatures.

It was very traumatic for me and I found it awfully difficult to settle down. There were a few girls at the school who used to bully me because I was Irish – they would taunt me and follow me home, and they made my life a misery. I hated it so much there was a stage when my parents thought they might have to go back to Ireland because I was so deeply unhappy and homesick.

I had to stick it out but it always left me feeling separate from the others because from an early age I was made to feel different. Eventually, I left school and did some part-time modelling for Patricia Platt's agency in Liverpool. They entered their models into beauty pageants so they could get used to an audience and increase their confidence. The Miss Liverpool contest was due to be held at the Locarno Ballroom in Liverpool and the agency suggested I enter along with a couple of the other girls. To this day, I don't know how I won it, but I did.

Shortly afterwards, I had the opportunity to go to London but my father disapproved. He was very old fashioned and you didn't argue with your parents in those days – you were told to do something and there was no discussion. He didn't think it was right and told me to find a proper job, something that would stand me in good stead. I began doing secretarial work in a travel agent's and ended up in a law firm. I've pretty much been in and out of law ever since.

It has proved useful because I've never been without a job, but if I'd had my way, I'd have gone off and become a professional dancer. I'd learnt all types of dancing by then: Irish, ballet and tap, and I'd got all my medals and cups for ballroom dancing. I loved it and that's all I ever wanted to do but you didn't say no to your parents. It ate away at me for years and years, but with maturity you look back and realise it wasn't to be, and at least I can say I've never been out of a job. I've always been able to support myself, even when I've been on my own.

Clothes and fashion enchanted me and I used to love to dress up to go out. I think people have lost the art now, which is a shame; they just don't seem to bother. I've always wanted to take care of myself and look my best; if I feel good, then I can take on the world.

Brian and I met in 1961 at the Downbeat club in Liverpool and, to this day, I'm still wondering how we bumped into each other because I was always on the dance floor and he was always at the back of the room with his friends. I remember I was wearing a sleeveless navy linen dress with a white scalloped pattern on one side. Back then, they had ultraviolet lights in clubs that would pick out the white and he tells me that's what caught his eye. I was collecting my coat to go home and he came over to chat but I was dashing for my bus so it was only a few words. He just asked why I was leaving so soon.

He was well dressed and looked a decent type. I suppose his height and his build struck me the most, and he was awfully handsome and smart in his collar and tie, but I thought, 'Who's this cheeky devil talking to me?' and fled to the bus stop. But he played on my mind a little bit and I was quite pleased when I saw him there again the following week. He made his way over and struck up a proper conversation and that was where it all began.

I was 19 and he was 22 and we both lived at home with our parents. He was already a footballer and had been at Everton for about four years, but the truth is, I didn't realise football existed as a way of making a living. I thought it was just a game lads played in the streets. He did tell me he played but I thought he just meant in the park, and it was only after I'd met him a few times that I realised it was his job. I had absolutely no idea.

After a number of dates, he asked if I wanted to go and see a match, and out of curiosity I agreed. Brian didn't drive a car until well into our engagement so anywhere we went was on foot or by bus. I remember walking all the way to Goodison Park and getting engulfed in the crowds and wondering what on earth was going on. There were masses of people, thousands and thousands of them, swarming their way to the game and I got swept along the road with them. I'd never seen anything like it in my life.

I finally got inside the ground and it all seemed to be going well. I was entering into the spirit of it but nobody had told me they changed ends at half-time. A goal went in and I was jumping up and down in celebration until I realised I was the only one, then the penny dropped. I always seemed to have the knack of turning up wearing the opposition's colours too. I can still see myself now, wearing my lovely red coat with a coal-grey fur collar as I walked down Goodison Road, wondering why everyone was looking at me. It was lovely and warm but I never wore it again.

After a couple of years, we got engaged, but while we were courting, my parents moved over to the Wirral and I went with them. I loved it over there and I never wanted to move back to Liverpool again. It didn't hold many good memories for me.

Saturday was the big night out and occasionally we would go to the Royal Tiger in the city centre, but Brian wasn't really a clubby type of person and most of our friends were outside of football. We would go to the usual places in town for meals; the Porthole was one of our favourites and we would go to the Golden Goblet for their big T-bone steaks. More often than not we would end up in Russell's, the cabaret club in Parr Street. I remember Bruce Forsyth being on one night, but my idol at the time was Sean Connery. *Goldfinger* had just been released and I thought he was fantastic. This one night we had our usual table right up by the dance floor when a big group came in and among them was Sean; he'd been playing golf with Kenny Lynch and Jimmy Tarbuck. I couldn't believe I'd met my hero that night.

Everton made it to the FA Cup final in 1966 against Sheffield Wednesday. It was my first visit to Wembley and I had a turquoise silk dress and jacket made especially for the occasion. Of course, Everton won, so I got to see Princess Margaret present Brian with the Cup – it was one of the proudest moments of my life. I looked at him and thought, 'That's the man I love,' and I felt like I would burst with pride. He says the Princess was beautiful and she had the most delicate skin. I got to do it all again in 1968 but there was no Cup for him that day and it was a long drive home.

There was a big build-up to our wedding and I daresay Brian will never live down the fact that he gave up his place in the 1966 World Cup squad to marry me. To this day, people believe I put pressure on him – in fact, I'm sure my own brother is still convinced that it was down to me – but it was Brian's decision.

He wasn't in the original squad until Jackie Charlton got injured and he was called up as his replacement, but he said he'd made his decision to get married and he was sticking to it. I won't say that if he had gone he wouldn't have got earache from me, but it was totally his choice. I have to admit that now, when I see the England team finally getting their honours and recognition, I still cringe, even after all these years.

The wedding was planned for the close season of 1966. It was at St Peter and Paul's in New Brighton, a beautiful big Catholic church and with the longest aisle you could ever imagine. Gordon West was Brian's best man.

We did meet with a lot of opposition along the way – various people were not happy about it at all, with me being Catholic, but he stuck to his guns. There was bigotry in those days, there really was. Most of the opposition was based on religion so it meant Brian had to take religious instruction and that any children in our marriage had to be brought up Catholic. It might be difficult to understand now, but it was very real and it did go on.

When Everton won the League in 1963, the club took the players and their wives to Torremolinos for a special treat. Because we weren't married, I wasn't allowed to go and I was so disappointed. It was just as foreign holidays were about to become fashionable and there were only one or two hotels there. It all sounded so exotic. Brian was only there for a couple of days before he had to join up with the England squad for an Eastern European tour anyway, so he didn't have the best time either. We decided to go back there for our honeymoon and we had a great time, it was just fabulous. A member of staff even recognised him from the first time around.

I wanted to stay living 'over the water' but it wasn't policy at Everton with the club houses, and most of the players lived around the Maghull area. Brian's teammate Dennis Stevens had been living in a house in Arrowe Park on the Wirral but he must have got transferred to another club because when we were looking, his house was up for sale. We weren't given much of a choice but luckily I fell in love with it and that was where we started out our married life.

Brian couldn't dance to save his life – he has two left feet – and though he could easily go out and play in front of 70,000 people, he was too self-conscious to get on a dance floor. He's very much a man's man and it wasn't his style. I can't say it didn't cause a bit of friction when we'd go to functions and he wouldn't budge. Luckily, we'd always go out with friends, so I would have somebody to dance with.

He only scored two goals in his career and I saw both of them. Both times it was amazing and I was absolutely thrilled. I remember him running down the pitch in celebration – I think he was as surprised as the rest of us. I was jumping up and down with delight. I watched him play all the time. I went to all the home games and, as they progressed in the FA Cup, I might go to some away games too, depending on whether I could get a lift, although it was nerve-racking to watch him play.

There were some great things about the football life but one thing I couldn't stand was the way the wives were treated as second-class citizens. There was no way I could accept that and I was like a suffragette constantly fighting for the cause. It was the way things were, but I resented it. There were no amenities for the wives or anywhere for us to go after matches and it used to infuriate me. They didn't even have a room where we could wait for our husbands. I often stood outside in the dark and rain waiting for Brian to finish, and it was only the kindness of a doorman who would let me stand inside that got me out of the cold.

The club was also very strict about late nights and drinking. The players weren't supposed to be out after midnight and they weren't allowed to drink after midweek, yet straight after some matches, the club would take the boys off for what they would term 'special training'. They'd go to Blackpool or wherever and it was just an excuse for them to let their hair down. It certainly didn't go down well with me because I thought it was double standards – it was all right to do it while you were away but not at home? I used to hate it.

It was a lonely life at times. During the close season, the team would go on tour and be gone for weeks at a time. When they came back, it didn't leave much time to have our own holiday before they were back in training.

When they went back after the summer break, Brian would really suffer physically. Even now, when we drive past the sandhills at Crosby and Ainsdale, he winces and tells me how Harry Catterick had the team running up and down them for hours on end, gasping for breath.

Initially, Brian didn't really do a great deal with his spare time as he threw himself wholly into football, but, latterly, his father established a central heating business, J. & B. Labone, and he started spending time there. He was going to take over when he finished playing, but it got too big for his father to cope with and he sold it. They're still trading under that name and are all over the country and in Ireland now, I believe.

I liked to maintain my own identity and earn my own money, and am very independent. I've always worked full time and I used to fit my modelling in during the evenings, the weekends and the holidays, and I loved it. I liked the beautiful clothes and the whole concept; it was the perfect job for me. Before we married, I still entered the occasional beauty competition and I suppose I would have continued down that road, but eventually it conflicted too much with my home life so I packed it all in.

At weekends, we would go out in the city but there came a time when we had to stop it. In our innocence, we would think we'd be able to spend some time together but it didn't work out like that. Brian was the club captain and was well liked, so it would end up that most evenings I would finish up on my own because all kinds of people would come over to talk to him about football. They were always nice people and very courteous, but the next thing you knew another hour had passed, the night was over and you hadn't had a chance to have your meal properly. We ended up having to give the city centre a miss and find somewhere a little quieter so we could spend some time together.

Brian bought a beautiful chestnut racehorse and named him Goodison – at one time he held the course record at Ayr. He was stabled on the Wirral at Colin Crossley's and we would go along every weekend and feed him Polo mints and make a fuss of him. He had nine or ten wins in his time but we never saw one of them. We did see him come second a few times, and it got to the point where people would ask us to stay away when he was running because we were such a jinx. He lasted for quite a few years and then came the fateful day at Market Rasen. It was his first or second time over the sticks and he fell and broke a fetlock, and they shot him on the track. We were devastated because he was such a big part of our lives. We didn't know until it was too late, but they're allowed to take that decision without the owner's permission. It depends on the break, but a horse can nearly always get better although it's a long process and it may never run again.

Unfortunately, a lot of people would just claim the insurance but Brian and I would never have done that given the choice. I remember he rang in tears to tell me what had happened. I was crying as well and, to this day, I swear that if we'd been asked, we'd have brought him home. He wasn't the most expensive horse but he had a big heart and he always gave everything.

In comparison to players these days, Brian didn't get an enormous amount of attention from other women, but he got enough. It didn't make me angry; it made me feel quite insecure. There were some footballers that liked that side of it but I can say with hand on heart that Brian was never a womaniser; he wouldn't even notice if someone was after him. He really was a one-woman man and I didn't have to worry about that at all. I was never that self-confident that I would feel totally secure, but I felt I didn't have to worry too much.

We'd been married for a couple of years when we went on holiday to Malta. We stayed at the Golden Sands Hotel at Golden Sands Bay and were having lunch one afternoon when the Prime Minister of Malta, Dom Mintoff, recognised Brian and came over to introduce himself. He invited us to spend the following day with him and his family and we had a lovely time. The press had come along to the hotel and took a few photos of us lying by the pool. Years later, friends of ours went there and said the picture was still there, framed and on the wall.

I like people to be genuine and I have no time for users. We were forever getting calls for tickets for games; we've often been woken up in the middle of the night by the phone ringing. People thought Brian could just put his hand out and pull tickets off trees. I was probably more wary of people than him and soon realised a lot of them were not genuine – I could pick up on things like that quicker than he could.

I don't really like using the word but they seemed like hangers-on and I would know they only wanted to be with us because of who he was. They couldn't give a damn what kind of a person he was, they just wanted to be in his reflected glory. I got very angry with that. He would shrug it off and say it didn't matter but it used to rile me. I was proved right when he finished playing: it was amazing the number of people who we suddenly didn't see any more.

Brian was away in Mexico playing in the World Cup in the summer of 1970 and I was at home six months pregnant. It was the best thing that ever happened to me and I absolutely loved it; I just bloomed. Like most footballers, he wanted a son. I thought it might have been a boy because the baby was never still but deep down I really wanted a little girl. I'd seen the most beautiful aquamarine and diamond ring in Pike's the Jewellers, which was absolutely gorgeous. Brian said that if I had a boy, I could have it – Rachelle weighed in at 7lb 12oz. on Sunday, 6 September but he got me the ring anyway because he was thrilled to bits.

My mother and Brian came with me to the hospital and Rachelle was born by emergency Caesarean. They were known as shock births in those days and you weren't able to hold your baby for 48 hours. The babies were fed, washed, dressed and changed within their special soft-canvas crib, so it was nearly two days before I could hold her. It was like a cruel form of torture. I couldn't believe the fear I felt, thinking that it was all too good to be true and that I might lose her.

One night, I woke up and put my hand out to touch her and she was absolutely stone cold. I panicked and screamed the place down; I was in floods of tears, saying there was something wrong with her. They took her away and when she came back they said she was fine and just fast asleep. I couldn't believe I had this beautiful little girl and she was going to be mine; it was just the most wonderful feeling in the world. I always say I only ever had one child because I couldn't improve on perfection. She is the greatest achievement in my life.

A lot about being a footballer's wife was fun and, as I'd always been more interested in the arty side of life, the spin-off – getting to meet celebrities – was certainly colourful. We met quite a number of showbiz people and that was what I enjoyed most. I once went to a party at the singer Frank Ifield's home and met Bob Monkhouse – he left quite an impression on me because he was the most charming man you could meet and so clever and quick. Another nice man we met was Frankie Vaughan, and when we moved over to our new house in Lydiate, Ken Farrington, who played Billy Walker in *Coronation Street* at the time, would stay with us whenever he was doing a play in Liverpool.

Rachelle had a pony called Smokey and the house was adorned with rosettes they'd won. We had stables at the back of the house and a paddock that Smokey shared with Peter the donkey. One Sunday afternoon, after Brian and his friends had all been to the pub and come back to the house, Ken thought he would have a laugh and try to ride on Peter but he threw him off and Ken ended up with a broken arm. His play started the following night and ran for two weeks so he had to do the entire run with his arm in a sling.

I always wanted to retain my own identity and joined with the Green Room Playgroup, a well-known amateur dramatics society. We staged a play called *Suddenly Last Summer*, which was performed at the Neptune Theatre in Liverpool. I was thrilled to bits when I got a really good write-up from the *Liverpool Echo*, and even more so at the after-show party when a woman was introducing us and she said, 'Oh, and this is Pat Labone's husband.' It was then I knew I'd retained my individuality. After all those years of being made to feel like a second-class citizen lurking in the shadows, it was a great feeling because I'd been seen as a complete person and not as an extension of my husband.

Brian was doing well at Everton and had been lucky enough to escape any major injuries but it was a collision with Gordon West, believe it or not, that put him out of action for a long time. It happened during a game in London and I had to go down there on the train to see him in hospital. That was when they discovered he had 'double kidneys' – I never found out if that meant he had four kidneys or just two that were twice as big.

That injury put him out for quite a while but, for somebody who was rarely on the sidelines, it is ironic that an injury ended his career. It was his Achilles tendon, although I think they can repair those quite easily now. My recollection of it was that all he needed was rest but he was never really given the time to heal. He wasn't forced to play but they'd give him a couple of weeks off then they would desperately need him back. He was the captain, so there was a big obligation there.

His football career ended in 1971 and he went into an electrical business with the cousin of a friend, but it didn't work out. Unfortunately, he'd gone into business with a disreputable person who took advantage of him. He was left with a load of debt, which he had to pay off, and the business folded. He had nothing behind him – football had been his life and, apart from anything else, there just wasn't the money. What he'd earned he'd given to his father to put into his business, so that was it.

He went into insurance and he's been doing that ever since. He did reasonably well but I always felt that in some ways Brian was wasted because he really could have done so much more. He's the Master of Ceremonies at Goodison on match days but I always think he'd have made a great TV pundit or a radio commentator. He'd have been brilliant. He had the flow, the patter, the ability and the brains to do something really creative and interesting.

We were married for 14 years and together for 19. There were some outside influences that were partly to blame and our marriage came to an end in 1981. My main concern was for Rachelle because I didn't want her to suffer. The nice thing about it all is that we've proved that it can be amicable. She never resented anything, she's never suffered in any way and we're all dear friends. We celebrate Christmas and birthdays together and there's always a lot of laughter – it's congenial and the kind of behaviour befitting the captain of Everton Football Club.

We had a meal together last New Year's Eve and, even after all these years, there's still never been anybody important in his life. He says he's like a swan and he's mated for life. He's not the most romantic of people, with flowery words and gestures, but when he does say something, it means so much.

Brian is an honourable and modest man, and I think that's what people admire about him. The one thing I'm really proud of is that I can honestly say I've never heard anyone say a bad word about him. After all this time and the sheer number of people we've met throughout our lives, I truly haven't. He's getting a bit crotchety in his old age, but he's still a nice man. He could mix with the highest and the lowest and treat them all the same. It was those traits that made me fall in love with him.

I don't know many other footballers who have put as much time and effort into helping others out, and he's never asked for a single penny. Most would want a fee but not Brian – he's given his caps and his medals away for auctions and charities, but that all goes unsaid and unsung.

I think I would handle being a footballer's wife much better now than I did when I was actually married to one, but you can't put an old head on young shoulders. When I look back, I can see there were certain areas that I had difficulty coping with and I don't think I was the best footballer's wife. I'm hoping I was a good wife, but I have this Irish thing inside of me that would always protest and have to question things.

Both my parents died in their 60s – Mum was 66 and my father was 69. He'd had numerous heart attacks then eventually one got him. I didn't have the best of relationships with my father. I can say that now – it took me years to admit it – but it's true and I think that's where my shyness and uncertainty originated.

Sadly, my mum died of the most horrible cancer. We were

devastated because we all loved and adored her. She was my strength, the only real certainty in my life. She'd be so pleased to know we're all still very close. My brother lives in Bath so we don't see him as much but thankfully my sister Linda lives nearby and she really is my dearest and closest friend. We have a really strong family bond that holds us close and we all rely on each other; it's a lovely feeling.

I still dance whenever I get the chance – even now my feet can't keep still when I hear music. I know that will never change, just like I know Brian and I will always be there for each other. The bottom line is we can't live together but we're star-crossed lovers and he'll always be part of my life. Even though he still hasn't learned to dance, I was his first love and his last.

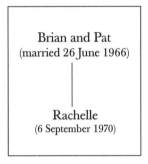

Brian and Pat
(married 26 June 1966)

Rachelle
(6 September 1970)

Everton Is Him And He Is Everton

Trish Lyons

Mike Lyons used to watch Everton from the terraces, when he idolised Jimmy Gabriel. A striker who converted to defence via the midfield, he signed as an apprentice in July 1969 and enjoyed a lengthy Everton career, playing 442 games and scoring 59 goals. He was captain during one of the leanest spells in the club's history, winning only a runners-up tankard in the 1977 League Cup final. Lyons represented England at Under-23 and B level before moving on to Sheffield Wednesday in 1982. He helped them to promotion and joined Grimsby in late 1985, where he had his only foray in management. He is currently coaching in Australia.

Born Patricia Maloney, 2 June 1957,
Dublin, Republic of Ireland

My dad was Irish and was over in England on business when he met and fell in love with my mum and eventually took her back to Dublin with him. He was a tailor by trade and owned a shop called Louis Copeland on Capel Street in Dublin. Louis was his business partner and the master tailor – he cut the cloth and was the real craftsman of the trade. The business was the most acclaimed in Ireland and it probably still is, because it's still running to this day. Mum was young and beautiful, and came from a privileged, horsey, 'green-welly' background and worked as a hairdresser.

I was born in Dublin but when I was about four, my parents separated. There was never any possibility they would divorce because they were staunch Catholics, so Mum returned to England instead and brought me with her. Dad was still involved in his business, but he followed us over to try to resolve the situation and from their reconciliation my two brothers, Michael and Brendan, were born. We lived in Crosby, north Liverpool, and my mum had a hairdressing shop called Pauline's in the city centre. It was a gift from her parents and she ran it and worked there full time. Life was good and we had a lovely, happy childhood.

Notre Dame on Maryland Street was a grammar school and I loved my time there. I really enjoyed learning and found it came quite easily to me. I was blessed with a strange combination of a very mathematical mind and an artistic hand. Numbers always intrigued me but art was the love of my life. Somebody once told me that was quite common in left-handed people.

I left school at eighteen with six O levels, three A levels and a master plan: I was going to become an actress. I'd started off acting in the church hall, went to drama school from the age of five then on to the Everyman, a youth theatre in Liverpool. I worked very hard and went on to become a member of the National Youth Theatre. We were semi-professional and I danced and performed on stage, and absolutely loved it. Laurence Olivier was there when I passed my audition for the Guildhall School of Music and Drama in London. I knew I would have to move to London to continue my education. Luckily, my Aunt Caroline was living in Swiss Cottage and had invited me to stay with her. I couldn't wait for my plan to swing into action, so in the meantime I had moved down in readiness and while I was waiting for the academic year to start, I decided to find a temporary job.

The Playboy Club was at 45 Park Lane. It was a fabulous five-storey building that overlooked Hyde Park and it was terribly sophisticated. One Saturday morning, they were holding auditions for waitresses and croupiers, so I went along. I don't think it would be allowed now, but in those days, you would have your interview and then you had to parade your figure in a swimsuit to see if you would look good in the Bunny outfit. It wasn't just about your bust size, though; I like to think it was a combination of personality, numeracy, appearance and dexterity. Two of us got jobs, a Mauritian girl called Mari and myself, and because I was good with numbers, I trained as a croupier on the American roulette tables. Casinos were very glamorous places back then and it really was another world, but I didn't get too carried away. I'd just turned 18 and was always mindful of the fact that I was going to be enrolled into the Guildhall in a couple of months and I was just trying to save money for the student years ahead.

The uniform was pretty standard, complete with cuffs, collar, bow tie and ears, but came in different colours. Mine was maroon velvet and my name tag said Bunny Patricia. I was chatting to one of the other girls as we headed off for a break when Michael heard my accent. Everton had been playing in London and some of the players had come into the club and were having a drink in the Playmates' bar. He came over and asked me whereabout in Liverpool I was from. I was quite perplexed because I didn't even know I had a Liverpool accent, but we exchanged a few pleasantries and I went on my way – it was strictly forbidden for us to fraternise with the punters.

He hung around the gaming floor and when he got the chance, gave me his phone number and asked me to ring him. I stashed it in my purse and the next time I went up to Liverpool to visit my family, I remembered how lovely he had been and how handsome he was so I rang the number, but he wasn't in. The next day he was there and was quite secretive about where he'd been. He said he wanted to see me again but it was difficult for him to get away and he asked if he could take me out the next time I came home. I said that would be lovely and headed back down to London with a spring in my step.

I couldn't wait to see him again and I'd never known the time to pass so slowly. It wasn't until the summer that I caught the train up to Lime Street. We met and he took me to a trendy little pub in Knowsley Village. I'd never drunk alcohol before and when he asked me what I wanted I asked for a packet of crisps and an orange juice.

He said he had to go away for a few weeks and was quite evasive when I asked him questions about how he earned his living. I began to think there was something suspicious about him. He had a nice car, he travelled abroad a lot and always had a few bob in his pocket, and then it dawned on me that he must be a drug smuggler – it was like a hammer blow, but it all seemed to fit. I was too scared to tell my mum about him in case he was a criminal and I thought I would lose my job in the casino, so eventually, with a heavy heart, I told him I didn't want to see him any more because I thought he was a bit odd. He assured me there was no shady business going on but he had to go away for the summer and there was no way he could get out of it. Then he came clean and told me he was a footballer and it was the pre-season tour. I didn't know anything about football but I was so relieved I almost wept because, by that time, I was quite smitten.

I was still based in London but, the way my rota worked, I was off at the weekends and could catch the train up to Liverpool on my days off. We spent more and more time together and I fell totally in love. He made me feel like I was in heaven. I adored him and within a very short space of time he asked me to come back to Liverpool so I could be nearer to him. There was another Playboy club in Manchester, so I requested a transfer and about a month later I was living back at home with my parents in Crosby and driving backwards and forwards to work until the club closed down soon after. That was when I got a job as a beauty consultant for Revlon in Henderson's department store.

My first experience of football had been when I was a little girl, but it was at Anfield because Dad was an avid Red. I thought it was boring. At half-time, I thought it was the end and we could go home. I couldn't believe I had to endure the same a second time. I never went to a football match again after that until Michael invited me to go and watch him play, and I took my dad along.

I was a 'happening chick' before I met Michael but after a few months, he asked me to marry him and I didn't hesitate to accept. It all happened so quickly and we were married just over a year after we'd met. It was a true whirlwind romance.

Our wedding was on Sunday, 18 January 1976, at the high altar in Liverpool's Catholic cathedral. He'd played against Norwich City the day before and they had drawn 1–1. I remember the commentator announcing over the Tannoy beforehand not to put Mick Lyons in the wall if Norwich got a free-kick because he was getting married in the morning.

Looking back, I suppose I was incredibly naive or just too consumed with what I was doing, but I had no idea so many people would be there. It was absolutely chaotic, chock-full of press and about a thousand Evertonians, standing outside in the freezing cold, had come to wish him well. It was a great big wedding and there were police everywhere, trying to hold back the crowds. It wasn't a great day – in fact, it was awful. We didn't get wonderful photographs because the weather was so bad and there weren't enough police to keep the people away. All the photos had to be taken indoors at Goodison Park, where we had our reception.

We couldn't go on honeymoon because it was mid-season but Billy Bingham gave Michael two days off from training and we drove up to Lake Windermere and stayed at a hotel called the Old England. It was in beautiful surroundings but it was very old fashioned and terribly out of date, and the wind was so horrific we couldn't go out.

Michael was the club captain then and earning £225 a week, so we thought we were absolutely minted. He bought a lovely dormer bungalow in Maghull and that was where we lived for about 18 months; then we sold it and bought a house in Sefton Village where we settled and I remain with the children to this day.

The directors of the club were good to me and gave me a job in the Littlewoods offices in Old Hall Street. I worked full time and really enjoyed it, and I stayed until 1978 when I became pregnant.

I went to all the games, home and away. Not an awful lot of the other wives wanted to do so much travelling, so I went on my own or with Lynn Hughes, a friend of mine who'd also been my bridesmaid. Michael would travel with the team on the coach and we would pick him up from Goodison, where they got dropped off. I began to understand the game after a while and could have a legitimate conversation and analysis with him about tactics and the way matches had panned out.

I remember going midweek to Maine Road one time to watch Everton play Manchester City; it was the era of the patchwork jeans and cheesecloth shirts. Michael was renowned for being the last one out of the dressing-room after every game and I always seemed to be waiting for him in the players' lounge. This guy with an entourage came over to me and asked if I wanted a drink. I declined but he started chatting to me anyway. I told him I was waiting for my husband and with that Michael appeared. He apologised to Michael and said he'd been chatting me up, trying to get me to go out for a drink with him, but George Best always did have a soft spot for blondes.

My best pal in those days was Lynn Stanley, Gary's wife. She lived in Childwall, but I had my car and could go and visit her, although I seem to have lost contact with her now. Ann and Billy Wright were great company and so were Dave and Ann Jones, who lived in Formby. We had a wonderful life and I loved it.

Saturday was our big night out, usually as part of a crowd to either celebrate or commiserate the result of the day, and we used to have lots of fun. We wouldn't necessarily go to a club, but we'd always go out for dinner as a group and usually stay in the restaurant for the whole evening. We'd go into Southport or Ormskirk or somewhere in the countryside. There would be a post-mortem on the game and the men would figure out what went wrong and what went right. Fans would often come up to chat and express their feelings about the match, but that was part of the job and it was what you expected to happen. I can honestly say that it never bothered me at all.

If we'd won, those Saturday evenings would be absolutely fantastic.

If we lost, Michael was awful to live with. He couldn't help it, he just loved the club so much. Everton is him and he is Everton.

He was extremely disciplined with his training and his lifestyle. Before a home game, he had a strict regime. He'd have something light for dinner on Friday night and go to bed at about nine o'clock. In the morning, he'd go for a very long walk followed by stretching, collecting his thoughts and meditating, then, at about eleven o'clock, he'd get himself ready to go into work. He didn't speak a word; he was totally focused on the game and psyching himself up. There was no sex before the match either – he would be in bed and straight to sleep.

In my role as the captain's wife, I did a few things. I would often go with him to Alder Hey hospital or to charity evenings and I did some fundraising with him, too. The club was wonderful with us and made me feel very welcome and included.

I didn't really mind people ringing for tickets or asking for autographs; it was all part of his job. It was when it got nasty and personal that I began to dislike it. Some terrible things happened when he became a target for the boo boys, but because it was unknown to me I just took it all in my stride. I remember once we had a tree snapped in the garden and another time people were chanting 'Mick Lyons is crap' outside the house. I wouldn't have minded except that I was in there on my own and he was out having a good time.

When Billy Bingham left in January 1977, Gordon Lee took over and Michael found in him a manager he really liked and deeply respected. He said nobody knew more about football than Gordon Lee and they got on like a house on fire. I think they both shared the same passion and work ethic.

Everton were doing really well in both cup competitions that year until referee Clive Thomas knocked us out of the FA Cup by disallowing a perfectly good goal against Liverpool in the semi-final. I still don't think Michael has got over that to this day. It took the wind out of everyone's sails but we had already got through to the League Cup final and I made my first trip down to Wembley for the final against Aston Villa.

All the wives went on the train and stayed in a really posh hotel just outside London's Kensington Park. I remember almost bursting with pride when Michael led the team onto the pitch. If I close my eyes, I can still see him now in the minutest detail. Luckily, I can't remember much of the game, though, because it was dreadful. It finished up 0–0 and there were two replays.

We were all in a buoyant mood when we got back to the hotel, optimistic that we'd win the replay at a canter. There was a huge dinner booked for that evening and a great time was had by all. I wore a beautiful dress; it really was something special and I must have looked so young. On the Monday, there was an article in *The Times* about the game and the journalist had written: 'Patricia Lyons could have graced the pages of *Vogue*, she looked so wonderful.' I was absolutely thrilled to bits.

The replay was at Hillsborough and ended up 1–1 and the second replay was at Old Trafford where we got beaten 3–2, although Michael had scored to make it 2–2 before they lost in extra time. It was heartbreaking.

We'd been married for 18 months when I fell pregnant. Michael Joseph was born in May 1978 at Oxford Street maternity hospital. I had to be induced but I remember, the day I went in, Sebastian Coe was running in the 800m at the European Championships so Michael asked if I would wait until the next day so he could watch the race. In the end, I drove myself to the hospital and met my mum there. I had a private room, but somebody must have been indiscreet because I left the room to go to the loo and when I came back my room had been ransacked. Everything I owned had been pinched: my bag, my keys, my purse, everything was gone and I had the police there taking fingerprints all night. It was the last thing I needed the day before my baby was born. Whoever it was must have lain in wait.

Everton always seemed to take the players away for long periods of time and I would get terribly lonely, but it was the worst at Christmas time. For me, the best days were in June during the close season because I would hardly get to see him at all in December. The team would often go to Alder Hey to see the sick kids, but Michael was there all the time anyway. In the summer, he must have presented more awards and visited more schools than anybody alive; sometimes he'd do three in one evening and he'd never ask for or accept a fee. He was wonderful in that respect and he still is. He always felt football had given him so much and the least he could do was give something back.

Michael was fantastic with young local teams, too, as he had come up that way himself. He went to the De La Salle school, the same school attended by Francis Jeffers and Wayne Rooney, and ran three teams in all, while I was team secretary. If he ever had any spare time, he liked to play golf and he's quite good at it now. He loved tennis, too, and Billy Wright was always his partner.

I remember him coming home from games with some terrible injuries. He was an extremely brave player and was always bleeding from somewhere. He had any number of cut eyes and eyebrows, and one time at Grimsby, Justin Fashanu elbowed his tooth out. I remember another time he got an elbow in his face and came off the pitch, had stitches and then ran back out to carry on playing. Once, he was in plaster up to his hip following a cartilage operation but the worst I can remember was after an away game when I went to pick him up to bring him home and he couldn't walk. He'd had a really vicious kick in the shin. Jim McGregor, the physio, somehow got him into the car and told me to take him back to the house. I got him into bed and he went delirious. The kick had poisoned his blood and made him hallucinate. He thought he was a soldier in the Second World War, fighting on the front line. The poison had travelled from the bottom of his leg to his groin. It was very scary. Eventually, he became so ill he had to go into hospital.

Francesca, our second child, was born on 26 July 1980. I know it sounds daft because she's a girl but she's the image of her dad – beautiful. She's Daddy's girl and he loves her to bits. My mum was absolutely fantastic when the kids were born. She would take both of them off my hands whenever I went to a match.

Michael's transfer to Sheffield Wednesday in August 1982 was a big shock to the system. Howard Kendall had arrived at Everton as manager and it was quite clear that Michael wasn't in his plans, so he was put on the transfer list. Wednesday were in the old Second Division at that time and Jack Charlton was their manager. He was a lovely man and he really admired Michael and came in for him. We couldn't sell our house, so Michael moved over to South Yorkshire and bought a house with Wednesday teammate Lee Chapman. Jack Charlton made Michael the captain and they got promoted the next season. It was a great big event.

The transfer was a good move for Michael and he made the most of it. He tried to pursue his career the best way he could but unfortunately it didn't really happen. He would drive down there on a Monday morning and come back again on the Saturday, after the game. Meanwhile, I was just looking after the kids. My family was nearby and they were very supportive so I started doing promotional work for different cosmetic houses.

Michael had a short spell as player–manager at Grimsby but wanderlust set in after he finished there and he went to work in the Far East and Australia in 1991. I travelled with him on and off but in 1999 I finally came back to our old house with the children.

We're separated now but we still have an amicable relationship and are in touch all the time. We spent so much time together it would be very strange if he wasn't still part of my life.

Our son Michael Joseph can play football – he's quite an adequate sportsman – but he's more academic and extremely gifted with his hands. He's very arty: a carpenter by day, a musician by night.

I'm so pleased when I hear people speaking well of Michael; I think it's wonderful. I know he's a living legend and, having known, loved and cherished him for all these years, I'm not the slightest bit surprised. He's a good, honourable man and he deserves all the recognition he gets. People go up to him all the time to ask for an autograph or to shake his hand, even in the depths of Borneo.

I did make sacrifices for him in many ways. Obviously, in a

professional capacity, but emotionally too, and so did the children. Having said that, I'd do it all over again. I always felt very lucky and privileged, and that feeling never left me all the time we were together.

If Michael Lyons hadn't walked into the casino that night, my life would have been so different. I'd have followed my dream and enrolled at the Guildhall and then gone on to study the art of acting at RADA. Nothing would have been the same, but I have no regrets. I had a great time and my spirit and love for the arts has always shone through.

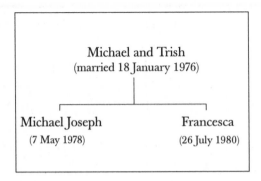

Michael and Trish
(married 18 January 1976)

Michael Joseph
(7 May 1978)

Francesca
(26 July 1980)

A Proper Glutton For Punishment

Rosemary Hurst

Signed in October 1964 as a centre-forward who had played for England schoolboys, John Hurst became the first Everton player to come on as a substitute when he replaced Fred Pickering at Stoke in August 1965. Hurst had already featured in Everton's 1965 Youth Cup-winning team and secured a regular first-team place in 1966–67, by which time he had found his optimum role, centre-back. Hurst played in the 1968 FA Cup final defeat and was ever-present during the following two seasons, the latter yielding a Championship-winning medal. He played 385 games with Everton, scoring 34 goals. He was transferred to Oldham in June 1976, where he played another five seasons before retiring, and is currently scouting for Joe Royle on behalf of Ipswich Town.

Born Rosemary Ingram, 15 September 1947,
Jersey, Channel Islands

My mum was born and brought up in Guernsey and her family were all Islanders, too. She had a great life and a good job, and remained single until she was 28, which was considered quite old back then.

Because she was getting on a bit, she met and married the wrong person, as often used to happen in those days, and, in 1939, my older sister Pat was born.

Guernsey was under German occupation during the war, so Mum and Pat were evacuated to Leeds; it was while she was there that she met my dad. At the time, he was an engineer in the royal navy and teaching at the naval college. They had a fleeting romance, fell madly in love and it didn't take her long to realise she couldn't go back to her husband. My dad had been married before, too, which was quite unusual in those days, and when the war was over they moved to Jersey, where they set up home and Dad started a building business.

In 1946, my sister Susan was born and I followed hot on her heels 13 months later. In 1949, baby Avril completed the quartet. We were blessed to have such wonderful parents: they were outgoing, romantic, modern and incredibly happy and we all loved them dearly. Both were in their late 30s, so were quite mature to have such a young family – we must have been exhausting at times. Nonetheless, it was an idyllic childhood and our house was always full of laughter.

Building restrictions on the island made it tricky for my dad to make a good living and they eventually decided there was more opportunity for his kind of work on the mainland and that England offered us all a brighter future. Mum wanted to live on the coast and Dad was a northerner, so they decided that Blackpool was the place to go. There was great excitement. We sold the house and moved in with an aunt for a couple of nights before we left – I can still remember us all being packed into her house with our new shoes under the beds, ready to start our adventure.

I was five and it was the first time I'd been on a plane. I spent the journey sitting on my dad's knee being violently sick.

Our new house wasn't ready, so we moved into a hotel. I must have been developing measles because the next thing I remember is a doctor examining me then being whisked off in an ambulance to the hospital where I was put into isolation. My poor mum – as if she didn't have enough on her plate. They put me in a bed with high sides which felt like a cot. I was broken-hearted because they thought I was a baby. When my parents came to see me, they weren't allowed in and had to look at and speak to me through a window. I'd never been away from them before and I was terrified that something awful was going to happen.

I missed my sisters terribly but was eventually allowed to leave hospital and the family took me to our new house near Stanley Park in Blackpool. They'd moved in and it all seemed so huge with its big new rooms. We settled in quickly and resumed our home life. Mum was always encouraging us to dress up, put on plays and all kinds of imaginative things like that. Each one of us had a different forte; I was always one for sewing and making things. I was very creative and must have inherited that from Dad.

My first school was Baines Endowed in Marton. I enjoyed it, but the teacher must have noticed that I couldn't see the blackboard so I was taken off to the optician's for an eye test, where they found my sight was failing. To my absolute horror, I was issued with a pair of the National Health wire-framed glasses that were indestructible and hooked behind my ears. They were awful. Mum took me to school and had to drag me out from behind her to go in the gates because I knew I was about to become an object of ridicule. It was horrible, but I think you learn to understand other people better when you've been made fun of. Kids can be very cruel, but when I look back, I think it stands you in good stead in later life. You become far more tolerant of people with difficulties.

Other than my dad doing the Pools every Saturday, none of us girls knew about football, but for some strange reason, when I was about ten, I pleaded to get a football game for Christmas. It was called Soccerette and consisted of a table marked out as a pitch with little legs about four inches high. The players had magnets underneath them and there were magnetic sticks that you put below the table to move the players around and try to score a goal. Why I should ever have wanted that, I just can't imagine, but there was something about the way it operated that captured my imagination. Sure enough, I got it for Christmas, but my mum and dad must have wondered what on earth was going on. The game was only manufactured for a few years before they stopped making it, but I loved it. To this day, I still don't know why I was attracted to it, but it was so bizarre considering the way my life turned out.

One of the most exciting memories of my childhood was the day I met Johnny. Us girls came home from school to find a tall, dark, handsome stranger in the house. He was about 24, crushingly attractive and he'd just spent five years in the army as a regular soldier. We were all instantly besotted. Then Dad told us he was our brother, his son from his first marriage, and I almost dropped dead. He was the image of Dad and we suddenly had an insight into how he'd looked in his youth. They'd spent years tracking each other down. We couldn't believe our luck; we'd always wanted a brother and now we had the best-looking one in the world.

In those days, there were still grammar schools, but my sister Susan went to the brand-new St George's comprehensive in Blackpool and, because we were so close, I wanted to go there too. I was in the year below her and had come top in the exams, so my parents were offered the chance to transfer me to the grammar school, but I wouldn't take it. I'd made friends and was settled. I didn't want to uproot and start again, much to the disappointment of my parents and my sister, who really encouraged me to go. I didn't have the confidence to go it alone; I always wanted to follow in Susan's footsteps. I was quite in awe of her and, because we were so close in age, we were best friends as well as sisters and we stayed that way right through our teens. As it turns out, if I'd left St George's, I never would have met John because he was a pupil there, too.

John was a handsome devil and had always been a star at school because he used to win all the sports competitions. He had quite a fan club – girls were always vying for his attention and that was the reason I always avoided him. He was a year older than me so we didn't socialise at all until he asked me out on a date through a friend. I took some persuading in the beginning because the last thing I wanted to be was some kind of conquest.

Eventually, we got together and started our courtship. At that time, it was only teenage stuff: we would go to the cinema or for walks or ten-pin bowling. He was great company and made me feel very special.

He'd had interest from football clubs right through school and had played for England schoolboys, so his parents had foreseen that his career would be in the game. Lots of clubs had tried to persuade him to sign, including Manchester City, Aston Villa, Wolves and, of course, Blackpool. I don't really know why he chose Everton but that was where he went as an apprentice at 15.

When he moved over to Liverpool, I thought that would be the end of it, but he asked if we could continue our courtship and he would ring me every single night from his digs. At first, he was in the youth team and his dad would drive though to watch him play at Bellefield training ground on a Saturday afternoon, then bring him home for the rest of the weekend and he'd get the 7.30 train back again on Monday morning.

I'd left school by then and was attending night school, learning shorthand and typing. I started working in a solicitor's office in Blackpool as an office junior and was hoping to work my way up to become a secretary. His parents lived near Stanley Park, too, so we could easily walk to one another's house. Then, to my horror, we sold our house and moved up the north shore to Cleveleys, which was at least two bus rides away. We thought it was the end of the world because we were quite in love by that time and didn't know how on earth we were going to be able to see each other. Neither of us could drive, but we soon passed our tests and I would borrow my dad's car or he would borrow his dad's.

When John was younger, his shoulder used to dislocate really easily and he had to have a big operation to fix it. They sent him to Broadgreen hospital during the close season when he was 17, and the operation was a great success. The next year, he went off to Australia for six weeks on a pre-season tour and to me it seemed like a lifetime. He asked if I would wait for him and I promised I would. When he came back, he asked me to marry him. We'd only just moved to Cleveleys and the front room hadn't been furnished properly; we had a three-piece suite but no carpet and there were boxes everywhere waiting to be unpacked. We were sitting in there having a coffee when he proposed. I remember putting a tea towel on the floor so he could go down on bended knee. Of course, I said yes straight away. We got engaged on my 18th birthday in September 1965.

I loved going to watch him play and loved travelling to Liverpool; everybody I met was so warm and open-hearted and had a wonderful sense of humour. I remember one evening there was an FA Cup match at Goodison against Liverpool and John asked if Susan and I wanted to come through. Susan had a Ford Prefect, her first car, and we were feeling adventurous, so we told him we would make our own way. We trundled through to Liverpool and parked in one of the little streets that led up to the ground. We'd arrived early, so we went and got ourselves a bag of chips and sat there waiting until it was time to go in. A lady came out of her house and asked us what we were doing. I told her we were waiting for the gates to open so we could go to the match. She said: 'You silly girls, why don't you come inside and eat your chips in here and I can make you a cup of tea?' We didn't go in because they'd opened the gates by then, but we couldn't get over it. We'd never met her before and she didn't know who we were, but she was prepared to let us into her house. I don't think it would have happened in Blackpool.

Our wedding was booked for 25 June 1968 during the close season, but Harry Catterick asked John to bring it forward because he wanted him to have settled into married life before the pre-season training started again. I don't know what they thought would happen to him once he got married, but they made a big deal out of it. We had to rearrange it for 25 May instead and reorganise everything, so I lost my photographer and had to send out all the invitations again – I can't imagine the club getting away with it today, but we just did as we were told in those days.

Things kept going wrong and there was a point when we didn't think the wedding was ever going to happen because Everton made it to the FA Cup final. They seemed to play lots of matches back then, much more than they do now. Just as they came up to the semi-finals, John was taken very ill. He phoned me to say he'd been hospitalised with suspected hepatitis and asked if I would go and see him and pick up his car. Then the phone got disconnected and I was absolutely frantic. The semi-final was on the Saturday and by this stage it was Monday, so I phoned Everton to speak to the secretary, Bill Dickinson. I explained that John was my fiancé and that we were getting married later in the year and that I had to go and collect his car, but he wouldn't tell me where John was. He said it was a sworn secret and that the press mustn't find out because they didn't want anyone to know what the team line-up was for the Saturday. I was pleading with him to tell me; I was so frightened.

I decided to take matters into my own hands and got on the train to Liverpool. I arrived at the club and asked to see Mr Dickinson – I was really nervous because it was so official and the wives and girlfriends weren't treated with any kind of respect. I went into his office and I can remember to this day sitting there and explaining that I'd come all the way from Blackpool, I had nowhere to go, no money and I didn't know anybody who could help me. All I wanted was for him to tell me where John was so I could pick up the car then I could get back to visit him. He refused point-blank. I walked out of the office crying and he still wouldn't tell me. He said it was an absolute secret and nobody was allowed to know. It was so barbaric. I still can't believe it to this day.

I didn't know Liverpool very well at all, but I managed to find my way to his digs at Pinehurst Avenue in Aintree, where he stayed with a wonderful lady called Mrs Barnes, who thoroughly spoilt him and was like a second mum to him. She couldn't have been lovelier if she'd tried. In fact, my children used to call her 'Grandma' when they were little because she was like a member of the family. I told her about my dilemma and then I had an idea. She didn't have a phone, so I went over the road to a phone box armed with pen and paper and rang directory enquiries. I asked them for the numbers of all the posh nursing homes in Liverpool – I said posh because I knew he would be somewhere nice.

They gave me quite a few and I started to work my way down the list until I got to Gateacre Grange. I think it's a private house now but then it was a nursing home run by nuns. For the umpteenth time, I explained who I was and who I was looking for and she said, 'Oh, yes, we have John here.' I almost wept with relief. For all their secretiveness, the club hadn't even remembered to tell the nuns not to mention it, or maybe she just felt sorry for me and couldn't bring herself to lie. I got into a taxi and went straight over. John was furious with the club for being so horrible to me.

He was very poorly all week but it wasn't as serious as they'd thought. What had happened was he'd become physically exhausted from overwork and had dehydrated. John is sallow-skinned – he tans very easily, but in the winter or if he isn't well, he looks quite yellow. Anyway, he didn't have hepatitis at all; he was just run down. He was absolutely broken-hearted that he wasn't playing in the semi-final but we sat there and listened to the game on the radio. We played Leeds and won 1–0, which meant the final against West Bromwich was on 18 May, exactly a week before our wedding date.

Because we weren't yet married, I wasn't supposed to go to Wembley as part of the official group but the club gave me permission. Maybe it was because John had been so ill and they took pity on us, but I remember Mo Harvey having to make her own way there because she was only engaged to Colin at the time. We stayed at the Waldorf and it was so plush and beautiful, but we were all devastated at the end of the match when we'd lost 1–0 after extra time.

Sir Alf Ramsey was at the dinner in the evening and he invited John to go on an England tour with the Under-23s the following Sunday. John explained that he was getting married the next week, so Sir Alf came over and asked me would I mind very much if John went away with them the day after the wedding. All the players and their wives were sitting there and there was nothing I could say other than of course I didn't mind.

John's career was everything to him and I would never have got in the way of that, but I couldn't help thinking it was pretty bad timing. Fortunately, Harry Catterick intervened and said that, because John had been ill, he didn't think it was wise for him to go, so it was taken out of my hands in the end.

Three weeks before the wedding, the shop that was making my dress burnt down and, to tell you the truth, I was beginning to think there was something standing in my way. It was unbelievable, just one thing after another, but we eventually married at St Paul's Church on Central Drive in Blackpool, the parish where we'd both been brought up. A friend took the pictures, so they were a little disappointing, but it was a lovely day and I was so proud to become Mrs Hurst.

I remember there being very little available on the market when we were house-hunting, so we decided to buy a little semi-detached in Maghull and the club told us to leave it with them to sort out. They got it surveyed and bought it, then we bought it from them. I don't think it was out of kindness – I think they just wanted to be sure John had somewhere to live. I know it sounds cynical but things were different in those days. The players weren't pampered to the same degree that they are now, especially the ones who'd been there since they were boys. Everything was regimented and the men played because they loved the game – money was never the driving force because they didn't earn that much more than your average man in the street. We were a bit better off but it wasn't silly money and you were never going to be set up for life.

We moved into our new house and I was suddenly on my own with no family, no friends, no support network and living in a strange city. I didn't really know many people but we moved next door to a couple called Dave and Mabel Nicholson and they were wonderful. We became very close and they were a great help as we settled down. They both had a fabulous sense of humour but I was always so slow – I became his stooge for years.

Just before the wedding, my dad was taken very ill. He'd been unwell for a long time and we knew that, but he was stoic and covered it up for the day. Shortly after, he was taken into hospital and had a big operation. He had a colostomy fitted but, because they wanted to protect me from worrying too much, I wasn't told that he had cancer for over a year.

He carried on for another nine years and when he finally lost his battle, it was a devastating time for us all. It was hard to be away from home then and that's why we valued Dave and Mabel so much. They always made sure I wasn't on my own and when John would go away on tours, they'd take me to the airport to meet him and bring him home again – it meant so much to us both. I owe them a lot because it was dreadfully lonely before I had the children, and they always looked out for me.

Gwen and Tommy Wright lived a couple of streets away, so we became friends and I was very close to Gordon West's wife Ann. She's the most fascinating person, she really is – vivacious, witty and so funny. She didn't give a damn about anybody, and she was fabulous company. She was an educated woman in her own right and a fantastic pianist. When we first got married, Gordon West used to pick John up when they went away so I could have the car. Pat Labone lived nearby, too. She was so stunning and we all looked up to her. She was beautiful and you never saw her when she wasn't absolutely immaculate. We went on holiday with Jan and Joe Royle a few times – we even ended up going on their honeymoon with them – and we're all still good friends to this day.

I didn't go back to work after I got married and it was quite a novelty for me to have spare time at first, because I'd worked since I had finished school. I was quite happy to be a homemaker, although I didn't have too much time to get used to it because I fell pregnant a year later.

Samantha was born in Oxford Street maternity hospital on 6 February 1970, her dad's birthday. I was overdue and they were going to induce me. I remember John was due to play the next day down in London and that the weather was horrific – we were snowed in so he took me into hospital on the Friday morning. The gynaecologist was a man called Vasant Kumar and he had said that he would have me in on the Friday and I thought that was fine because John would be away playing. John kissed me goodbye and went off to the match and I didn't expect to see him again until the Saturday night. I was excited and frightened, but I was prepared to get on with it. Then, at about 3.45 that afternoon, John walked through the door. The match had been called off, so he was able to be with me after all.

He was adamant it was going to be a girl and wouldn't even choose a boy's name because he wanted a daughter so badly. He was from a family of three boys and they'd always longed for a sister. I was convinced it would be a boy but he didn't waver once. When Sam was born, he was elated; I'd never seen him so happy. It was a wonderful day. He said it was the best birthday present he'd ever had.

John had some funny pre-match superstitions. He would only ever eat poached eggs on toast on the morning of a game and, if Everton were in a Cup run, he would never wear anything but the clothes he'd worn for the last round, and that was right down to his underwear. Another thing I noticed was, once he got on the pitch, he would kneel down and re-tie his laces. He did it every game without fail.

We moved to Ormskirk in 1974. They say new house, new baby and sure enough Alexandra was born in November 1975. She was another late delivery and the gynaecologist had agreed to induce her on the Sunday so John could be there. I was booked in at Park House in Waterloo, where a lot of the Everton babies were born. It was a natural birth but they started off the labour by drip. John and Sam took me in at lunchtime and at 12.50 they set off home again to wait for the call. At one o'clock, I got the first pains, so as soon as they got home they had to turn around and come back again. Alex was born an hour later. There was no messing around with her, and John and Sam just made it back in the nick of time.

I used to go to all the home games. John's parents would come through and I'd go to the match with his dad, and his mum would look after the children. I would sit back and watch and feel so proud. It was almost surreal because at home he was just John or Dad and was an ordinary chap, but when he was on the pitch, wearing his kit, I could feel the importance of it all and it would give me butterflies. There were thousands of people who'd paid good money to watch and, whenever he was on the ball, I just knew they were willing him on.

John was a dedicated player: he'd have died for Everton. He was incredibly loyal and was always getting injured one way or another, but it would have had to be really serious for him to stop playing. I remember one time he had a split eye and his head cut open. He went off and had stitches and came back on wearing a skullcap. He was a proper glutton for punishment.

The worst injury he came home with was when he was at Oldham and he did his Achilles tendon. He was really in agony. One of the other players brought him home and he collapsed in the hall. He was never a wimp – he was as tough as they come – but the pain was so severe he literally passed out. But he recovered and I suppose he was lucky because he didn't really suffer anything too serious and nothing that kept him out of the game for any length of time.

He only ever thought about football – it was his whole life. It took a long time for him to wind down after a match and he wouldn't sleep well at all. He used to say you never needed anyone to tell you if you hadn't played well because you were well aware of it. If he did have a bad game, it would really bother him and he would often re-live the match in bed at night. I had plenty of bruises from that because he would get quite physical. He's always been a quiet person and very deep. I sometimes thought it would have been better if he'd not kept everything bottled up inside. It might have made it easier for him if he'd lightened the load. It was the same when he was nervous about a match; he'd go very quiet and uptight and it was a bit like walking on eggshells.

Our home life was just the same as everyone else's. People imagine it would be different but it wasn't. We were just normal, working-class people. We never played it any different because we both knew that when he was in his 30s, his career would come to an end. If you believed the things that were written and allowed it to interfere with who you were, you'd have been very disappointed when it was over. I saw it happen once or twice when people found it very difficult to adjust.

John's always been a family man and the only thing that ever came before us was his football, but we didn't mind at all. People ask if it made me mad when he went away or missed Christmas, but I always said that people married sailors and they were away all the time. Christmas was the players' busiest time of the season – on the morning of the 25th, they would go straight into training then off to Alder Hey hospital to see the kids. When he came home, he could never eat his dinner because he was so upset after visiting the sick children. The club would then take them away every Christmas afternoon so they could prepare for the Boxing Day game, so we were always alone then, but we just accepted it as part of the job.

In a way, anybody who gives up working when they get married makes some kind of sacrifice and I was sometimes a bit frustrated that I never really finished my education. Although I attended night school, I always felt as if I wasn't fulfilling my potential. I didn't really make many sacrifices as such; I kept busy at home sewing and upholstering furniture and looking after the girls. I had no family nearby, so I couldn't seriously think about returning to work because there would have been nobody to look after them. I was lucky that John's job allowed me to be at home and I had the choice. I'm so glad I didn't miss a minute of them growing up. We had great fun, always inventing things to do and games to play.

John would be at home during the close season, so he was with us then. We had a wonderful family life. There are lots of young girls who I work with now at the local council who had no choice other than to go back to work as soon as their babies were a couple of months old. I was at home till Sam was eleven and Alex was five, so I had all those years with them. They were wonderful.

John's quite a homebody and has lots of hobbies. He doesn't like the winter because it keeps him indoors and he loves to be outside. He's always been mad about gardening and loves bird-watching. We've got more bird tables in our garden than they have at Martin Mere – sometimes I think we could start up our own wildlife sanctuary. He would do his share around the house and spent a lot of time with the girls, and he loved taking long walks with our dogs.

We still live in Ormskirk and it still surprises him that he's recognised in the street because those heady days of fun and football were a lifetime ago. John and Joe Royle have worked together a lot since then. They never let go of football and he would die without his teletext and the long conversations with Joe about Ipswich Town. He's still deeply involved with it mentally and would never be able to let it go. Football made him the man he is.

We might not have had as lavish a lifestyle as the players have today, but it was twice as exciting because it was all so far from what we knew. We had no idea how things should or shouldn't be; it was just how it happened. I wouldn't mind being a footballer's wife now – not because the spoils are better, but because it was a wonderful experience.

The last FA Cup final I went to was in 1995. It was a long time since I'd been to one and we were participating in a different way because John was involved with the coaching side of it then. I think you need to be involved in it to understand the importance of it, though. I was so sorry my girls had never experienced the thrill – everybody should feel that excitement once in their life. When your man walks out onto the pitch at Wembley, the pride overrides anything to do with money or status. There's nothing that can touch it and when you come home again you re-live those moments and that's when you realise how privileged you've been.

If a spectator can feel that, imagine how intense it must be for the players, and how hard it must be for them when it starts to leave them. I remember John saying he knew he was getting old because players would start running past him. That was when it started to sink in and that was the hardest time for John. Football is a gift for all of the players, like any other talent, and you can only really enjoy it if you can take it for what it is.

I don't think that would be any different today, unless the financial rewards have overtaken the love for the game. I can't comment on present-day players because I'm not part of it any more, but they seem to be pampered and, from what I can gather, only communicate through their agents. The managers barely speak to the teams these days.

When John started playing, it was like joining the army – the discipline was so strict and so regimented. There was a huge amount of respect for other players and the manager, and there wasn't all this publicity. The little things seemed very grand to us.

Just after the 1995 Cup final, John had a heart bypass operation. He hadn't been well but he never told me. We'd gone to the Charity Shield and after the game John was in another bar with the YTS boys he was coaching. Joe came over to me and told me not to worry, that John would be fine. I didn't know what he was on about so when I got home, I asked him whether there was something wrong at the club. I told him what Joe had said but he shrugged it off because he didn't want me to worry. They'd noticed he wasn't well when they were training and sent him for an angiogram. Within two months, he was back in Broadgreen having a bypass. He was in the best place to get something like that sorted and, even though Everton parted company with him when Joe left, I was really grateful because if they hadn't taken fast action, anything could have happened.

I lost my mum in 1995; that's why my sisters and I all make a special effort to keep in touch. Time passes so quickly and life gets in the way. We're still very close and meet up every couple of months for a boozy weekend, although Avril lives in South Africa now and we've not had the chance to go and visit her yet. It's hard to coordinate time off with the others, but we'll get there eventually. She has a ranch with horses in a conservation area near Hoekwil in the Western Cape. We're all desperate to go and see her.

I wouldn't have missed being a footballer's wife for the world. I look at my girls now and they have children of their own. Alex has a daughter, Katherine, and Sam has James, our first grandson, who'll soon be three, so we're all watching him closely. He seems to be left-handed and maybe he'll be left-footed too. John bought him a set of miniature golf clubs as soon as he was born. He won't be able to use them until he's about nine but they're there, waiting for him.

I've had a lovely life with all the great people that we've met and our family life was wonderful, and it's all because of football. We went to some fabulous places, met people we're still friends with to this day and did things we could only have dreamed of. I still can't believe my luck.

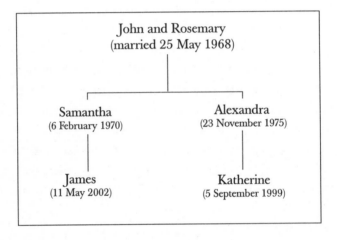

He Took My Breath Away

Celia Morrissey

So incensed was Bill Shankly when John Morrissey, then 22, was sold to Everton in 1962 for £10,000 without his say, that the Scot threatened to quit Anfield. Morrissey went on to carve out a decent career at Goodison Park, playing 311 games at outside-left, scoring 50 goals and collecting Championship medals in 1962–63 and 1969–70, and an FA Cup losers' medal in 1968. He is a successful property developer today and lives in Blundellsands, north Liverpool.

Born Celia Collister, 4 April 1941, Douglas, Isle of Man

There were four girls and two boys in our family but we were born in two batches, so Mum was a housewife who really had her work cut out for her. Lionel, Patsy and Gordon were quite grown up when she had my twin, Angela, and me. We're not identical, we don't even look like sisters; and then came the baby of the family, Betty, 18 months after us.

My father was a jack of all trades and master of none; he worked as a painter and decorator more often than not, and kept himself busy the rest of the time. I went to St Mary's Catholic school in Douglas, a mixed school where the teachers were nice to me but, to be honest, I wasn't really in love with it and always looked forward to leaving.

I was very much a homemaker. Mum would go to work in the summer because trade was, and is, very seasonal on the Isle of Man, and I was the one who would be at home doing the cleaning for her and tidying up after everyone. When she came home she would be so delighted, she'd say: 'You're the only one who ever helps me in this house.' None of the others would bother, but I was a home bird and always loved cooking, too.

John was from a family of Reds, and had signed for Liverpool not long before I met him. He was 17 when he came over to Douglas on holiday with his mum and an uncle. I was 16 and had been working in the Scottish Wool shop since I left school a year earlier. Our mothers were distant relatives, so Aunty Nelly arrived at our house to visit with John in tow. He was so handsome, the first time I saw him he took my breath away.

We went to the pictures together that evening and I suppose that's where it all began. After he went back to Liverpool we wrote to each other for months and he would phone me about twice a week. When the football season finished he came back over to the Isle of Man and it was lovely to see him again. I travelled back to Liverpool with him on the ferry, met the rest of his family and they invited me to stay for a while.

When we were apart, I missed him terribly and, after much pleading and cajoling, Mum eventually agreed that I could go over to Liverpool and lodge with John's parents at their house in Athol Street off Scotland Road so we could continue our courtship. I was 17 when I arrived.

John has three sisters and they all spoilt him rotten and all still lived at home. Both sets of parents were very old fashioned, so we didn't live together as a couple because that was completely out of the question. But there was plenty of space in the house, so we had separate rooms and some nights we would go to the pictures or dancing at the weekend.

He was a really dedicated player who loved football and took it very seriously. He hardly drank, never smoked and was always in bed really early, so sometimes I'd go out dancing with his sister Kitty. All we used to do was dance – we didn't even start drinking until we were about 21. John likes a drink now, but still goes to bed early.

John's dad was a docker and had opened a shop on the Wirral selling bits of furniture, and his mum bought a grocery shop on Scotland Road, around the corner from the house. I would help her out from time to time to earn a bit of extra money, and give her a hand around the house whenever I could.

In the summer of 1962, Everton made John an offer he couldn't refuse. Bill Shankly was away scouting in Scotland and when John returned to Anfield after a training session, there was a message that Harry Catterick was waiting to speak to him in Shankly's office. Catterick told him Everton had put in a bid of £10,000, that they would increase his wages from £17 to £20 a week and that he would be guaranteed first-team football starting the very next Saturday. They agreed the deal and John was told to go to Goodison that afternoon, where he would be unveiled to the press.

Shankly returned shortly afterwards and was so furious the deal had been done without his knowledge that he threatened to walk out. He rang John and told him there had been a mistake and that he was part of his plans for Liverpool's future. He told him to ring Everton and tell them he had changed his mind. There was a bit of to-ing and fro-ing but there was no going back and John became a Blue that afternoon. For the next few years, whenever he played against Liverpool, the fans would shout 'Traitor' and 'Judas' at him but it was nothing he couldn't handle. As soon as the wage cap was lifted in 1962, his money rose to £35 a week.

As promised, he made his Everton debut against Sheffield Wednesday the next Saturday, in August 1962, and they won 4–1. I was at that game with a Liverpool reserve player who used to be John's room-mate called Alan Jones. It was a bit strange to watch him play football – I'd never been to a match before – but all the same I quite enjoyed it, even if I didn't really know what was going on.

I didn't go to many games; Saturday was the day I would get my hair done, but I used to look forward to the match finishing because that was always a big night out. We'd usually go the Lord Nelson for a meal and some weeks we'd meet up with Pat and Jimmy Gabriel then we'd all go to the Royal Tiger Club. It was the time of Beatlemania and, even now, when I hear a Beatles song, it reminds me of those days. We'd be on the street waiting to go in and the music would be belting down the stairs. We used to love dancing. Not many of the players would get up on the floor but John was a great mover.

I wasn't allowed to join the players and their wives on their trip to Spain in celebration of their 1963 League win because it was in May and we didn't get married until June. The club didn't want to be seen encouraging that kind of behaviour, but I did go to Wembley with them, twice.

The first was in 1966 and I was there again two years later. John didn't play in 1966; he'd injured an ankle and wasn't fit, and neither was Fred Pickering, so they swapped the side around a bit and brought in Mike Trebilcock, who ended up scoring twice. Who knows what would have happened if John had played. The history books would have been written differently, that's for sure.

The men had gone down to London on the Thursday so they could get settled in and the wives went a day later. We travelled down on the train from Lime Street and were booked into the Waldorf, which was a beautiful, majestic place. We went for a meal and to watch a show at the theatre on the Thursday night. I remember spending most of my time with Gwen Wright, Tommy's wife.

John and I got engaged when I was 20 but my mum died tragically young a year later. She was the person I had most time for and it broke my heart that she didn't see me married. We had a white wedding, five years after we met, on 22 June 1963 at St Anthony's Catholic church on Scotland Road and we had the reception in the Lord Nelson. A few players were there, Alex and Jean Parker, and Nancy and Alex Young, and my little sister, Betty, was my bridesmaid.

After the wedding, we moved into our first house in Aintree Lane. It had three bedrooms and cost £3,500 and we really thought we'd made it to the big time. At the same time, we were worried we'd be paying off the mortgage for the rest of our lives. Pat Gabriel lived round the corner and so did Alex and Nancy, before they moved out to Aughton. Pat and I had our babies around the same time so we'd sometimes see each other at the clinic and have a natter.

Our first son, John, was born in March 1965 at Park House nursing home in Waterloo. He was due on the Sunday but arrived on the Monday night. John Snr wasn't at the birth – the men didn't do things like that in those days, they just dropped you at the hospital and off they went to wet the baby's head.

John didn't have much spare time because he had a little newspaper shop near Oriel Road in Bootle. He'd go training and then he'd pop into the shop and see if anything was happening or needed doing. He was very hard working and ambitious, and always wanted a better life. He was very sensible, considering he was so young.

On the pitch, John had a reputation for being a hard player and he often came home badly injured. When he was still with Liverpool, he got involved in some kind of a scrum against Portsmouth: there were fists and boots flying and he ended up with a broken jaw. He's also had teeth knocked out and his nose was broken two or three times. One time was against Leeds, courtesy of Norman Hunter, and another was when he played against Liverpool in the FA Cup semi-final in 1971. He was caught up in a mêlée so he wasn't sure who was responsible, but when the dust settled Larry Lloyd and Chris Lawler were closest to him.

I suppose we were quite well off at that time, but it was nothing compared with what they earn today. Towards the end of his playing days, John was earning £100 a week. Everton were known as the 'Mersey Millionaires' and they had 50,000 or so fans paying in every week, but I think it was the club that made big money, not the players. There was a crowd bonus and a bit of extra money for winning the game on top of the basic, so I suppose we were quite comfortably off really.

It was a penalty in the semi-final against Leeds that got us through to the 1968 FA Cup final. I was pregnant with Stephen at the time, but I was at the game. Alan Ball was injured and Harry Catterick told John that if there were any penalties, he'd be taking them. I remember sitting with my head in my hands when the moment arrived because I couldn't even look. It seemed to take the longest time and I only looked up when I heard the screams and knew it had gone in. A newspaper photographer came to our house on the Sunday morning and took John and young John down to the canal. The next day's papers were full of pictures of them with a little tiddler in a jam jar.

Aunty Nelly looked after John Jnr when I went in to have my second baby. Stephen was born on 9 November 1968 and weighed in at 8lb 9oz. It was a Saturday morning and Everton were playing Ipswich at Portman Road – the match couldn't have been further away. They drew 2–2.

John phoned Park House before the game and the sister told him he had another son. He didn't get to see us until the Sunday because Ipswich is so far away and they didn't get home until really late at night. The nuns were lovely to me: Mother Monica was a beautiful person and Sister Celia was lovely as well. She took me up to the operating theatre and made me feel really at home, which was just as well because you had to stay in for a fortnight in those days after a Caesarean.

I was lucky we didn't need to move house because we stayed in the Northwest when John finished at Everton in May 1972, and he played a season with Oldham before retiring. After his success at Goodison, his interest wasn't there any more and he only played a handful of games before he hung up his boots in the summer of '73. The passion was gone and it made training and recovering from injury that much harder. He still follows football, loves watching it on the television, and we watched young John play professionally all the time. It's a little bit unusual for a footballer to have a son who can play too.

John Jnr signed for Everton as an apprentice when he was 17 but he was only there for a couple of years. Howard Kendall, the manager at the time, released him in 1985. Although he signed up with Wolves, John had to commute every day and his dad told him to move down there or leave. He used to get up at 6.30 in the morning to get to Wolves in time for training, and that was the same every weekday. He was spending so much time on the road, it was taking away from his game.

He went to Tranmere and ended up staying for about 12 years and playing almost 600 games; he really loved it. We would go on a Saturday to watch him and really enjoyed it. I preferred watching him to watching John because I wasn't as keyed up about it. Stephen was also on Everton's books for a short time, but they both work with their dad now, buying and selling property.

When I weigh everything up, I don't think I made any sacrifices for John's career. I've always been the motherly and homely type. When I look back, I think if I had my time over, I'd have liked to be a beautician or something like that, but even so I've had a good life and I'm happy with my lot. I loved being at home, bringing up the children and cooking nice meals. It suited me down to the ground.

Given the chance, I don't think I'd like to be a footballer's wife now, though. There seems to be an awful lot of pressure on the players and the wives. We were lucky in the '60s because football gave us a great start in life. Now, we have a place in Florida and usually spend four months a year out there, on and off, between October and March, and that way we miss the worst of the English weather.

No matter where we go, though, somebody will recognise John even though his hair is completely white now. Of course, now they're all of a certain age, but it doesn't matter where we are in the world, there will be somebody who wants to shake his hand or come over and say hello.

We were in Disney World in Orlando with my son and two of our grandchildren a while back and somebody shouted over to him. It doesn't really surprise me, because Evertonians are like that – they remember everyone who played for them and they cherish them. I think John quite likes it when it happens. It makes him smile.

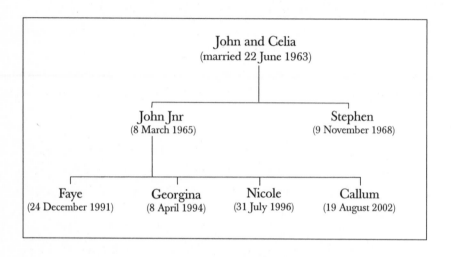

John and Celia
(married 22 June 1963)

John Jnr
(8 March 1965)

Stephen
(9 November 1968)

Faye
(24 December 1991)

Georgina
(8 April 1994)

Nicole
(31 July 1996)

Callum
(19 August 2002)

Music Was My Heartbeat

Ann West

Gordon West joined Everton from Blackpool for £27,500 in March 1962, 'a world record that will never be broken', according to the press, as the miner's son from Barnsley became Harry Catterick's first signing. Athletic, agile, determined and composed, West played in goal 399 times for Everton and collected a full complement of medals before leaving the club in 1973. Tempted back out of retirement by Tranmere Rovers in October 1975, he played 17 games in total and provided first-team cover for four years before calling it a day. He appeared three times for England and it would probably have been more but he withdrew from the 1970 World Cup squad for family reasons. He now lives in Waterloo, Liverpool.

Born Ann Pickup, 10 August 1942, Blackpool

Collegiate Grammar was an all-girls school in Blackpool; I was quite academic, enjoyed it very much and left with five O levels, two A levels and a scholarship to the Royal College of Music (RCM). The great love of my life was music and I've often wondered why.

My mum was six and Edie, her youngest sister, only five when their mum died and they went to live in Blackpool with their older sister Emmie, who was nineteen. Mum was quite musical and would have loved to have followed that path but there was never any spare money. Instead, she resolved that when she grew up she would have a daughter named Ann who would play the piano. I went to ballet lessons, like most little girls do, and think I was given the choice of ballet and piano. Fortunately, I chose the piano because, the size of me now, God help us all.

I was born in Aunty Emmie's guest house during the war into a nearly all-female household: Aunty, her husband Walter, their two daughters, Marie and Dorothy, my mum and Edie. Mum managed a tobacco and fancy goods shop at the time and Dad was doing his national service. He saw me the day after I was born then was posted to the Middle East, Greece and Italy. The next time he saw me was in January 1946 when he was demobbed and resumed his job as a carpet and furniture salesman.

I was five when Mum and Dad bought the guest house next door to Emmie's and that was about the time I began studying piano. As far as I can remember, I was a conformist and a very well-behaved child who only became noisier with age.

There was always lots of family around; my grandparents and Dad's sisters, Elsie and Hilda, lived two streets away and we had a constant stream of visitors from Easter until the Blackpool Illuminations ended in November. Everyone in my family could turn their hand to anything, from waiting on tables to peeling potatoes, washing up, making beds and cleaning. We offered three cooked meals a day for 10/6 and had a hectic life, with Dad staying up to serve biscuits to anyone who wanted them and redecorating during the winter break, all the while holding down his full-time job. We all developed a strong work ethic because we never stopped. They were happy days and we laughed a lot.

Music was my heartbeat. I played a lot of duets with my friend Valerie, who travelled on her own from Preston to Blackpool for piano lessons from the age of nine, and we shared our first attempt at smoking after winning five Woodbines on a slot machine and carefully cutting them in half. It was a bad move – she still smokes to this day and I only gave up in 1995. I accompanied the Blackpool Girls' Choir from the age of 12, played a Mozart concerto with the National Youth Orchestra of Great Britain when I was 13 and played live on television at 15. We even did concert tours of Norway, so I've actually played on Edvard Greig's piano – it was quite something to be allowed to do that and I felt incredibly honoured that I was granted permission.

I was 13 when my sister Susan was born – now there was a surprise for us all. Like me, she was born in Emmie's guest house but she arrived in September, during the Illuminations, when it was packed with visitors. I was absolutely thrilled to bits to have a sister because it was so unexpected. It had never crossed my mind I might have any siblings.

Sue was a breath of fresh air, turned life upside down and didn't sleep through the night until she was about four. She was a complete tomboy who always seemed to be standing on her hands and causing ructions. She was very musical, too, but, unlike me, she had a wonderful voice and sang solo with the Blackpool Girls' Choir, also live on television. She was very temperamental and didn't like performing. I can remember her throwing a complete wobbly before an event, then singing beautifully, as if nothing had happened. My poor mum.

There's such an age gap that we never fell out and Sue can't even remember me living at home. She was my bridesmaid when she was six and she's actually closer in age to my kids than to me, so she was very much like their big sister and they were very close. I remember when Alan Ball lived over the road from us in digs in Blackpool and he used to knock round for Susan to see if she was coming out to play.

My family all liked football; Mum and Dad even went to Wembley when Blackpool beat Bolton in the 'Stanley Matthews Final' in 1953, so I suppose when we heard these friends of ours had young footballers – Gordon West and Malcolm Starkey – staying at their guest house, it seemed like quite a good idea to go and have a look at them. I'd left school by then and I think I was just killing time before I took up my scholarship at the Royal College of Music in London the following month.

It was Gordon's great sense of humour that struck me the most. I was quite enchanted. He was so charismatic, good-looking and different from anybody I'd ever met before. I was 17 years old and had been surrounded by academics, musicians and people from completely different backgrounds all my life, so his individuality played a big part in the excitement and the attraction. He was 17, too, and we had our first date in August 1960, shortly before I left for London and four months before he made his Blackpool debut in December.

While I was at the RCM, I shared a flat with a girl from the Wirral and travelled home on the train at the weekends so Gordon and I could continue our courtship. I wanted to enter into the spirit of things, so I supported Tottenham Hotspur for one game because I thought it would be like going to watch Blackpool but with a few more people, and I went to see Gordon whenever he played against a London club. He would get me a ticket and I would meet him briefly before the match then wave him off on the bus afterwards.

After a year in the Smoke, I transferred to Manchester Royal College of Music, which was much more enjoyable, and it meant I could live at home. Gordon and I would go out for dinner to the Lobster Pot in Blackpool, where they served the finest scampi and steak, followed by a visit to the Clifton Hotel opposite the North Pier, where we'd drink Pimms.

When we got engaged in January 1962, Gordon moved into my parents' guest house. He did his share of helping out and the long winter nights would see us in front of the fire with Gordon making lamps from empty liquor bottles. He used to love the mixed grill that my mum served up when I got home from college in Manchester. A fine offering of steak, chops, mushrooms, bacon, sausages, egg, liver, beans, tomatoes, fried bread and chips. When his dad visited, he would request a special serving of it for him, too. It was fit for a king.

After about nine months in Manchester, I decided I'd had enough of college so I packed it in. I'd always played the piano at concerts and found when you go to college that stops because you're too busy learning your trade and there aren't the venues available. I'd been so used to playing all over the place that I found it quite strange not to be performing. Looking back, I think what I needed was a gap year, but they were unknown back then; you just had to get on with it. I didn't give up music for Gordon; I just stopped because I'd had enough.

Harry Catterick had come to watch him play a few times and in March 1962, backed by John Moores' millions, signed him for £27,500, making Gordon the most expensive goalkeeper in the world. Catterick wanted all his players to be married and settled, so he actively encouraged it and we were wed in June 1962. It took us six weeks to organise the wedding – I don't know what these people who plan them for months and months in advance are thinking about, they must be mad.

The wedding was wonderful. I'm a bit of a showbiz-type person so getting done up in a wedding dress was fabulous. We married in the Holy Trinity church in South Shore, Blackpool. It was quite a big bash – we had about 100 people there and, although that's nothing to how they are today, we had a nice do at the Cliffs Hotel in Blackpool then flew from Manchester to Paris for a week's honeymoon. We were both 19 and it was the first time I'd ever flown.

Nearly all the Everton players lived in Maghull and we moved into a nice three-bedroom semi at 81 Claremont Avenue and I thought it was wonderful. Micky Lill was an Everton player and he had lived there before he'd been transferred to Plymouth. Micky and his wife must have taken in lodgers because Jimmy Gabriel's name was on a shelf in the airing cupboard. After the bright lights of Blackpool, Maghull was a real shock to my system. It was like living in a backwater and, although it was only an hour away from home, my mother always used to protest that it was too far.

Beryl Harris, Brian's wife, and I became great friends and we were very close for a long time. I must have driven her mad because, having given up everything to be Gordon's wife in Maghull, I had nothing to do – I used to pop round there every morning to visit her. She lived a bus ride away in Lydiate, near the Coach and Horses pub, which was very handy for Brian, and he often used to pop out for a 'shovel full of coal'. She had a son called Mark, who was a baby at the time, and a few years later had Ian, and I would be there all the time. The other person I was really very close to was Rose Hurst. We were both from Blackpool and spent a lot of time together. We saw quite a lot of Pat and Brian Labone, too. We didn't do anything spectacular; we just went round to each other's houses, had coffee, chatted and looked after the kids. I liked a lot of the other wives but I didn't see much of them other than at the match.

I was at a terrible loose end and, three months after I married, I started my professional career when I was asked to play at the Blackpool Music Festival as an accompanist. From then on, I worked freelance.

Just before we arrived at Everton, there was a ceiling on wages of £20 a week. Shortly afterwards, they lifted the cap and they were hailed as the £100-a-week footballers. I think Gordon's new contract gave him £45 a week but that was a lot then, and there were win bonuses and extra money for big crowds, so it did add up, especially if they were on a winning streak and the supporters were pouring in. In 1963, they were earning significantly more than the average man in the street. I look at it as being £100 a week when the normal man's wage was about £10, so we were very well off.

It was nothing to what it is today and, if you want my opinion, I think it's immoral and obscene and it's not doing these kids any good at all. That they can earn in a week what a nurse earns in five years. It just can't be right and it's spoiling football. They're no longer interested in winning and they can't be disciplined because, even if they're dropped, they still get paid these extortionate amounts. There can't be any incentive for them to win any more.

I was about five months pregnant when we won the League in 1963 and the club took us to Torremolinos. I was so cheeky. I'd been invited to do a concert that clashed with us being away, and I asked John Moores if he would pay for Gordon and me to go separately so I didn't miss it. He said no and we all had to go together. Looking back, it was a bit of a liberty, but you're like that when you're young.

Torremolinos was very interesting. Can you imagine it in 1963? It was nothing more than a building site. We stayed at a beautiful hotel called Las Tres Carabelas, but when I went back 20 years later, I didn't recognise the place. It was horrendous. We had a lovely swimming pool and there wasn't a lot to do besides sit around the pool, eat and drink, but how luxurious to be taken away for a fortnight. I was quite big by that stage and I'll always remember one of the reporters ringing up for some reason after Stephen was born and telling me that he hadn't realised I was pregnant. He must have just thought I was fat.

I would go to all the home matches and when I had the children they would go over to my mum and dad's quite a lot of weekends. They were fantastic grandparents and Steve and Mark have great memories of their time with them and their cousins, Jonathan and Daniel, who lived close by. I can only imagine the mischief they got up to with Sue, only eight years older, joining in too.

It wasn't really strange to watch Gordon play. I was used to performing myself, so it was second nature to me and I don't think I let myself in for anything I couldn't handle. I felt very proud of him, though, and I can remember the first England cap he won. I flew from Speke airport to London and went to watch him at Wembley. They played Wales and I don't think there was a big crowd but I felt enormously proud watching him when the national anthem was played.

A lot of the players would go out to clubs on a Saturday night but we weren't into that scene at all. I liked to have a drink, but I didn't go to nightclubs. I suppose the local pubs were the Punchbowl, the Meadows or the Coach and Horses. We'd go for a meal or to the pub but I was never part of the Royal Tiger scene. The Tiger was a club in the city centre, where loads of the players and their wives went most Saturday nights.

I'm a very sociable person, even more so now than when we were married, but I think what really bothered me was that I was never sure if people liked you for who you were, or if it was for what you were. I didn't like that uncertainty. I'm sure a lot of them were genuine and good people, but if you went out for a meal with non-footballers or as a couple, then people could be rude. I think they should leave you alone when you're out privately. We weren't bothered that much but it was always in the back of my mind that people wouldn't have been there if Gordon wasn't an Everton player. Having said that, we did have some very good friends: Vera and Tony Pope, and Gwen and Eddie Owen, and lots of neighbours who I hope liked us, too.

Gordon did get very uptight and nervous before a game and I think that's well documented. The players and coaching staff didn't know much about digestion and diets back then, and they used to eat the wrong food – their pre-match meal was steak and toast. He used to get very anxious before a match because he is a nervy kind of bloke – I think it's folklore now about how ill he was – but that's the way it should be. Nerves play a big part when you're a performer and it puts the edge on your game. I don't think you should be there if you're not nervous and I believe that even Stan Matthews used to throw up before games.

I can remember Gordon getting very annoyed one night because he had a match and people were coming over from Blackpool to watch, so they would be coming back to the house afterwards for supper. I wasn't a great housekeeper and I thrust a vacuum cleaner in his hand and asked him to get the lounge smartened up a bit before we went to the game. I don't think he had too much time to let his nerves get to him that night. Looking back, it was terrible of me but it was a job that needed to be done and I was often on my hands and knees cleaning the kitchen floor before playing with the Liverpool Philharmonic, if people would be coming back to the house afterwards.

Whether he had any superstitions in the dressing-room, I can't say, but he had none at home. He wouldn't have worn the same clothes for

ABOVE: Rosemary and John Hurst

INSET: Rosemary Hurst with her first baby, Samantha, in
Oxford Street maternity hospital, February 1970

ABOVE: Brian and Pat Labone
with their racehorse, Goodison

INSET: Brian and Pat Labone at the races

Michael and Trish Lyons, 1980

Gordon and Irene Lee, St Luke's Church in Cannock, September 1955

Gordon and Irene Lee at home in Lytham with their children (from left): Christine, Gary and Sharon (© *Daily Star*)

Torremolinos, May 1963 (from left): Jimmy and Pat Gabriel and Johnny Morrissey slake their thirst (© Jose Antonio)

John and Celia Morrissey, St Anthony's, Liverpool, 22 June 1963

'I think he's found the fountain of eternal youth': Brenda and Dave Thomas, 2003

Dave and Brenda Thomas on their wedding day at Romaldkirk, North Riding, Yorkshire, December 1972

'Alex was demobbed on the Friday night and we married the next day, in Newtongrange church': Alex and Nancy on their wedding day, 15 July 1961

Nancy and Alex Young at Butlins in Ayr, July 1957

Ann and Gordon West at Holy Trinity, South Shore, Blackpool, June 1962 (© Blackpool Gazette & Herald Ltd)

Ann and Gordon West with two-week-old Stephen at home, October 1963 (© Newspix)

Tony and Marina Kay,
Parsons Cross, Sheffield,
28 September 1957

Marina and Tony Kay celebrate
their last night in Sheffield before
his transfer, 1962

Tony Kay with Toni, Russell, Jamie and Ricky at home in Aintree, Liverpool
(© DC Thomson)

Carole and Martin Dobson marry in Burnley, June 1987

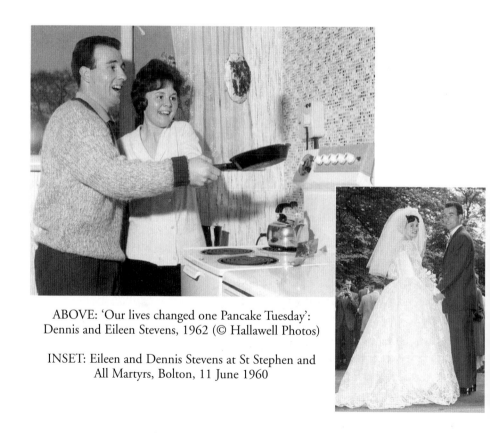

ABOVE: 'Our lives changed one Pancake Tuesday':
Dennis and Eileen Stevens, 1962 (© Hallawell Photos)

INSET: Eileen and Dennis Stevens at St Stephen and
All Martyrs, Bolton, 11 June 1960

Joe and Janet Royle at St Mary's
in West Derby Village,
Liverpool, June 1970

Joe and Janet Royle with Lee, aged two
weeks, April 1971

'They all love their football and they're all Evertonians':
the Royle family, 1995 (© Gemini Photography)

ABOVE: Jimmy and Pat Gabriel step out before an all-star cast (left to right): Alex Young, Bobby Collins, George Thompson, Alex Parker, Roy Vernon, Billy Bingham and Micky Lill

INSET: Pat and Jimmy Gabriel shopping in Edinburgh

Jimmy, Pat and Karen Gabriel, 1963 (© DC Thomson)

consecutive matches because they were probably still in the laundry basket.

Typical boys, my sons were both born on really inconvenient match-day Saturdays. They were both born at home because my mum had her children that way and I saw no reason not to carry on the tradition. I was very lucky, looking back, but you don't consider any risks when you're young. It's only as you get older you start to think more about situations.

Stephen came into the world on 5 October 1963. I'd taken cod liver oil on the Thursday to try to bring on the birth; I needed him to come because I was due to start work a fortnight later. I don't think the cod liver oil worked – all it did was give me terrible stomach ache – and he decided to be born on the Saturday lunchtime, by which time Gordon had gone off to play at Birmingham. Derek Temple and Tony Kay scored that day and we won 2–0.

Mark was even better. Again, Gordon was away because Everton were playing Liverpool in the fifth round of the FA Cup at Goodison the next day. I went to stay with neighbours, so I wasn't on my own and I got up the next morning, went home, lit the fire and thought 'I'm having this baby'. I rang my friend, who was a nurse, then rang the midwife and she suggested I might just be excited because it was a match day. I told her no, so she told me to get into bed and headed over. Mark was born about two hours later. The match was an evening kick-off on 11 March 1967. Gordon rang up before the game and I told him he had another son. Alan Ball got the winner that night and Mr Catterick very kindly sent me a bunch of flowers.

Other than occasions such as that, I don't know that I ever had many dealings with the club. The fact that there was no players' lounge and the wives were left standing out in the street did used to bother me a little, but I don't remember being furious about it.

I remember once Yorkshire Television came over to film our lives and showed it on television, and another evening when we were watching *A Question of Sport* with the kids and a picture of Gordon and I came on. Strangely enough, they didn't get Gordon and they thought I was a model.

We were quite happy to get the kids to bed at 7.30 and sit in chatting or watching the television. In the beginning, we spent a lot of time going over to Blackpool at the weekends because there was so much more to do there but, as Gordon got used to Liverpool, he didn't go to Blackpool as frequently. I still went over most weekends for piano lessons and to take the kids to see their grandparents. I'm sure Gordon socialised more in his later years but not early on and, in those days, he actually didn't drink very much and neither did I. We'd get the kids to bed, make a cup of coffee and watch the telly. Looking back, it seems pretty boring.

The team didn't go away too often pre-season, not like they do now, but I remember when they went to Australia for six weeks when Stephen was a baby. I would have wished he hadn't gone for so long, but more often than not they used to go to Llandudno or Blackpool for weekends of 'special training', and I didn't mind that at all, it was just part of the job.

Going to Wembley was absolutely great and I remember real excitement at the thought of it. We all went on the train together from Lime Street station, then we were herded into the hotel and went to see the Joe Brown show in the evening. I don't think clubs would get away with shunting everybody around like that now, but it was all part of the excitement then and we were so young we didn't question very much.

We were 2–0 down and suddenly Mike Trebilcock scored two. It was unheard of. He'd hardly had a game before that and was only brought in at the last minute when Fred Pickering was injured. When Derek Temple sealed the victory, we were shrieking with delight. I've still got the photo of Princess Margaret presenting Labby with the Cup and Gordon is beside him – that was a fabulous day. We had a good night, too, but I seem to remember we had an even better night two years later after we'd lost. I think we drank more and tried harder to compensate for the bitter disappointment.

The second time we got to Wembley, in 1968, we stayed at the Waldorf again, and it was still as posh. After our night out, we all went back to my room for a drink. I remember ringing down to the bar to ask them to bring a bottle of something up to the room and being politely told that we might have had enough already. I think it was done in a nice way but they made themselves clear. We weren't over the top or anything, because in those days you didn't do such things, but they thought we'd had enough and, to be honest, they were probably right. Still, we got the bottle we wanted in the end.

I remember us ladies sitting around talking about the dresses we were going to wear for the after-match dinner. I'd bought mine from Lytham in Lancashire and it cost 25 guineas, which was quite a lot in those days. Maureen Temple started to describe hers and it dawned on me that it was exactly the same only in a different colour. I thought I would go out on the Saturday morning and try to find something different but I couldn't, of course, so we just kept well away from each other.

I'm sure Everton did a lap of honour as losers in 1968 – the first time it had happened – and Gordon led the way. I can also remember Alan Ball throwing his losers' medal on the floor. It was the most wretched feeling you could ever imagine.

I decided to go and teach music in Seaforth, north Liverpool, for a while and did a bit of 'concerting'. Then I decided that I wouldn't mind playing with the Liverpool Philharmonic Orchestra, so I went and auditioned with them and did two concerts. I didn't make any sacrifices for Gordon's career and he wouldn't have wanted me to. I did keep a scrapbook of our achievements and I've still got it now. It's a bit tatty but it's still here. In it are newspaper cuttings from when Gordon declined to go to the 1970 World Cup in Mexico. I don't know why he made that decision, but he did and it was totally his choice.

The England squad went to Mexico for ten days or so the year before, to get the players acclimatised. Gordon Banks's dad died and he was sent home so Gordon played, but he injured his shoulder and Peter Shilton was flown out to replace him. When Gordon came back, he made up his mind that he wouldn't be going the next year and it absolutely amazed me.

In a way, I was pleased that he didn't want to go but I'm not sure he gave the real reason for his decision. He didn't like being away from home for that long and, again, I guess nerves played a part in it, because that really was the world stage, but he made that choice. I daresay it wasn't the best decision he made in his career but you can't turn back time.

He was second to Gordon Banks and they were in their prime at the same time but, on his day, I think Gordon West was much better. It was hard for him to break in and when he had that chance, he could have made his mark but he chose not to. If he'd decided to go, we might have seen a different set-up altogether, but we all know that hindsight is a wonderful thing. Gordon Banks didn't have too many bad games and was less flamboyant, but Gordon West was a great keeper and I suppose that decision practically finished his international career.

I don't know whether he regrets it, but I suppose he does now. I know I got blamed for him not going and, thinking back, there were times when I asked him not to go on tour. Who would want their husband to go away for a long time? But, to be honest, I'd have been quite pleased for him to go. So, next time you see Labby, tell him to stop making up stories about me.

I didn't hate anything really about being a footballer's wife, but I've been ex-directory since we got home from a derby game where we'd been beaten 5–1 and somebody rang up and shouted 'Thanks, Gordon!' and hung up again. We had a couple of calls in the middle of the night, too, and that was quite menacing, but as far as people knocking on the door, that didn't really happen apart from the young kids knocking round for Stephen and Mark to go out to play.

In 1971, we decided that one of us needed to get qualified in something because his career would eventually come to an end and he wasn't qualified in anything other than playing football. I encouraged Gordon to try and get into teaching because he was a really hands-on father and very good with kids, but I'd already got A levels so I could go back to college or university easily to gain some qualifications.

A bloke who taught at CF Mott training college in Prescot said they had a beautiful Bosendorfer piano from the BBC Manchester studios at the college and asked if I wanted to go and see it. It was wonderful and I fell in love with it. I knew a lot of people at Liverpool University and when the professor there knew I wanted to go back into education, he said I could go there, but I felt that was going to be too academic for me – and they had this beautiful piano at CF Mott. In the end, that was the deciding factor. So that was where I went to train as a teacher. The day I started teaching in 1974 at St Dominic's Catholic school, I had to ask for the morning off to go and get divorced. My lifelong friend Joanne, who's a professional singer, accompanied me to the court for moral support, and I've accompanied her in a musical capacity ever since. I had no concept of how awful divorce was and the terrible effects it can have on a person's life, and it took me a long time to get over it.

I taught for 20-odd years, initially in Huyton, where I stayed until 1977, then I married Ray and moved to the Isle of Wight. He was teaching craft, design and technology when we met at St Dominic's. I brought my parents from Blackpool to the island in 1998 so they'd be closer to me.

Sue went over to Australia in 1977 for three months for a 'look around' with her fiancé Paul and they've been there ever since. They've been married for 25 years now and have two teenage children, Ben and Louise, and have settled in Mount Lawley, Western Australia. In spite of the distance, we're still very close. I've visited seven or eight times and in 1992 I went out there for a year on an exchange. My parents loved Australia, too, and I go back as frequently as I can. It's like a second home to me.

Ray got a job teaching in the international school in Papua New Guinea. They wanted us to go as a couple but my mum was unwell then so it wasn't a good time for me to leave. I went over there a couple of times when I retired from teaching, though. An exciting, if rather terrifying, thing happened one time I was there. I was booked to play an outdoor concert and was just about to sit down at the piano when, in true Hollywood style, a gun was fired just outside the venue. It turned out to be not too serious, just an attempted hijacking, which was quite run of the mill in Port Moresby.

Mum made her recovery and things were looking up, then a routine operation went wrong and had to be repeated and I lost her in 2003. It was totally unexpected and I still find it hard to believe she's gone.

Where my boys are concerned, Steve is a mad Evertonian and Mark used to say he supported Liverpool, but I think that was just to cause trouble. In fact, he had a season ticket for Southampton a couple of years ago. I think he loves football but nobody in particular. They both play a lot of football, both in goal, and I think they could have been professionals if they'd had the dedication but I imagine it was too demanding because it takes over your whole life.

They didn't do music and I didn't force it on them at all. Stephen did start to learn the piano and now, like everybody, regrets not having continued. He seemed to have a natural talent for it and he also started learning the violin and the oboe, but I'm sure he wouldn't like to be reminded of that. Mark is married to Lisa and they have children of their own now but he played and trained for Lancashire at tennis before we left the Northwest for the Isle of Wight, and went on to do the same for Hampshire for a time. I think going across the water on the ferry to training on cold Friday nights really tested his dedication. It became too much for him in the end, but they both play a very good game. They were very sport-minded and I thought that would always keep them off the streets. Snooker, cricket, golf, football, anything to do with sport they had a love for, but Stephen's true passion is Everton. He travels the length and breadth of the land following the Blues and in 1985 he travelled to Czechoslovakia. He's made it his business to follow them everywhere; he's just mad about them.

It doesn't surprise me that Gordon still has legendary status because Evertonians remember everybody who ever played for them, so he's in the right place to have that sort of recognition. He was pretty famous at the time and, wherever we went, people would recognise him. I remember on holiday in Spain and Italy people came up to him in the street – in fact, I've just returned from Madeira, where I bumped into an Everton season-ticket holder and it took only moments before Gordon's name was mentioned. It's probably because his career was cut quite short that his name isn't the first one that springs to mind when people think of a goalie – they think of Banks, Shilton and Bonetti – but when you go back into the record books, he did have a very good career.

I wouldn't like to be a footballer's wife now, although I would like the money, but not really for myself. I would give it away so my family had mortgage-free houses. I'm happy just settling down to be a quiet-ish 60 year old. I still can't get over the sheer delight of being a grandmother. The fair at Ryde is not quite Blackpool pleasure beach but it provides Mark's kids and I with endless hours of fun.

I'm sure the current footballers' wives love it but some of them are famous in their own right so they're not short of a few bob either. They live a completely different life now, and I'm absolutely sure they wouldn't live in a three-bedroom semi in Maghull. I can't say that I'd like to be a part of what it's become now, but I have very few regrets, and I really mean that.

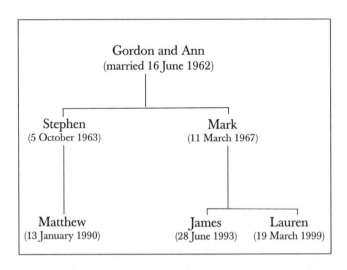

Gordon and Ann
(married 16 June 1962)

Stephen
(5 October 1963)

Mark
(11 March 1967)

Matthew
(13 January 1990)

James
(28 June 1993)

Lauren
(19 March 1999)

They Were The Best Years Of Our Lives

Norma Vernon

A fiery Welshman, who Everton rejected as a schoolboy, Roy Vernon, 'Taffy', eventually signed from Blackburn for £27,000 in February 1960 and finished as top scorer in each of his four seasons, captaining the 1962–63 Championship-winning side. In all, he played 200 games and scored 110 goals at Everton. Vernon fell foul of the disciplinarian manager, Harry Catterick, on several occasions and in March 1965 joined Stoke for £40,000, where he spent five generally productive seasons before finishing his career with a handful of games for Halifax in 1969–70. Nobody can recall him missing a penalty – even in training – and he was capped 32 times by Wales. Sadly, he died in December 1993.

Born Norma Tierney, 26 July 1937, Darwen, Blackburn

There were little benches behind the goals for the kids at Ewood Park in the old days and my sister and I would sit over the wall and watch the game. With my dad being a market trader, we didn't get to go very often, so when we did, we really enjoyed it.

Blackburn was a huge, bustling market town back then and one of the biggest events of the year was the Easter Fair. The fairground was set up right in the town centre on the square; it was so exciting and the whole town would turn out to go on the rides. I was 17 and went with my friend Marian, and Roy was with his friend Pete. They spotted us, made their way over and paid for us to go on the speedway. What struck me about Roy was his confidence; he was by far the most self-assured boy I'd ever met in my life.

I didn't realise it at the time but Roy had seen me before. I'd left school a year earlier and started work in the offices of the Gas Board, where I was trying to learn shorthand and typing. He was in the youth team at Rovers but was sent to technical college because he still had to finish his education. His lodgings were in Darwen, a bit further on from where I lived, so we used to catch the same bus home.

He came from a little Welsh mining town called Ffynnongroew and went home to see his family for the close season but we met again in the September at King George's dance hall – everybody went there on a Saturday evening. I think it was the day he made his debut for Blackburn's first team and he came up and asked me to dance. When the dance was over, he just kept hold of my hand. As far as he was concerned, I was his girlfriend and that was that. He never really let go of me again.

My parents were market traders doing house clearances and selling antiques, and they brought my sister and I up to be very independent and to learn about life as we went along. They worked hard and thought that sending us to a decent school would make up for the time they didn't have to spend with us. I was five and my sister Liz was seven when we started at the Catholic convent and we stayed until we were sixteen. Our parents were very quiet people and were happy with anybody we brought home as long as they were decent and respectable.

Roy had four sisters and he was his mum's pride and joy. She didn't want us to get married because he wasn't 21 until the April and it meant she would have to sign for him. I got on well with her so it wasn't that she disapproved or didn't like me but she'd been the same with her daughters; she just had a thing about signing them away. It was only a matter of two months, so it was a bit strange, but she refused point-blank and his father had to give his permission instead.

Roy was Church of England, which didn't help matters, but he was taking instruction so he could change religion. The parish priest was a Rovers supporter so every time he went for his lessons they just ended up talking about the match. By the time he was supposed to have learned all his religious instruction, he hadn't done anything at all. The priest asked if he really wanted to become a Catholic or if he was just doing it so he could marry me. Roy confessed and the priest just said, 'Then be a good man in your own religion' and that was it.

It was a bitterly cold day when we got married in February 1958. It was a Monday because it was during the season but, as fate would have it, Rovers had drawn in a Cup game on the Saturday so the replay was on the Wednesday night and he had to be back at training the next day.

Liz and two of Roy's sisters were our bridesmaids, my brother was our best man and one of Roy's best friends was an usher. His parents came up from Wales and we had a big white wedding and our reception in the High Lawn Hotel in Darwen, Blackburn. All the press came because Roy was an established player by then. It didn't bother me, but my father was very apprehensive because he was so shy and quiet and I felt quite sorry for him. My mum took things in her stride, but Dad didn't like a fuss.

We went to Blackpool for our honeymoon and stayed overnight at the Butlins' Metropole Hotel. We didn't have a car, so we got the train back on the Tuesday morning and Roy went off to the training ground.

Rovers were playing Wolverhampton the day my first boy, Mark, was born. Because it wasn't very far away, the team usually travelled on the Saturday morning, but the forecast was for fog and they decided they would have to go the night before and stay over. The baby was overdue so I went to my mum's and, of course, I went into labour. Roy rang at lunchtime and I'd left instructions to tell him I'd gone shopping. I didn't want him to know I'd gone into hospital in case he worried and it distracted him from his game. I needn't have bothered because they were beaten 5–0 that day.

He got home from the Midlands at about eleven o'clock and went straight to my sister's to pick me up but I'd already had the baby and was in hospital. He was annoyed with me for not telling him because he'd got off the bus early and had to walk home, and he didn't even have anybody to share his news with.

The manager at Rovers was Johnny Carey and he had said Blackburn should never part with Roy, so when Johnny moved to Everton, he went back and got him. I think Everton had rejected Roy when he was a schoolboy because he was so small and slight, but he grew taller when he was about 15. He was very wiry and muscular, and stood about 5ft 10in., but he looked taller because he was so slim and strong. He was like whipcord.

When we moved to Everton, we lived in a three-bedroom semi-detached in Ridgeway Drive in Lydiate. Bert Slater, the Liverpool goalkeeper, lived across the road and Ron Yeats, the Liverpool captain, was around the corner, so we were surrounded by good friends and had a great support network. It wasn't too bad for me because I was quite close to Blackburn, so if Roy went away for any long spells, I would go home to my parents. I never used to ask if I could go; I would just announce that I'd be there the next day and Mum took it all in her stride, although she had four foster children at the time.

Everton were always good to us. Blackburn was only a small club and by comparison Everton were enormous. The first Christmas, Roy came home with a hamper full of goodies – a turkey, mince pies and a Christmas pudding – and inside the hamper was a Stratton powder compact for me. It was a lovely surprise.

I remember Roy phoning me up from Honolulu, where they had gone on a tour. I was in tears on the phone because I was pregnant and a bit weepy. He said: 'There's no point in me ringing if you're going to cry.' I used to miss him so much when he was away but that time I think it was my hormones making me upset.

He had a sardonic sense of humour, a quick tongue and was very temperamental and feisty. If we ever had a row, it was quickly over, I always knew he didn't mean it and that it was just his 'Welsh' way. He would be making me laugh the very next minute.

My second son, Neil, was born in October 1960. I was due and Roy was playing for Wales in Cardiff. He didn't want me to be on my own so he arranged for me to stay overnight with Micky Lill and his wife Paddy. Jimmy Gabriel was a lodger with them and he was away playing for Scotland at the same time. The team travelled back overnight and got home in the early hours. Roy got into bed and a little while later I felt the first twinges. I woke him up to tell him the baby was starting and he said, 'Could you not just have another couple of hours' sleep? I'm shattered.' He didn't panic at all.

We got up and Jimmy was there, grinning all over his face. He was so excited because he was going to be the godfather. Paddy and Micky Lill were great; they looked after Mark for me while I went in. Mark was only 20 months old at that time. When you've got no relatives nearby, it's quite isolated, but football communities all rally round and help each other.

I was so happy when Jimmy met Pat; they were so well suited. She was a Liverpool girl and she met Jimmy on a blind date through another teammate, Bobby Collins. We went to their wedding and they're still together to this day.

Nancy Young was my best friend. They were in a hotel when they first arrived so when Alex and Roy went training, she would come round and help me look after the boys. She always said I couldn't cook very well and we would survive on tomato soup or eggs on toast. I was only married 11 months before I had Mark and I was pregnant with Neil when we moved to Lydiate, so it was all very sudden and I had to learn quickly.

My boys were mischievous – they used to call the eldest one 'Fingers' because he had a really inquiring mind; he had to know how everything worked. I remember him letting Ron Yeats's tyres down once on a match day. They could be a bit of a handful at times.

I went to most of the games to watch Roy play, especially at Goodison Park. I think Wolverhampton beat Everton 2–0 on his debut but I remember Johnny Carey telling me how pleased he was with Roy's performance. We didn't get any special treatment as wives, but we did get a ticket for the match and we would stand outside in the street like everybody else, waiting until we could go in.

I was fortunate that I had brilliant neighbours and babysitters. I was so grateful for that. The people next door were absolutely great and we had a good friendship. My babysitter lived round the corner and I would take the boys there on a Saturday lunchtime so I could go to the game and she would bring them back on Sunday morning. Her name was Mrs Johnson but we called her Aunty Ann.

Saturday nights out were our big treat and we'd all go to the Royal Tiger Club or the Pink Parrot, but the Tiger Club was our favourite. I wasn't used to going to nightclubs and one of the first times we went it was about eleven o'clock at night and everybody started panicking and running around. We were downstairs and there was a right old commotion. I thought it was some kind of a raid, like in the films, but it was because somebody's wife had turned up and her husband was in there with his girlfriend, so they had to usher this woman out.

Because Roy was the Everton captain, I was once asked to open a table at a casino. Roy told them it was a bad idea because I've got no coordination. I'm left-handed, so when I threw the dice, one of them went up in the air and the other one went somewhere else. I think they're still looking for it now.

Roy wasn't superstitious at all – he was super-confident. He had his own way of doing things and his own mind. One of his sayings was: 'You eat to live, you don't live to eat.' He didn't have a big appetite and he smoked like a trooper, so I don't suppose that helped, but what he ate was good food. He'd have steak and egg or boiled ham and tomato, and some nice bread. He was a meat-eater but he only ate dainty little portions. If you put a huge plateful of food in front of him, it would overwhelm him and put him off. He was naturally slim and slightly built but he was a hard worker; he trained really hard and he was as tough as old boots.

He was the only man who could smoke in the shower. He would sit in the bath washing his hair with a cigarette in his mouth and it never got wet – I don't know how he did it. I think his smoking was a nervous thing really; he didn't even seem to inhale, he just puffed away. He would even have a cigarette in his hand as he ran down the tunnel and stub it out just before he got on the pitch. I've got a lot of photographs of him and he always seemed to be holding a cigarette. Even when we won the League in 1963 and he was getting presented with his medal, he had one. I imagine he had it secreted on his person – unless one of the fans had given it to him on the way up to the balcony.

That was the best day ever and the best night too. The last match to clinch the title was against Fulham and Roy scored a hat-trick. It was the proudest moment of my life. For Roy to get three and to captain the team was just beyond belief. It was the absolute pinnacle of his career.

As a special treat, the club took us all away for a fortnight in Torremolinos. It was almost unheard of to go to Spain back then and we felt so sophisticated. The hotel had just been built so there wasn't much to do besides lounge by the pool in the sun and eat nice food. There was a lot of building going on around us; the tourist industry was in its very early stages then. I remember my suitcase got lost somewhere for the first two days – all the girls were in their swimsuits and I was wearing a dress! It was a beautiful hotel and we felt so privileged; we had the time of our lives.

Roy was mad about horse racing. He would go to the races with Alex Young and when the Grand National was on, we used to end up with all kinds of stable lads coming to stay with us. I didn't appreciate it very much at the time but that's the kind of man Roy was. I laugh about it now when I think back.

We were very naive, us wives – we were so young and innocent, they would often be at the races when we thought they were training. Roy and Alex were 'men's men'; they liked the kind of companionship offered by the match and the horses. I've got a photograph of them both judging the Miss New Brighton beauty pageant. The girls are like beauty queens used to be, so glamorous in their one-piece swimsuits, whilst Roy is so dark and brooding, and Alex is so fair – they were like chalk and cheese. They got on really well on and off the pitch, and were great friends.

The players were often taken away on 'special training weekends', which I think were just authorised drinking and bonding sessions. It didn't bother me too much because it was part of the job and, if I did mind, I just had to get over it. I don't think any wives like to think of their men going away, especially if you've got kids, but the perks of the job made up for that.

I always had lovely clothes, although I'm only 5ft tall, so I could never buy anything off the peg and would always have to have it altered. Roy would take me shopping in Blackpool and I always had to have my hair done at the hairdresser's. I remember doing it myself once and coming downstairs feeling quite proud of my creation. I asked Roy what he thought and he said, 'Nice try, love, now go and book an appointment.' He liked me to look nice. I think all the lads took pride in their wives' appearance.

We'd moved to Stoke when my youngest son came along. It was July 1969 and Roy was away in America with the club. Maurice Setters' wife Kathy came and sat with me every single day so I wasn't alone and she was dying for the baby to be born. I was so overdue that she had to go on holiday and, of course, I went into labour almost immediately. Young Roy was born in the old North Staffordshire hospital. One of the staff said if I'd have waited another month, I could have gone to the new hospital instead.

Roy didn't make it to an FA Cup final. He left Blackburn and they made it to Wembley; he left Everton and they won the Cup; he went to Stoke and, after he left, they won the League Cup final. He played in the early rounds but it was never his destiny. All he won was his Everton Championship medal in 1962–63 and 32 caps for Wales.

There was nothing I disliked about being a footballer's wife. We didn't get pestered that often and the people who did come and see us were usually very nice. I didn't like it when I was sitting in the stand watching the game and I would hear the fans shouting bad things at the lads. 'Ooh, he's a dirty devil' or 'He's always like that . . .'. I don't think they knew who we were, but it used to irritate me because I always thought Roy was a fantastic player and I wanted to leap to his defence.

None of my boys plays football; they say they inherited my genes when it comes to coordination. Mark likes motorbikes, Neil plays golf and Roy likes to watch Rovers when he can, but he's in the retail trade so he's at work most Saturdays. They all blame me for their lack of sporting ability – but maybe it will skip a generation or two.

I lost Roy in December 1993. His smoking finally caught up with him and he died of lung cancer. They'd found a tumour a couple of years earlier, so he had one lung removed and really believed he was getting better. I knew he wasn't because the doctors had told me, but I didn't want Roy to know. He asked if there was something I wasn't telling him and I said no. He told me that football had given him the best life he could ever have hoped for. He was from a mining village and, by tradition, he would have worked down the pit like his friends and his family. Instead, he'd travelled, been to some of the most amazing cities in the world, made a good living and met some of the finest people. We had one last holiday together in Spain. Neither of us said a word but we both knew. He was 56 when I lost him. Jimmy Gabriel was the caretaker manager of Everton then and he came to the funeral with Colin Harvey and Nancy and Alex Young. Alex Parker and Fred Pickering were there, too. It was a good turnout; he'd have been so proud.

I've got six grandchildren and one great grandchild; they range from twenty-seven to one year old but there's only one boy. When my little granddaughter was at primary school she had to do an essay about what made her proud. She wrote how her granddad had been a footballer. Jimmy Gabriel sent her the most marvellous letter praising Roy and saying how he was the best footballer he'd ever played with. She was only about ten at the time and I was so happy.

Roy's memorabilia is in the Legends Bar at Goodison Park and I was invited over to the opening and another time one New Year. I took my son and his wife and we met Joe Royle, had something to eat there and went on a tour around the stadium. We had a lovely day.

I live back in Blackburn now. After Roy died, I started going to Ewood Park again to watch Blackburn with my daughter-in-law for something to do and to give me an interest, but then my grandchildren started getting interested in ponies so they're down at the farm every weekend now. My son has a business and they have a few season tickets for the clients, so I still go occasionally if they're not being used.

I always look out for Everton's results and when they were struggling the other year and fighting relegation I was as anxious as anybody. When you've been there five years, there's a great bond. We both loved every minute of being at Everton; I suppose they were the best years of our lives. The people were brilliant, we had fantastic neighbours and made great friends. If Roy was here now, he would say exactly the same.

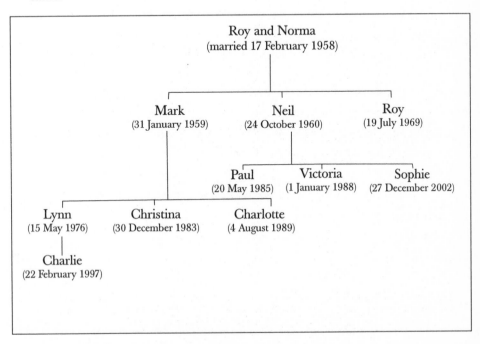

He Wouldn't Pull His Socks Up
Brenda Thomas

A jinky winger, born in the Northeast and spotted by Burnley's almost legendary scout, Jack Robson, Dave Thomas began his career at Turf Moor in 1966–67 before signing for QPR in 1972–73. He achieved the almost unique feat of banking promotion bonuses from both clubs that summer, as they finished first and second in the old Second Division. He signed for Everton in August 1977 and appeared 84 times for the club. Gifted in the extreme, Thomas could cross with either foot and played a major part in helping Bob Latchford hit 30 top-flight goals that season and collect the £10,000 prize from the *Daily Express*. A disastrous £420,000 move to Wolves followed, although it opened the door to a spell with the Vancouver Whitecaps in the old North American Soccer League, before he wound down his career with Middlesbrough and Portsmouth. Capped eight times for England, Thomas now works as a PE teacher in Chichester.

Born Brenda Blackbell, 5 September 1950, Sunderland

It was a beautiful summer evening in July 1970 and Dad had sent me down to the village pub early so I could save his seat. Although I was born and bred in Sunderland, my parents owned a cottage in Cotherstone in the North Riding of Yorkshire for years and my older sister Jill and I had spent our weekends and holidays there for as long as we could remember.

Dave lived in West Auckland but his parents were away so he was staying with Roy Long, his old school friend, in a nearby village called Whorlton. Roy and his friends Joe and John Richardson were farmers and Dave had been helping on their farm. They'd all come into the pub after a cricket match and I noticed Dave the second he walked through the door. What initially struck me about him were his lovely bright eyes.

I vaguely knew one of the guys they were with and he came over to say hello. Dave was with him and, before I knew it, we got chatting. I thought he was rather nice. I noticed he had a lovely smile and those big, white, tombstone teeth, then I looked down and he was wearing Barker shoes. They looked quite expensive and were immaculately polished. I always thought you could tell a lot about a man by his shoes. Dad's shoes were always smart because he'd been in the army, so I was impressed.

I would never have recognised Dave, but I had actually seen him before because I'd been to Roker Park with Dad to watch an England versus Scotland Under-23 match and Dave had been in the England team.

Dad was a regular at Roker and had tickets right in front of the press box so he could just turn round and ask for the half-time scores from everywhere else. He was an architect by profession and did a lot of industrial work – mapping out factories, schools and hospitals – but he designed houses too. He served his time with a company called Messers W. & T.R. Milburn, then set up his own practice after the war in John Street, Sunderland.

A great friend of Dad's was Jack Ditchburn, whose father had been the chairman of Sunderland FC. Uncle Jack was a solicitor and he later became vice-chairman and latterly president of the club. He was always a dear friend of the family.

Mum didn't work when we were kids and we had a privileged upbringing, although you're not really aware of that as a child. I suppose you tend to just think everybody's the same. In 1953, Mum bought the cottage, which was run down and very old-fashioned, but we did it up over a period of time. Alan Berriman was a family friend and a builder, so they shared the cottage with us, we renovated it together and the families had half each.

We were lucky because we got the end with the stable, so we would keep ponies. When we weren't there, the ponies would stay on a farm in Barnard Castle with Dick Wilson, a former jockey who used to work renovating the castle and also kept a pub. We started with one little black fell pony but there was endless fighting between Jill and I so we also got a piebald called Scout, and he was mine.

I spent my life looking after him but would ride horses for other people too. I literally spent my childhood on farms; all I wanted was to be a farmer's wife, surrounded by chickens and animals. I was the horsier of the sisters, as Jill was four years older and she grew out of it and became more interested in boys.

The Sunderland Church High School for Girls was very posh. I started at the prep school when I was five and continued as a pupil there. I liked all the lessons except maths – in fact, I still feel mentally scarred from being whacked over the knuckles with a ruler during one lesson. I've never forgotten it.

It was a lovely little school, though, as the classes weren't that big and most of the pupils were well-behaved young ladies. I left with the statutory amount of O levels and won a scholarship to go on for A levels in art, English and history, but I left in 1966 and went to Sunderland College of Art and Design to do a foundation course. Because I'd been educated in such a protected environment, I found the college quite a culture shock. Suddenly, I was thrust into this strange environment and everybody just seemed to sit about. There were some very nice people there but it all seemed very disorganised to me, coming from such a disciplined background.

I didn't complete my course. Before the year was up, I went to

Monkweirmouth College and did a shorthand and typing course. I was always interested in the arts and had an opportunity to go down to London and study fashion, but it really wasn't my thing. I just wanted to try all different areas to see which I was best suited to, but by then I'd decided I wanted to teach. In those days, you could do three years' teacher training and if you wanted to do a degree you could stay an extra year, but I thought it was more important to go out there and get a job. I was offered a few but chose to work at Hedworthfield comprehensive in Jarrow.

Dave's exactly a month younger than me and was born in Kirkby in Ashfield in the Nottingham area, where his mum came from. She moved up to the Northeast when she married and they moved in with her father-in-law, David Rhys Thomas. A film called *A Captain's Tale* was made about the team that won the first ever 'World Cup' competition with West Auckland Town, the team that represented Britain against Juventus in the 1909 final. Dave's granddad was in the team and spent hours teaching Dave to play football. His mum tells the tale that his first pair of shorts were made from blackout curtains.

Dave had been at Burnley since he was 15 and lived in digs with a wonderful couple, Winnie and Walter Edmondson, who spoilt him rotten. He and I got on like a house on fire in the pub that night and he asked if I would go out with him the next evening. I told him I couldn't possibly because I already had a boyfriend and he was actually in the pub at the time. He was chatting to my friend over the other side of the bar, so it must have looked as if I was on my own. We settled on meeting for a coffee the next morning, then went for a walk and that was it really – we just clicked. He had to go back to Burnley soon after but from then on he phoned me every single day, sometimes twice a day, until we got married two and a half years later.

Geographically, it wasn't the easiest of relationships to conduct but that was probably a good thing because it meant I could concentrate on my new job and he could keep his mind on his football. The miners did us a huge favour by going on strike, though, because some days there was no heating and the schools had to close down –

whenever we didn't have to be there, weekdays or weekends, I would shoot off to Burnley. If the weather was too bad, I'd catch the train, otherwise I would drive over in my clapped-out red Mini van. It was quite a hairy journey because the route passed over the moors and there were some very isolated roads out there. Looking back, my poor parents must have been worried sick about me but the car only broke down once. Another time, I fell asleep at the wheel and ended up in a grass verge.

Dave was very happy at Turf Moor. He'd been there on schoolboy forms since he was 15 and, at 16, he was the youngest player to make his debut in the First Division for Burnley. On his 17th birthday, he signed as a full-time professional, although shortly before that Don Revie had come in with a very tempting offer for him to go to Leeds. Dave's parents had both a verbal agreement with Burnley and the moral fibre to turn down the Elland Road manager's almost legendary suitcase full of money. Dave was brought up with those same strict working-class values and they have stood him in good stead all his life.

I'd watch him play every Saturday and it was scary and exciting at the same time. You're always wanting them to do well, but mindful that anything could happen. He didn't get many injuries – he was extremely lucky in that respect, as I can think of one or two of our friends whose careers were finished because of them. I guess nobody could really catch Dave.

My parents were out in Majorca in the summer of 1972 when he rang them to ask for permission to marry me. They said yes straight away. Dad was chuffed to bits with Dave being a footballer and, as my sister's husband was a rugby man who'd played for Durham City, he had his bread buttered on both sides.

During the 1972–73 season, Dave was transferred from Burnley to Queens Park Rangers and going to London was quite a shock to the system. He'd been at Turf Moor since he was a teenager and was quite a country boy at heart, so to be suddenly thrown into city life took his breath away. He went into digs with another lovely family, Mr and Mrs Parvin in Shepherds Bush. Luckily, my sister was working for an airline at the time so I could quite easily get a standby flight from Newcastle to London and sometimes he would fly up to see me.

We married at Romaldkirk church in December 1972; the most beautiful church I've ever seen, with a little village green. The only footballer who came was Bobby Kerr, who was married to a friend of mine and I'd been a bridesmaid at their wedding. Bobby was the captain when Sunderland beat Leeds in the FA Cup final a few months later in May 1973, when the manager Bob Stokoe ran onto the pitch in his famous celebration. Dad and I went to that game, too – we were Mackems through and through, and I can still name the team.

It was mid-season so Dave and I couldn't go on honeymoon immediately. He hadn't even booked anywhere for our first night, though, and we ended up driving twice around Harrogate in thick fog. I kept thinking he was having a laugh and would pull up outside a wonderful hotel, but no chance. We ended up in the Selby Fork motel and it really was as bad as it sounds. To this day, whenever we drive past it, our girls shriek with laughter and make us re-tell the tale. To compensate, we went for two weeks in Majorca the following close season and it was much better. In fact, we returned last year and retraced our steps. We went to the same hotel in Deia and, would you believe, the same bloke was on the reception desk.

When he was at QPR, we found a house in Wokingham, in Berkshire, which cost £14,950 – an absolute fortune, as we'd been looking at houses in Burnley for half the price. I had some savings because my granny had died and left me a little bit of money, and we pitched it all in for the house. As a teacher, I was earning £60 a month and Dave was earning around the same per week.

Joyce and Fred Warren lived nearby and they really took us under their wing. If it hadn't been for Joyce, I don't know what I'd have done because when you're so far away from home and family, you're in trouble if anything goes wrong. Dave and I met Adrian and Janet Whittle there, too, and I think Dave would still class him as his best friend. He tragically lost Janet young and with four children to bring up.

That season, Burnley and QPR were both promoted and during training one day Dave was asked if he would be entitled to two bonuses, but it hadn't crossed his mind. Terry Venables was a teammate and the PFA representative at the time, and he said he would fight the case for him, so they had to take on Bob Lord, the hardline chairman of Burnley. Of course, Terry won and, by way of a thank you, we took him and his wife out for a meal.

Since we were strangers in town, we asked Terry to book it and he arranged a table at the Sportsman club. We had a fantastic meal and after we'd eaten, he took us around the gaming tables. All of a sudden, Dave stopped dead in his tracks because there at one of them was the famous gardener, Percy Thrower, with a pile of chips in front of him. It looked so out of character – you would have thought Percy would be at home sitting in front of the telly with a cup of cocoa. Dave's image of him was shattered.

His other hero was Geoffrey Smith, who fronted a television programme called *Mr Smith's Favourite Garden*. John Motson was interviewing Dave at Everton for *Match of the Day* one afternoon and asked what ambitions he had. I think he meant in football but Dave was on a different train of thought altogether and said that he would like to meet Geoffrey Smith. He lives in a place called Kettlesing, just outside Harrogate; good old John Motson arranged it and we have kept in touch with Geoffrey ever since. He's a genuinely lovely guy.

We were at QPR for five years and both our girls were born in that time. Helen arrived on 2 August 1974, and Dave was at the birth. I can remember him sitting there with tears in his eyes, saying, 'It's a miracle.' Polly was born 13 February 1976. They are both sporty and have played hockey and tennis for West Sussex.

The whole transfer from QPR to Everton was strange because, only a few weeks before it happened, Dave had signed a three-year contract; the next thing there was a phone call saying Everton had come in for him. Dave Sexton had been manager but he'd left QPR to take over at Manchester United and Frank Sibley had come to manage at Loftus Road. It wasn't long after that the offer came in and I suppose

£200,000 was too good to refuse. Dave spoke to Gordon Lee and the next thing he was in the car, heading north. We were on our way.

George Wood, the Blackpool goalkeeper, arrived on the same day and the headline in the *Daily Express* was: 'MERSEY MILLIONAIRES SET UP BIG DOUBLE TRANSFER DEAL'. They made their debut on the same day, too, against Nottingham Forest in August 1977. I was very excited about moving up to Liverpool because it was such an interesting city, with beautiful buildings. I'll never forget the first time I drove up there. Dave had been put in the Holiday Inn and I couldn't find Paradise Street to save my life. I finally stopped the car and asked two blokes who were walking down the street. They said they were going that way so they hopped in and I gave them a lift. I was eternally grateful. I'd been doing circuits of the city centre for ages.

I have mixed memories of the Holiday Inn. I had my car broken into in the multistorey car park next door, but the hotel manager was a chap called Jack Ferguson – a lovely man who was very keen on his football – and he loaned us his car for a few days so we could go and look at houses.

We teamed up with some people who were also staying there – one guy, Arthur Rothwell, was a troubleshooter for Ford and had come up from Dagenham. He and his wife Jean had three daughters who played with our two. The youngest one was called Tasha and, very sadly, she had leukaemia and lost her fight with the disease. It was the saddest day I can ever remember and, as young parents ourselves, it really hit us hard. We still keep in touch with the Rothwells and they're living in Ormskirk now. The other couple that we've remained friends with is Marina and Kenny Dalglish. He'd been transferred from Celtic at about the same time and they had their kids, Kelly and Paul, with them. We all used to have good fun together, though I could hardly understand a word he said. He isn't as dour as some people seem to think. Dave and Kenny still play golf together and Marina and I keep in touch, too.

We moved way off the beaten track to a place called Dalton near Parbold. It wasn't the typical place for a footballer to live, but I suppose neither of us really fit that stereotype anyway. Our house was interesting, but it was rather close to a pig farm. It was quite small when we got there, but the farmer went into intensive farming and it grew rapidly, which didn't help when we came to sell the house. But it was a lovely place, with views over open fields, and most important of all, we had the most wonderful neighbours. Eileen and Les Earle lived next door and were absolute diamonds. I would never have survived as a footballer's wife if I hadn't been gifted with the best possible neighbours wherever I lived.

I think Dave was on £200 a week at Everton but all his bonuses went straight into a pension scheme – we never took them there and then because a bonus is just that. We were quite sensible with money; we knew his career would probably be short-lived. I remember when Bob Latchford scored 30 goals in Dave's first season and won £10,000 and everyone at the club got a £192 share. Dave says he's still got his. His trophy from the '70s sports show *Superstars* is still in our cabinet, too. It's the ugliest thing you've ever seen but he was in the canoeing, cycling and running, and he did ever so well.

We didn't really have much of a social life and I didn't know many of the wives because we lived in such a remote place. The only time I got to see them was at a match. I was friendly with Lyn Pejic, Mike's wife, who bought Kevin Keegan's house and lived near Mold in North Wales. I'd see her on a Saturday at the game or at any of the club dos but that was about it really. Dave enjoys the odd glass of wine now, but when he was playing, he was a complete teetotaller even though there was quite a drinking culture then.

I would go to as many home games as I could but the kids always came first. Polly was eighteen months old and Helen would have been three when we moved to Everton, so I wouldn't want to leave them with anybody for too long. Another fabulous neighbour, Jenny Cosgrove, or one of her two sisters, would sometimes look after the kids and I'd go to the match but then we'd pretty much come straight home.

I used to cook a lot and often entertained. I remember arriving at Anfield for the derby one day and had just sat down in my seat when

I got the most awful feeling that I'd left the soup on the cooker. I was panic-stricken and simply had to phone Eileen immediately to get her to go and check. It was such a palaver to even get to a phone. I couldn't get out of the ground, but I eventually found a policeman and explained my story to him. He took me into the surveillance room and announced my dilemma in a really loud voice to all the staff. I felt like such an idiot. Needless to say, I hadn't left the soup on at all. The match ended 0–0.

Dave was difficult to live with from Thursday onwards as the mental preparation kicked in and he started getting focused for the match. He'd always take a while to wind down after a game too, and would often re-live games in his sleep. One night he knocked my front tooth out with a flailing limb and I had to have it crowned.

He only scored six goals for Everton but he teamed up really well with Bob Latchford and it was far easier to just knock them over to him. The strangest goal I remember him scoring was for QPR against Sunderland after they'd won the Cup. The whole of Roker went completely silent. I think I was the only person in the whole stadium who stood up and cheered.

Everton were superb, probably the best of all the clubs because of the way they treated us. They put people at our disposal to help us and to come and check properties with us – the club were so professional in everything they did.

If anything wound me up, it was newspaper reporters ringing up and speaking to me as if I was a complete bimbo, or being far too familiar with me when I'd never even met them. I hated to be thought of as a typical footballer's wife. People have an awful stereotype of women who marry footballers and I don't think I ever fitted that bill. I used to shop at Chorley market and Lada sponsored Dave's club car.

Dave's transfer to Wolves was a disaster, really. I know we wouldn't have lived in a lot of places if he'd not gone there, but I always think it was a shame we never stayed longer at Everton. The main reason he left was because he was in a contract dispute; he didn't think he was earning as much as he was worth and asked them to review his salary. Bill

Shankly was at Bellefield one day and gave Dave a bit of advice about money not being everything, and I suppose he was right, but Dave was quite a sensitive kind of chap and his mind was made up. His timing could have been a bit better, though, because shortly after he shook hands on the deal, which had still to be signed, Dave Sexton from Manchester United came in for him. We went and looked for a house in the Midlands but there was nothing we fancied so we stayed put in Dalton. With hindsight, I suppose it was just not meant to be.

He never made it to Wembley with a club but I did go there to watch Dave play some of his international games. He won schoolboy, youth, Under-23 and full England caps. I went to every match I possibly could and felt incredibly proud of him. An even better feeling, though, was when he was invited to play in an Old England versus Old Scotland match.

They played it before one of the Euro '96 games and our girls were there with me. I always thought it was a shame that when he was playing professionally the children were too young to understand or realise the importance of it. They're so proud of him now, so to actually see him in action was wonderful. He is their idol and it's lovely because he thinks the same of them. There's such a great rapport between all three of them.

John Barnwell, now the chief executive of the League Managers' Association, was in charge at Wolves when it all went pear-shaped for Dave. It turned sour for two reasons – first, because Dave refused to wear boots with studs, and second, because he wouldn't pull his socks up. This was before they had to wear shin pads and Dave found them very awkward so he ended up falling out with the coach, Richie Barker, over it. Dave teaches at a school now and realises what a brat he must have been, but, by that time, he'd played for England and in hundreds of First Division games and couldn't understand what the problem was.

They told him if he didn't pull his socks up, he wouldn't play another game for them. It ended up with Dave taking his boots off at half-time and throwing his shirt at Barker. He didn't go back out for the second half of the match and that was the end of that. Of course, that was 1980, the year Wolves got to the final of the League Cup so, although I'd already bought my outfit for Wembley, I didn't get to wear it. Dave was stuck in the reserves for a long time as punishment.

We heard the Vancouver Whitecaps were on a recruitment drive and wondered what life would be like on the west coast of Canada. We went together to negotiate the deal for Vancouver and met the men in a hotel somewhere in Birmingham. I really didn't like one of them but Dave knew the other guy, Tony Waiters, who had been a goalkeeper at Burnley. Bruce Grobbelaar was playing for the Whitecaps then, but they were selling him to Liverpool and trying to take Dave over from Wolves. A three-year deal was pretty much agreed right there but we got Uncle Jack to look over the contract and make some adjustments.

Johnny Giles was the Whitecaps' manager and had arranged a promotional tour en route, so Dave flew out via Ireland in February 1981. Terry Yorath, Alan Taylor, Peter Beardsley and Barry Siddall were already in Canada and there was quite an established expat community. They all tended to live in condominiums but Dave wouldn't stay on his own, and he didn't want to go to a hotel, so they found him a brilliant family called the Mazzuccos, who he moved in with. There were four boys, and the dad looked and sounded just like Sylvester Stallone.

Before I could join him, I had to tie up some loose ends and have my wisdom teeth out – that was one of the rules, as medical treatment was so expensive there. Originally, we were going over lock, stock and barrel, but our house sale fell through so we had a last-minute change of plan and it stood empty. We gave Dad power of attorney and the girls and I flew out from Manchester airport on 12 April, with my parents there to wave us off. It was the last time I saw Dad alive; he died of a massive heart attack a month later. That rocked my world to its foundations.

We rented a town house in Burnaby, Vancouver, and the girls went to Stoney Creek school. From time to time, I would go there and help the teacher out. The directors of the club were great people and our life was idyllic in patches but mine was lonely when Dave used to go away for long periods.

The North American Soccer League was just getting established and George Best was out there, as were quite a few others towards the end of their careers, but then they changed the rules and clubs weren't allowed to have so many foreign players in their team. Dave had signed a three-year contract but the change came eighteen months after we went, so the last in were the first out. That was fair enough – they were trying to get the game off the ground in North America and the local lads needed to have a chance to make their mark.

In some ways, it might not be a bad thing if the same happened in England now. How else are young British lads going to get a chance competing against all these talented foreign players here? There aren't too many opportunities for them to break through any more.

We came back to England and Dave went to Middlesbrough for a short spell. So we didn't have to uproot the girls again, I stayed in Dalton and Dave stayed at the cottage in Cotherstone. I would drive over on match days to pick up his parents and take them to the game. Boro said they would give him a two-year contract but they only offered him one year. At about the same time, Portsmouth came in with a two-year offer so we went for the security of the longer contract. At the start of the 1982–83 pre-season, we finally sold the house after four years on the market and moved to the south coast.

Portsmouth were supposed to organise a house for us to move into but they forgot. We had nowhere to go and the removal people needed an address to deliver our furniture, so we sorted ourselves out with a rented house the day we arrived. Part of the deal was that the club would pay the rent for six months, but we were always getting the phone cut off or receiving final demands for the overdue rent. It was very unsettling and embarrassing.

One morning, I went out to buy some mushrooms at the farm shop and I saw the most beautiful wisteria-covered cottage in one of the small villages. I couldn't get it out of my mind and dragged Dave along to have a look. Thinking we would be able to sell it quite easily in two years when his contract was up, we bought it. That was twenty-two years ago and we've been there ever since. I guess Hampshire is home for us now, and the girls have spent most of their lives here.

After my dad died, Mum handed the Cotherstone cottage over to Jill and I. After a time, Jill wanted to get her cash, so it had to be sold. My heart still breaks when I think about it.

In 1986, when Dave finished playing, he was asked to join the coaching staff at Pompey. He loved that, he really did, and was so happy with his lot, coaching the reserve and youth teams. Initially, Bobby Campbell was the manager, but Alan Ball took over and told Dave they weren't going to run a youth team any longer and that his services wouldn't be required. A few weeks later, Alan Ball recruited his mate Peter Osgood as youth coach.

Bruce Rioch, who knew Dave from his Everton days, invited him up to coach at Middlesbrough, where he was manager, but Dave was still smarting from the slap in the face from Portsmouth. We were settled in the south and the girls were at school, too.

I went back to teaching and he opted out of football and started a little gardening business. He'd really had enough and he needed a break from the game. He did some garden maintenance and the local people were brilliant. He went to work for a chap called Mr Shand and they had a great relationship. As well as teaching Dave an awful lot about gardening, he got him back into fishing again. It was perfect because it got him through the rough patch.

Mr Shand had the most wonderful garden laid out by a top-notch designer and Dave helped him maintain it. He loved spending time with the old man, who was a lovely character and reminded us both of my dad. He also died quite suddenly, though, and Dave was devastated but he kept the garden going all the time Mrs Shand continued to live there. The new people who moved in have maintained it too, which is a relief as it's too beautiful to be left to go to rack and ruin.

I'd been working part time in the farm shop for a couple of years and one of my neighbours kept telling me to go back to teaching because the school was desperate for supply teachers. I went there for a quiet chat with the headmaster and finally left nine years down the line – I only resigned when I heard of another job in a private school over in Chichester. They wanted somebody to sort out the art department and I was ready for a change by then. I spent another nine years there and left in 2001.

Dave got back on his feet, doing match commentaries and analysis on the radio, and he just loved it – I hadn't seen him so animated for years. He worked with a guy called Peter Hood, who did the commentary while Dave did the analysis. He was really good at it, but sadly the local radio station lost the contract. He did go and work for another regional station but they wanted a Southampton player really, so that was short-lived. He was also doing some work in London for a digital channel called VNL but they went bust. They put the match out 'as live' 10 minutes after kick-off and he did the commentary. He absolutely loved it and that's what he'd like to get back into, but in the meantime he's a part-time PE teacher at Bishop Luffa school in Chichester. He likes the people he works with but he needs a new challenge. We both feel we're ready for a new horizon and he keeps mentioning that it might be a good idea if we sell up and go and live in Majorca, but I'm not so sure. I think he just needs something to fill his time. I think he could still play, if the truth be told.

Dave goes to watch Bognor in the Ryman Premier League now. He's a big friend of Jack Pearce, an all-round great man, who's been there for 28 years and remains on the management committee. It's a real family club and they play attractive football. He still goes to Portsmouth to watch the occasional game, too. Harry Redknapp is wonderful to him; he always manages to get him tickets for the game. Harry's very likeable, very open and well respected.

Our daughter Helen lives in Epsom and teaches French and Spanish at Epsom College. She's married to Chris, who's a physio and former hockey player, and they've got a son called Tom, our first grandchild. Polly is football mad and works as the exhibition manager for Wiley, the publishers, in Chichester.

It always saddens me a bit when I see sportsmen out of work. I wonder how we can allow people who were good enough to play for their country to be wasted. Dave's so good with the kids at school and I've seen the way they react to him. They just love him.

Dave doesn't regret much in life but going to Wolves at the eleventh hour and turning down Manchester United is his big one. Wolves led to all kinds of other things for us, so you can't have too many regrets, but he sometimes can't help thinking he made a bad call.

I don't think I'd like to be a footballer's wife now, but I suppose it depends on how you deal with it. I think it's very intrusive and that everybody is entitled to a private life. In my opinion, there are still some private players around today but people do court the limelight. I'd like to think that, if we were earning that kind of money, we'd do something useful with it and share it about a bit. It's a lot to be paid for entertainment.

We've had such a great time, we've been extremely fortunate and football has given us a lovely way of life. People still recognise Dave but that's not at all surprising because, apart from a sprinkling of grey, he looks exactly the same now as he did when I met him. I think he must have found the fountain of eternal youth.

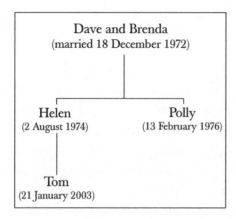

Dave and Brenda
(married 18 December 1972)

Helen
(2 August 1974)

Polly
(13 February 1976)

Tom
(21 January 2003)

The Time Goes By So Fast

Pat Gabriel

Signed by Johnny Carey from Dundee for £30,000 in 1960, Jimmy Gabriel was the most expensive teenage player in the country. An integral part of the Championship- and FA Cup-winning sides of 1963 and '66 respectively, Gabriel played 300 times for Everton and scored 36 goals. He joined Southampton in July 1967 and played for five seasons before moving on to Bournemouth, Swindon on loan and then Brentford. Capped twice for Scotland, Gabriel is now a soccer coach at the University of Seattle.

Born Pat Gaskell, 3 October 1942, Walton, Liverpool

Granddad was a coal merchant and my dad and his brothers started out their adult lives working for him and eventually took over the business. My mum's side of the family was really arty and creative, and ballet dancing was the love of her life. She was from Sheffield and had been a ballet dancer in her youth, even going on to teach it while she was still quite young. They were both on holiday in the Isle of Man with friends when they met and fell in love, and she eventually moved over to Liverpool when they married.

They went into the photography business together and would travel to Port Sunlight on the Wirral, where they used to take photos of babies at the clinics. Other times, they would photograph weddings or go to dance halls and take pictures of the American GIs with their sweethearts. Dad was a good provider and Mum was a wonderful, sweet woman, the mainstay of the family.

My life started out in Willowdale Road near Walton Hospital in Liverpool. I was one of four children. I had two older sisters, Kathleen and Janet, and David was our little brother. The house was always noisy and full of kids. We moved to Brook Road in Bootle for a few years and when I was about 12 we went to Aintree, where we finally settled. I loved living in Aintree. We moved into a new house in Altway, near the Blue Anchor, and I thought we were so posh.

Dad started up in business as a moneylender. He began doing it by chance really: when we lived in Brook Road, one of our neighbours was short of cash and asked if she could borrow a tenner if she paid him back over the odds.

We had a colourful and interesting childhood, with plenty of happy times. On Sundays, we would all go out for the day to a beautiful place in North Wales called Rhydymwyn. It was near a stream and we'd cross to the other side and have picnics. Dad would tie a rope to a tree and we would swing from it. They were memorable times, and Dad really did well and worked hard to give us a good life.

I went to Ormonde Drive Secondary Modern in Maghull. I worked hard and did the best I could, but I didn't find it easy. I remember when I first started there and we were doing fractions with Mr Thomas, a maths teacher from Wales. He used to get the students to stand up and explain what was on the board. I hadn't done fractions at my old school so I couldn't solve the problem and in front of the whole class he said: 'Pat Gaskell, I think you'll be better off in a "B" class.' I almost died of embarrassment and I went home that night and told my mum and dad that if I had to go back, I would run away from home because he'd humiliated me so much. I did go to a 'B' class and eventually came top but it took a lot of hard work on my part.

Tommy Steele was my idol when I was younger – I had a real crush on him. When I was about 15, he was appearing at the Liverpool Empire in *Goldilocks and the Three Bears.* A photographer friend of my dad's took me backstage and I had my picture taken with him and was thrilled to bits. He was blond and gorgeous; I must have had a soft spot for that kind of look.

I stayed on an extra year at school to learn shorthand and typing, and when I left I went to work in the office at Kirby's garage and car dealership on Northway in Maghull. They had branches in different parts of Liverpool and I did general office work, mainly in the invoicing department alongside the bloke who priced the jobs, and occasionally on the switchboard to relieve the operator. I quite liked it and it was a good feeling to have an income and to be independent. I felt very grown up.

Bobby Collins was playing for Everton at that time and he'd bought a couple of cars from our salesman Bill Basnett. Bobby told Bill that Jimmy Gabriel had moved down from Dundee and was really missing his family and was terribly homesick. He was only 19 and from a really close-knit family, with four sisters who thought the world of him. He'd recently moved to Claremont Avenue in Maghull to lodge with another player, Micky Lill, and his wife Paddy, and Bobby wondered whether I would like to meet up and go out with him so that he at least knew someone in Liverpool.

My dad wasn't a real football watcher and never went to games, but if he had to choose between Everton and Liverpool it would be Everton, but that was all down to my brother. David was two and a half years my junior and a fanatical Blue. His bedroom was covered in Everton stuff; he had pictures of Dave Hickson on the walls and blue-and-white scarves and rosettes hanging everywhere. I came home from work that night and told him I had a date with a footballer and made him guess who it was, but he couldn't. When I told him it was Jimmy Gabriel, his jaw dropped. He thought I was kidding, but I told him that Bobby Collins had fixed us up and went into all the details of his transfer and his homesickness until he finally believed me.

Bill and Bobby decided we should meet at the entrance to the Mersey Tunnel, just over the road from the Royal Tiger Club. I didn't drive and neither did Jim so Bill taxied me down there, introduced us to each other then left us to get on with it. Jimmy had been in the newspaper as the most expensive teenage signing in the country so I knew he was blond and good-looking, but he didn't know what he was going to get with me. Anyway, we went for a coffee in Bold Street, then on to the Downbeat Club, but he spoke so quickly and with such a strong Scottish accent that I could hardly understand a word he said and spent most of the date saying, 'Pardon?' He brought me home in a taxi and that was just the swankiest thing ever. We went into our house and all my family were sitting there, waiting for us to come home so they could meet him. David was absolutely gobsmacked and chuffed to bits.

I thought Jimmy was gorgeous. I'd had a couple of teenage crushes but that was all. I was terribly shy and hadn't done any dating or anything like that. He was a lovely guy – he was wonderful company and we always had great fun when we were together.

I hadn't been to a football match either so it really was the start of a completely new life for me. I still didn't drive, so my dad started coming with me. One time, we went to an away game at Turf Moor and my dad tells this story of a Burnley supporter in front of me giving Jim a bad time, shouting, 'Gabriel, you dirty bastard!' He says I clonked him on the head with my umbrella! I loved going to the match; it was such an exciting atmosphere, especially at Goodison. At first, it was strange to see him run out onto the pitch but you were so proud because there he was in front of such a massive crowd and to perform as they did was fabulous to witness. There would be 60,000 people there on an average week and the noise was just incredible.

We got engaged in the July of 1961. My mum told me I was too young to marry at 19, but I was having none of it and we booked the wedding for 4 December 1961 at the Holy Rosary in Altway, by the Old Roan in Aintree. The reason it was so quick was because he was still in digs and wanted a nice home environment to help him settle in, so we thought we should just do it.

We couldn't get married on a Saturday because he was playing and football was always his priority, so we arranged it for the Monday. Everton had played Manchester United on the Saturday and had beaten them 5–1, so we got off to a good start. He got a day off from training and all the players were there: Alex Young, Bobby Collins, Micky Lill, Roy Vernon, Billy Bingham, and Alex Parker was our best man. It was a white wedding – I had three bridesmaids and the reception was at the Melody Inn in New Brighton. Then we went on to a nightclub called Mother Red Caps, which was down in a cellar with a fantastic pianist, I suppose a bit like The Cavern used to be. It was a lovely day and everybody had a good time. Of course, we couldn't have a honeymoon but we spent the night at the Adelphi Hotel and thought it was the poshest place in the world. The next day, he left for Wrexham to meet up with the Scotland Under-23s to prepare for a game against Wales on the Wednesday. I travelled to the match with an uncle of mine and they drew 1–1.

Everton owned a few houses and either rented them out or sold them to players and, in a strange coincidence, we moved into the house that Bobby Collins had lived in with his wife and son. It was a small two-bedroom place, which was nice and cosy, and that was where we lived the entire time he was at Everton. It was in Wrekin Drive, the next road from Altway where my family still lived, so I could go shopping and pop in to my mum's for a cup of tea and a piece of her chocolate cake. She made the best chocolate cake you've ever tasted. We were only married a month before I became pregnant and Karen was born in October 1962, the season we won the League. Our second child, Janet, came along the season we won the FA Cup. It was a great way to commemorate the children coming into the world.

Karen was a good baby and so gorgeous. I had her in Park House nursing home in Waterloo, the usual place for the Everton babies to be born. She came into the world on a Friday night, before a match, and I've got photos of me from the newspaper that were taken in the hospital. Jimmy played the next day, of course. There was nothing on this earth that would make him miss a game.

I'd only been abroad once before – when I went to Switzerland with my friend Irene – when Everton took us all to Torremolinos to celebrate their League win. It was all terribly exciting. Karen was only about eight months old so she stayed with my mum, who was great like that and loved to have the children. Torremolinos was fabulous and we had a great time.

I became close to Nancy Young because she lived just up the road from me in Bullbridge Lane and if we went out, we would meet up with Ray and Pat Wilson, Brian and Pat Labone, and Johnny and Celia Morrissey. We would usually go to a restaurant for a meal then on to the Royal Tiger, or we'd go to the Downbeat. It was the Beatles era and wherever you went they were playing the Fab Four and the Merseybeat sound. We would sometimes have a little dance, but we mainly spent the night standing around chatting, and, of course, you'd get all the fans coming over and wanting to dissect the match. It got on my nerves a little bit because you felt like you shouldn't be there and invariably ended up in the background.

Janet was also born in Park House, on 27 August 1965, just at the start of the season. I had to go in late at night and Jimmy sat outside the labour room. I remember him saying afterwards that we weren't having any more children because he'd heard me in distress and felt so helpless. When the nurse showed me the baby, the first thing I said was, 'Oh, she's so like Mr Gabriel.' I always called Jim's dad Mr Gabriel. I know it's formal but that was just the way it was then. She was all screwed up and wrinkled but she was the image of him. Karen favoured my side of the family, with her dark brown hair and eyes, but Janet was very fair, with blonde hair, and very much like her dad.

Jimmy didn't have much spare time; they used to train an awful lot back then. Now and again, he would go horse racing with the guys. He wasn't really that interested in it initially, but he became friendly with Roy Vernon and he liked to have a bet. It comes to the point where you can get too involved with it and lose a lot of money and that was a phase he went through, so he started giving it a miss. When we moved to Southampton, he and Terry Paine bought a share in a racehorse called Scaramander. I'm not sure if it ever won a race but Jim said he owned the back leg when it was racing and the mouth when it was eating. He didn't really have that much to do with it other than go and see it a few times in the stables, and I guess it was more of an interest than anything else.

He liked to play golf as well and on a Thursday night the boys would all go out for a beer; the wives would have their big night out with them on a Saturday. I can't remember him having any particularly strange pre-match superstitions but he would have to eat steak on a Saturday morning and he always fastened his left boot first.

The people at Everton were always nice to us; they sent flowers when the children were born, at Christmas we'd get a hamper of goodies and when we made it to the 1966 FA Cup final, they took us down to London, which was amazing. We went on the Thursday by train and they took us to see Joe Brown and the Brothers then out for dinner on the Friday. We stayed in the Waldorf and went off to Wembley on a big bus. It was so exciting but nerve-racking too. We were all on edge and wanted them to win so badly. It was like a physical pain.

By half-time we were 1–0 down and the wives were crying with disappointment but after Wednesday scored another goal, they came back and scored, and then they scored again . . . that was when the infamous Eddie Cavanagh ran onto the pitch and, as the policeman grabbed him, he somehow wriggled out of his jacket. The policeman fell on his face and Eddie was off again. I don't know how he did it, but he must have planned it because he was out of the jacket like Harry Houdini and the policeman was on the floor clutching an empty coat. We were all roaring with laughter.

Once again, Mum took care of the girls and I remember her telling me that she put Janet in her pram in the hallway with a tin full of chocolate biscuits to keep her quiet because she and my sister were watching the final on telly and getting really excited and screaming, which frightened the baby and made her cry. When Mum went to check on her, there she was with chocolate all over her face, clothes, pram and wall, but she didn't mind because it kept her happy.

Winning the FA Cup was a different feeling to watching them win the League; we were looking at the points all the time and working out who could catch us and where we were likely to pick up points along the way – when you think back, it was quite stressful. It really affected Jim if they lost. He'd come home and be really down, and it rubs off on everybody, so you'd have to try to stop it having a domino effect. When you're on a high and winning and playing in all the competitions, there's nothing that can beat it, but if you're not on form, you don't know if you're even going to be picked for the team and it can breed all kinds of insecurity.

Jim was quite a physical player so he often sustained injuries. I remember he had a really bad gash on his shinbone once. It was L-shaped and he had to have it stitched but there was no flesh there so it must have been terribly painful. Another time, he had a groin injury and it became infected and poisoned his system. He was really ill then and went into hospital. They never let the press know because they were at a crucial stage of the season. He was on strong antibiotics every four hours, but he had the constitution of an ox and he was soon up and running again.

Considering he wasn't a striker, he scored quite a lot of goals and he saved the day a few times. I can't remember any specific occasions but he can recall them all as if it was yesterday. He's had his nose broken a fair few times, too. Gordon Banks elbowed him once when he went up for the ball, although I don't think it was deliberate.

When he was asleep he was fine apart from the odd nudge when he was re-living the game; far worse were the nights when he couldn't sleep because he was worried, or if he'd had a bad game. That preyed on his mind terribly and it was awful for us to see him feeling so tortured. When the club went through a bad patch, it would really bother him because it was his whole life.

On the odd occasion, we would get people knocking on the front door but it was mainly young kids looking for an autograph. They'd see you walking down the road and know where you lived but that was all right; we could live with that and I can't think of anything I hated about being a footballer's wife. I disliked the interruptions when we were out for an evening and people would come over and sit themselves down. You can understand that they wanted to talk to their heroes so it didn't infuriate me, but it did make me roll my eyes now and again. Of course, you got the floozies that were out to try and get your man but it was something you had to be strong about and I just had to trust him.

We had such a good time at Everton and things went well until Harry Catterick started bringing younger players in. Jim was in his late 20s by then and he didn't see eye to eye with the management on all things. Mr Catterick mentioned that Southampton had shown an interest. I wasn't sure about moving because it meant I would be leaving Liverpool, where I'd been all my life. Jim would be going to a group of people who would be his colleagues and his teammates, but I was going with two small children to a place where I literally didn't know a soul. I wasn't really the type of person who would go out and make conversation or chat with anyone either, so it was hard because I had to start over again. Meeting people and finding my way around was quite daunting and it could feel lonely at times.

His transfer to Southampton was in July 1967. I had to stay behind and organise the packing and sort stuff out, and the girls were only little so it was a full-time job looking after them. Karen was five and just starting school and Janet was two and a half. It was a wrench to leave my mum, too, because I'd never been very far from her in my life. It was exciting because it was a new phase, but it was hard – you had to adjust. There was no time to pine or feel sorry for yourself, you just had to get on with it. It was the life we'd chosen and you had to take it all in your stride. We stayed at Southampton for five years in all and it was a lovely place and we had a great time. Bournemouth was another fantastic place. Jim played there for two years.

By this stage, he was about thirty-four and coming to the latter part of his career. We met John Best, a native of Merseyside, who had played a few games for Liverpool and had been in America since the '60s. He was scouting for players to go to the States because they were starting a new football club called the Seattle Sounders. Although football is quite popular on a participation level in the States, they don't get the big crowds like they do in Britain, so he was recruiting players to make up the team and asked Jim if he'd like to go over. The States seemed so fantastic and we were really excited. Jim travelled over with the other players for the 1974 season that started in April but, because the girls were in school, we followed him out a few months later. We moved into a wonderful apartment with a swimming pool and we just felt as if we were on holiday all the time. We still live in Seattle now.

We got through the season and John asked Jim if he would like to come back and be his assistant coach, so we went back to Bournemouth and arranged for our belongings to be shipped over to Seattle. Although we had people who came and actually packed the stuff for us, I had to sort everything out. We couldn't use our electrical stuff and we sold a lot of the big furniture because it was ridiculous to haul it 6,000 miles. We really just shipped over the small personal things like china and irreplaceable items.

We'd wanted a third child when Janet was a few years old but it never worked out that way and it must have been the change of scene that did it because suddenly I was pregnant again. Of course, we were hoping to have a boy because all footballers want a son, but it never happened and Samantha was born in Seattle in 1975. We loved the song 'I Love You, Samantha' from the musical *High Society* and named her after that.

Jim and I have been together for 42 years now, quite literally a lifetime. I was thinking about it the other day and it sounds like ages ago that we met, but it doesn't feel like that long. The time goes by so fast, it's like it was last week. My mum and dad are no longer alive. Dad died in 1972 when we were in Southampton. It was an awful shock. He was 56. My mum passed away in 1994, so I was actually there to help and be her support towards the end, after all she'd done for me. She was diagnosed with breast cancer and she was 78 when I lost her. She came and stayed with us after she had the mastectomy and I was able to help her out as much as I could, but it had gone too far.

These days, one of my sisters lives in Sheffield and the other in North Wales. David hasn't lived in England for a long time; he's a heating engineer and has a place in Jakarta, Indonesia. He works in America sometimes and called me a few months ago to tell me he was in California. He travels around a lot and was home in Liverpool with his family for Christmas. He's always off somewhere or other but he's still a fanatical Evertonian.

Karen was twelve when we moved over to America and Janet was nine, and they've been here ever since. Our children are American citizens and when we went back to England in 1986, they stayed in the States and they've never really returned to the UK, except on vacation once or twice.

We've got quite a dynasty now, with nine grandchildren; and, of course, they're American too. Karen has four boys and two girls, and Janet has two girls, and they're all into baseball and basketball. They play a bit of soccer but the interest isn't really there. We do have one who we think might have a little bit of his granddad in him – that's Samantha's boy Jamie, who's six. Jim thinks he's got a few good touches, so he takes him out in the garden and passes the ball and plays with him a bit. He thinks he might have some promising techniques. So out of the nine there might be one who can play but we don't care; they're all wonderful and we love them dearly.

Since we came back to America, I've had a couple of jobs. Initially, I worked in a department store because I wanted something to do. I'm not a person to sit down and read a book; I'm more of a mover and I like to be kept busy. I enjoy pottering about in the garden and I don't look at it like a chore, but I'm the homemaker and the one in charge of the house. Jim might cut the grass now and again, but he's not that bothered about it.

I started my own business not so long ago, and it doesn't sound very glamorous, but I do home cleaning. Before, I was working at Gap and was so bored waiting around for customers; people would come in and look at clothes and then throw them down again and I would have to pick them up and refold them and put them back in the right place. That was all I seemed to be doing and it was incredibly dull.

My daughter Janet had a lady who used to come and clean for her. She wasn't too happy with the set-up and she knew I wasn't too happy with my job, so she asked if I would like to go and clean for her and that's how I started. I'm only a one-man band and I could have more customers but I don't want to make a million dollars – it's just something to do. So I have thirteen customers and I go out for maybe two or three hours in the morning and again in the afternoon. I could do more but I don't want to kill myself. I go into some lovely houses – they're just gorgeous here – and that's my job. It's not very prestigious but I really enjoy it.

There are a lot of big cleaning companies here, teams of people who go out in force, but I'm just one person and, with all the clients I've got, I never feel like a stranger walking into their homes. I was recommended by word of mouth so it's all on a very personal level.

Lifestyles now are so different from then. I thought I had a wonderful life; it was so exciting and interesting and, although you went through your bad patches and your worries, I wouldn't have changed it. We've been to places we would never have gone if Jim hadn't been a footballer, so there's been a lot of experiences I might never have had.

We were at an Everton dinner back at the Adelphi in Liverpool in 2001 and it was amazing when Jim walked into the room – he got such a loud cheer. It's wonderful to hear that and it surprises me in a way to think that he enthrals the fans even now. It's been almost 40 years since he left but the Evertonians have so much love for him. He was always a popular player and I think it was because he always wanted to win so much that it showed, and the fans loved him for that. They used to say he played the way they would have played; he would spill blood for the cause and that was the kind of commitment they liked to see.

Looking back, I think maybe I shouldn't have given up work when we first got married. At the time, it was great because I didn't have to get up in the morning and go and stand in the rain at the bus stop, but in hindsight I think I maybe would have gone part time or something. I didn't have to stop work, but Jim was on £20 a week, which was a good wage, so there was no need for me to go and I wasn't career-minded at all. I think I maybe gave up a bit of my own personality and my independence. I became quite isolated because Jim was training every day and if you're getting up and going out to work you can retain your individuality a bit more. Maybe if I'd stayed at work a bit and kept myself involved in the day-to-day aspects of life and the workplace, it would have given me more self-confidence. I think I gave up my individuality and gave everything I had to the marriage. With me being so young, I thought it would be great not to have to go to work but, as you get older, you realise there's a lot to be said for it.

I think football is very different now – it's more business than sport – but I don't know any other life. In my day, the men were out on the pitch playing football and the women held it all together and were very much in the background. My role was as wife and mother. It was a really important job but the men were the stars and they got the accolades.

We've had our ups and downs and our insecurities over the years, as well as our share of lows when Jim's been out of work, but we got through to the other side and we've had a great life. I loved being a footballer's wife and I'm so glad it worked out the way it did.

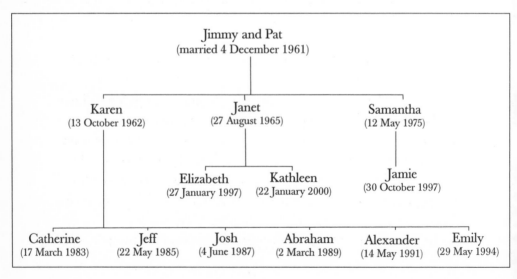

We Were Treated Like Royalty

Annette Scott

A teenage prodigy at Rangers, Alec 'Chico' Scott signed for
Everton in a £40,000 deal in January 1963. Dubbed 'The
Flying Waiter' by teammates because of his habit of running
with one arm held in a way that was only missing a tea towel,
he made 176 appearances in the royal blue and scored 26 goals.
He won the Championship title with Everton in 1963 and the
FA Cup in 1966 but left for Hibernian in September 1967,
later signing for Falkirk. Alec played 16 times for Scotland. He
died suddenly in September 2001. Much missed.

__Born Annette Buchanan, 20 May 1937, Falkirk, Scotland__

It was a very happy and carefree time to be growing up. My dad was
in the building trade and worked as a slater, and Mum was very
modern because she worked when nobody else's mum did. Originally,
she was part time in the office at the Prudential, then she joined the
Provident Clothing Company, which was a huge credit organisation
for people who didn't have much money and needed to buy clothes on
tick.

She started with a book of virtually nothing and ended up making a fabulous wage. In fact, she was earning more than my dad in the end. Eventually, she built up such a huge run that Dad had to drive her to collect from her customers; they all paid in sixpence a week. She only really worked on Friday and Saturday, and on Mondays she had to add it all up, calculate the tax, take off her wage and pay it all in. She was very small and slim, immaculately dressed, a wonderful woman and years ahead of her time.

We moved from one house to another in Falkirk and were the first people I knew to get a car – it was all very exciting. My brother Alex was three years older than me. We had a very happy childhood and in those days you could run free and nobody bothered about locking their doors or anything like that. They were great days and we couldn't have wished for better.

I'm not saying I did well at school but I absolutely loved it. I went to Falkirk Technical School and was crying when I had to leave – which sounds ridiculous because almost everyone I ever spoke to said how much they hated it, but not me. I was going to go back for my fourth year but all my pals were leaving and getting jobs and I thought I would be the only one, so I saw a job as a secretary in an accountant's office advertised, applied for it and got it.

I knew Alec by sight because he was in the year above me at school but I actually met him properly at Doaks Ballroom, the local dance hall, when I was 18. He came over and asked me to dance and that was it really. It was in the days when you could actually speak to the person you were dancing with, so I asked him what he did and he told me he was a footballer. I wasn't really impressed because it didn't mean that much to me. He asked if he could have another dance and he didn't seem to let me go. Later on, when he was leaving, he said goodbye and that he would see me the next week. We didn't go out on a date straight away, it was just a gradual thing over two or three weeks, and when he finally asked me out, we went to the pictures.

Alec was incredibly kind, good-hearted and generous to everybody. It was just part of his personality. He was always lending people money if they were short of a few bob and that was something that never changed throughout his life. Even when he was in the pub trade, people used to say they would get a 'Scott loan' because he was renowned for being quick to put his hand in his pocket.

He was a big Tony Bennett fan, loved Nat King Cole and the song he always sang was 'Walking My Baby Back Home' – that was his party piece. He wasn't the type who would want to be on the dance floor all night but if we were ever anywhere, all the ladies at the table got a dance from Alec. He would make sure nobody was left out, but he liked to stand and chat with the men, too, make no mistake.

He'd provisionally signed for Rangers when he was 16 and was almost immediately called up to the first team. It was unusual for that time because they normally had to work their way up and serve some kind of apprenticeship, but he must have just been in the right place at the right time.

My dad was a football fan and followed Falkirk but I'd never been to any games or anything like that and I didn't know much about it, though I soon learned. Once I started courting, my dad would take me to the Rangers game every week to watch them play. He started to follow Rangers but deep in his heart he always supported Falkirk.

I started keeping all the newspaper clippings of Alec's career and putting them into scrapbooks. I ended up with loads of them and still have them now. It was wonderful to watch him play and Rangers were the top team at that time, winning every single domestic honour and playing regularly in Europe. Alec was often flying out to Russia, Italy, Sweden, all over the place. He used to bring me fabulous gifts when he went away, beautiful rings and really unusual presents. He had really good taste. I don't know if he was getting guidance from anybody but everything he chose was lovely, even the clothes, and when the kids were born he'd bring lovely presents for them. It was great to see them dressed up in things you would never see here.

He was awfully generous – the kindest person I'd ever met. Rangers were making a fortune because of their success and Alec was getting paid much more than the English players because there was a cap of £20 a week on the wages down there. In Scotland, they got a higher basic plus bonuses. His was £22 a week and that was a lot of money in those days, and there were the summer and winter bonuses, which boosted the earnings right up. Crowd bonuses hadn't come in, or cash for scoring goals, but it wasn't far away, and it all happened when we moved to Everton. The block was lifted in 1962 and Alec got the benefit of that too, because he was already well established.

We married locally in St Modan's parish church on 24 June 1959, when I'd just turned 22. Evelyn was my best friend and my bridesmaid, and we're still best friends to this day. Reporters and press photographers were there but so much was happening I didn't really take much in. It didn't bother me, them being there, but it did get intrusive at other times. I don't know how they put up with it nowadays, I really don't.

Alec had two brothers and a sister; both boys were footballers, too. Jim was his best man and played for Newcastle and Crystal Palace, and Robert went to Bury in the lower League. Their dad was a very talented player but he wasn't really interested in it enough to make a living from it.

We had a week in Jersey for our honeymoon. We flew down from Glasgow and it was the first time I'd been on a plane. Of course, Alec had travelled extensively with Rangers but I got a real taste for it and after that we were abroad at every opportunity.

He wouldn't dare stay out late the night before a game; he'd always be in by ten o'clock. I remember a couple of players at Everton getting warnings about drinking – the fans would phone Mr Catterick and tell him that they'd seen them out late or drinking too much. When we were young we never drank alcohol, not ever. We went dancing but we would never dream of going into a pub. It was completely alien to us and never even crossed our minds. The first drink I ever had was at a Rangers do; it was advocaat and it was vile. They asked me what I wanted to drink and when I said I didn't want anything, they looked at me as if I was mad. The way we'd been brought up, the only time you had drink was in your house at New Year and once it was gone, it was gone.

If you were doing an apprenticeship in those days, you wouldn't get called up for national service until it was over. Alec wanted something to fall back on if his football suddenly came to an end and was doing his training in engineering. When it was completed, he was eventually called up but fortunately he got stationed at Edinburgh Castle and they released him every weekend, so not only did he keep playing for Rangers, he also got to stay at home, though he had to catch the train there every morning. The colonel was awfully good to him because he was into football, so I'm sure that helped.

Alec was a supreme athlete but that was his natural talent; he only trained like everybody else and wasn't obsessive about it. He didn't have much bother with his weight during the close season and pretty much stayed the same all year round. He was very sport-minded, though; he loved tennis and played all the time in the summer when we were up in Scotland, but not so much in England because there was nobody for him to play against. He loved golf, too; he looked after himself but he wasn't a fanatical trainer at all, it was just his gift.

When I found out I was having twins, I nearly collapsed. I went to the antenatal class and they looked at me and said I was too big for three months and that maybe I'd mixed up my dates, but I was sure I hadn't. They did an X-ray and told me I'd have to go back for the results the next week. I was on tenterhooks wondering what was happening and then they dropped the bombshell. I broke the news to Alec while we were driving down the road and he almost crashed. When I think about it, I should have picked a better moment.

I was awfully worried that they would be born while Alec was away; he was scheduled to go abroad when I was due and, of course, there was no question that he wouldn't be travelling with the team, so the doctor said he would induce them and the boys were born on 1 February 1962, a few days before Alec went away. The midwife said 'You've got two boys and one is the double of your husband', but I couldn't see their resemblance to either of us.

I'm very small and slim and I remember my mother-in-law saying that she was so worried they would be wee midgets because I'm so little, but they were both big, healthy boys: Alec Jnr weighed in at 6lb 14oz. and David was 6lb 14½oz. They didn't need to go into incubators or anything. They're not identical, but they were very alike as babies. They were very individual, though, and as the years went on, they started to look different.

It took a bit of getting used to, that's for sure. It was hard work at the beginning because you literally needed two pairs of hands – one was wanting to be fed and the other was crying, and if there was nobody there to help, it was a nightmare. When I look back, I wonder how I coped but when you're young you don't ask questions, you just get on with it. The worst thing was the pram. I had one of those beautiful chrome Silver Cross twin prams that weighed more than me. I don't know how I managed to hold onto it sometimes, especially going downhill. I would take them out and after two minutes all the covers would be on the floor after one of them had kicked them off. Never once did I have a nice tidy pram, all neatly tucked in.

We never bothered moving because Glasgow was only a 25-minute train journey before you jumped on the Tube and it took you straight to Ibrox, so there was no point in moving. Alec could get to work faster than some of the players who actually lived in Glasgow because of the traffic. Everything was convenient for us in Falkirk and I had my parents on hand to help me with the boys. The crunch came when Alec got transferred to Everton in February 1963 and they were 13 months old.

Spurs had been after him too, but the deciding factors were that his brother Robert lived in Bury, so at least we'd have one person we knew relatively nearby, and, of course, it was far easier to get to Scotland from the north of England, so we could go home for the weekend and see my mum and dad.

The transfer was with immediate effect, so he had to go ahead of us. He would drive back up to Falkirk after the game but then he would have to go back on Monday morning for training. We lived in rented property so we didn't have to sell up to move, but we'd started up a grocer's shop that my and Alec's mum worked in, so they took that over and I started going back and forwards from Scotland on the train to look for somewhere to live.

He moved into the Lord Nelson, a hotel right near Lime Street station, while we looked for a house and one morning we were in the dining room having breakfast and a couple of tables away were Eric Morecambe and Ernie Wise. It was before they were really famous and you only vaguely knew who they were, but that was our claim to fame.

I'd never been to England before and I didn't have a clue what it would be like. Everton gave us a list of houses in Maghull to take a look at and we could decide which one we wanted. The house we chose was in Kendal Drive, a newly built semi-detached with a curved bay window at the front. I couldn't get over the houses being just plain brick – it looked really peculiar because the only houses I'd ever seen had been pebbledashed.

I went to all the matches at Goodison and my neighbours, Enid and Bill Bailey, would look after the boys for me. It was the highlight of my week and I really loved watching the game. Some of the wives went purely for the social aspect and just wanted to chat, but I genuinely wanted to watch the football. I loved watching the match and I still do.

I was alone with the boys for a lot of the time and homesickness hit me really hard. Enid and Bill had a daughter, Jan, and she would come and babysit and let us get out from time to time. That made a big difference because, before that, I couldn't go anywhere and I was really tied down.

John Moores owned Everton then; he was very generous and such a lovely man. You would expect him to be aloof but he was just a wonderful, warm person and from the school of thought that if you were happy at home, you were happy on the pitch. He was charming to everybody and was just one of many. When we moved down there, we had a driver at our disposal from the Littlewoods headquarters and he'd take you to go and get furniture or to choose wallpaper. You were allowed so much in a furnishing budget and it was lovely.

Sandy and Jeanette Brown moved down from Scotland in

September 1963 and we socialised with them and Derek and Maureen Temple. Occasionally, we met Pat and Jimmy Gabriel, but we were also friends with two couples who were nothing to do with football, and it was quite refreshing to have a change of scene and conversation.

We liked to go out to eat. The Lydiate Country Club was one of our favourites, which wasn't as posh as it sounds. It was just up the road and you'd get a huge big plateful of food and the fellas loved the big steaks in those days.

Sometimes we would go on to the Prince of Wales on Lord Street in Southport but mostly we'd go to the Sands in Ainsdale. We'd have a meal there, a few drinks and some of the others would normally come too: Pat and Ray Wilson, and Alan and Lesley Ball, and there would often end up a big crowd of us. Once I met some people, my homesickness subsided a lot and it was much easier.

We'd been abroad on holiday quite often by the time we won the League in 1963 and the club took us to Torremolinos. I always remember that the hotel was in the middle of nowhere. It wasn't the Costa del Sol as we know it now, that's for sure. We thought it was a desolate place, although our hotel was wonderful and everything was laid on for us. It was about a mile from the village and it was very poor around there. There was one nightclub and I can remember the girls were told that if we went to Malaga we were to cover up and mustn't wear shorts. It was very prim and proper in those days. The women were chaperoned but we had a lovely time and were treated like royalty.

In the summer of 1964, the club took the players to Australia for six weeks in pre-season. I wasn't very well while Alec was away and I felt so isolated. Of course, he would write and I always wrote back, and by the tone of his letters, I thought we would be emigrating there, he really loved it. I told him he was looking at it from a different stance. They were getting wined and dined and taken out on yachts and really living the life of Riley; it would have been a different story if you were to actually go there to try and make a living. But he kept going on about what a wonderful place it would be to bring up the children and to be in the sunshine all the time, although nothing ever came of it. He came home with badges and souvenirs from every club and place they visited. It was lovely to have him home again; I'd missed him so much.

Some of the local wives thought the way we were treated by Everton was terrible, but I always thought I was treated well compared to when we were at Rangers – we were lucky if we got in the door at Ibrox. Everton were far more generous to the wives and the players. The players were better thought of, too, and I always used to remark on the difference because, at Rangers, it was as if the players didn't matter at all. The board came first and that was it.

I remember when Everton sent us an enormous Christmas hamper with booze and goodies and lovely stuff, and there was even a present in there for me. It was a dressing-table set; a matching brush, comb and mirror, and it was nice to be remembered. There was an enormous turkey, too, but we'd already bought ours so Alec got in the car and took it to a nearby children's home – otherwise it would have gone to waste.

Everton was a much better place to be and although there was the rivalry with Liverpool it was absolutely nothing compared to the bigotry between Rangers and Celtic, which could turn really nasty. The most wonderful thing that will always stick in my memory was when they won the FA Cup in 1966 and the team were driving back into Liverpool. We were on the outskirts of the city and everywhere you looked there was a sea of blue, white and red. There were as many Liverpool fans out on the streets to welcome the boys home as there were Evertonians. All the Liverpool supporters had decorated their balconies and windows, and there were flags flying wherever you looked.

Ken Dodd was a well-known Liverpool supporter and I can still see him now, standing on the pavement on his own, waving like mad; he was so thrilled that the Cup had come to Merseyside, regardless of which team. If that was Glasgow and Rangers had won, you wouldn't have seen a bit of green anywhere, not even a blade of grass. I thought it was wonderful and there was great banter between the clubs, which was something I'd never experienced before.

We were so excited about going to Wembley. Jeanette Brown and I went down to London on the train to buy our outfits and came back home again the same day. I wore a cerise coat and dress with navy accessories. There was to be a big dinner in the evening and I had a navy chiffon dress to wear. The wives were all discussing their outfits and I can't remember who it was but one of them described her dress and I realised it was the same as mine. I almost died on the spot – of all the dresses we could have picked. Because I was so small, I'd already had mine altered so she said she would go and buy a new one because I couldn't take mine back.

We got phone call after phone call from people asking for tickets for the final. There was all this talk that the players would get a hundred tickets each but the chairman of Sheffield Wednesday was a bit of a churchgoer and he put a block on the number the players from both teams were allowed and they ended up with five. We had a friend who worked in a factory office and everybody knew she could get Wembley tickets from Alec Scott without a problem. I don't remember how much the tickets were but she was gathering in all the cash in advance and she had a biscuit tin full of money. She was just waiting for Alec to hand over the tickets and she would distribute them among her colleagues.

Of course, the bombshell fell and you should have seen the carry on as people were desperately trying to get sorted out. Even immediate family couldn't get to the match; it was ridiculous and nothing short of a disgrace. The spivs always managed to get hold of tickets, though. I could never quite work out how, but they always did.

I think coming from behind to the win the FA Cup 3–2 was my proudest moment because we were on a low, thinking we'd never come back from two down. To cap it all, it had been billed as an uninteresting final and it turned out to be one of the most exciting ever. It was just wonderful to witness.

The boys all got presented with gold watches and the wives got boxes of Belgian chocolates, which weighed a ton; they were the heaviest I'd ever come across. I found the menu from the dinner recently. We've got so much stuff from those days, mainly from Rangers because he was there for eight or nine years, but some lovely things from Everton too.

I don't suppose many of the players got to see that entire Cup final again, but we did. A cinema in Falkirk arranged for us to watch it with the Provost – the Scottish equivalent of the Mayor. It was quite strange really, the three of us sitting in the empty picture house watching the game. Then they presented Alec with the Pathé newsreel in a huge can. I don't know what we were supposed to do with it and I imagine it's obsolete now, but it's still here.

Alec didn't have any superstitions or rituals and, even if he lost, he wouldn't be whingeing or depressed. He obviously wasn't very happy if they had been beaten but he never brought it home with him. I've seen some of the players with their faces tripping them up but he would just say they were beaten by the better team on the day, or they were unlucky, and that was where it ended.

He was very fortunate with his injury record; he never sustained anything too serious. The worst he had was when he was playing abroad for Rangers. He was running at full tilt when somebody fouled him but he was going so fast he went headfirst into the stone wall around the edge of the pitch. He managed to get his head down but he was completely out for the count and was carried off on a stretcher. He came home with stitches and a huge bandage around his head like a turban. Another time, he got a knock on the head and began hallucinating and talking gibberish, but he was all right in the end.

I saw him play for Scotland every time I could and it was wonderful. There's nothing like the atmosphere of being at the game, and to see him play for his country made me feel so proud. The fans used to call him 'Chico' and to hear them chanting his name around the ground was just amazing.

He often used to re-live games in his sleep; he would sit up and stick his hand out and shout, 'Goal'. He used to talk in his sleep, too, and I could literally hold conversations with him. He'd start off quite sensibly then it would turn to gibberish. I'd try and remember them for the next morning but I never could. I should have written it down just for the comedy value.

I don't think I made any major sacrifices for his career other than leaving Scotland to go to Everton, but I didn't look on it as a hardship; it was actually quite an adventure and, once I got over the homesickness, I really enjoyed it. It was quite daunting with the boys being so young, but I knew Alec would be there so it wouldn't be too bad.

I loved my time in Liverpool and we really did think of staying, but we had the business at home and I had a dress shop that I'd opened up in Falkirk, so it made sense to go back. If we'd started a business down in England, we would have had no support network and what if one of us took ill?

We could have happily stayed in Liverpool without a doubt, though. We liked the people – they were friendly and always good to us, and the fans loved Alec, who was very well thought of. We left England in September 1967, when he was transferred to Hibs, and he ended up at Falkirk, so he went full circle and retired in 1972.

When I was in England, the only thing I really missed was a dance. They had a get-together with the FA Cup win but that was it. At Rangers, they had one every year and we were all invited to a dinner and then on to a dance. Whenever they won a cup or a trophy, there would be a celebration for the players. At Christmas, we would be taken to a show of some kind at the theatre. I remember Everton had us back to Goodison for drinks when we beat Manchester United in the semi-final of the FA Cup. Everyone was on a high because that was them through to the final, but they didn't have an annual party and that was the one thing I really missed.

If I had the chance to be a footballer's wife now, I don't think I'd take it. In our day, there wasn't so much pressure on the players and they didn't live their lives under such scrutiny. It all seems so different now. They still seem to come from ordinary working-class backgrounds but they're suddenly flung into this artificial world with vast amounts of money that some of them just can't handle and they seem unable to live a normal life.

I'm sure there are hundreds of players and their families who are more normal but I think these enormous amounts of money bring their own problems. The money they earn is beyond comprehension. They'll never have to work again, that's for sure, but the fact is, it's ruined the game.

All the teams you thought would be there forever have gone. Look at Leeds. Who would ever have believed this could happen to a club of that stature? It's all wages and transfer fees and this carry on with agents. We'd never even heard of agents. It's quite sad, in a way. They're under the microscope all the time – their lives and everything they do – and then stories appear in the papers and you don't even know if they're true. I feel sorry for David Beckham and his wife; the press were just sitting there waiting for something to go wrong. They love it when that happens because it sells their newspapers. It makes me sick.

We didn't spend the money Alec was making because we didn't have a lavish life. We had a car and that was it. I was always of the opinion that he could go out on the pitch and break a leg and that would be the end of his career, and then what would we do? So I saved the money and banked it and that's how we built up enough to get a pub.

We went into the trade with his brother Jim when he finished football and they built it between them from scratch. The pub was in Falkirk and called the Hurlet, which is an old Scottish word that means a building on a corner on a hill. At first, I was doing everything – working behind the bar and in the kitchen – then I had to call a halt to it.

It was all right, but I wasn't ecstatic about it. I was hardly there in the evenings, as I was at home with the boys, but if I was there at night, I was on the other side of the bar. We had some great times and made lots of friends. I retired from my pub duties before he did. I always had plenty to keep me busy – we had the dog that always needed walking and I loved to be in the garden. Alec worked there right up until he'd had enough.

We sold the pub and Jim opened a very small bar in Falkirk and Alec would go in and give him a hand for two or three hours a couple of days a week. It kept his hand in and structured his day. He was a very sociable person; he could meet everybody, catch up, have a natter, hear some new jokes and he still had time for his golf. He loved that. He didn't like sitting around but he wasn't a DIY person or anything like that. I was the one in charge of that side of things.

We didn't really know Alec was ill until he was in hospital and from the time he was diagnosed with cancer to the time he was gone, it was only two or three weeks. I lost him on 12 September 2001, the day after the planes crashed into the World Trade Center in New York. I was sitting in intensive care at the hospital when I heard that news and it seemed as if the whole world had gone mad. Alec never regained consciousness, so he didn't get to hear about it. It was the most awful time and what magnified it was I'd lost my mum six months before and was only just starting to accept that. It really was devastating; we'd been together our whole lives.

His funeral was awesome. Hundreds of people were there – I couldn't believe the turn-out. I didn't even see half the people who came to pay their respects because I'd have been there all week. There was no room at the crematorium; everyone was standing outside and it was impossible to get in. There were so many familiar faces and dozens of Rangers players from the old days. Gordon West, Brian Labone and Derek Temple all drove up from Merseyside to see him off, too.

My boys still live very close to me in Falkirk: five minutes in each direction. David played a bit of football but he was very injury prone so he went into the pub trade with his dad. Young Alec went off to university but he hated it so he went into the fire service instead. They both got on so well with their dad and would go all over the place with him playing golf. They really enjoyed each other's company.

We had so many plans and we were going to travel much more

when he retired, but it wasn't to be. I console myself with the knowledge that he didn't suffer and was never in pain. We lived a charmed life and we were very fortunate, but I miss him so much and miss not hearing his jokes.

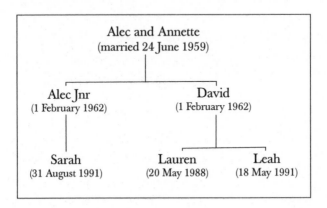

Nothing Really Daunted Us

Carole Dobson

For five seasons, Everton's midfield was graced by Martin Dobson, another record signing at £300,000. Expectations were high when the 26 year old arrived from Burnley in August 1974 and he rose to the occasion, going on to make 230 appearances and netting 40 times before his return to Turf Moor for £100,000 in August '79. He won five England caps and went on to play for and manage Bury before a spell in charge of Bristol Rovers in 1991. Dobson is now settled in Bolton, scouts for Ipswich and writes a column for the *Lancashire Evening Telegraph*.

Born Carole McManus, 6 May 1949, Burnley, Lancashire

Catholic nuns ruled Paddock House Convent Grammar in Accrington with a rod of iron and, although my parents were absolutely thrilled that I passed my 11-Plus and had won a place, I have mixed memories of my time there. My brothers all went to St Theodore's High School in Burnley but my sister Linda followed in my footsteps. It was a good school, the sort of education parents were grateful for, and it prepared you well for life, but it was awfully strict and I was ready to leave when

I did. I finished at 16 then went on to college, where I studied art and design.

There were five children in our family and I was the oldest. Dad was a steam-engine driver for British Rail and during the holidays we would go with him when he was taking a train to the seaside. As a special treat, we could go on the footplate with him. It was awe-inspiring and I've got great memories of days out in Southport and Blackpool. We'd spend the day on the beach with Mum then get on the same train Dad was bringing back home. It was real story-book stuff. Mum was kept very busy when we were young but she was a confectioner by trade and was always making cakes for special occasions. Later on, she had a part-time job and Linda and I had to help with household chores and do some of the cooking, which stood us in good stead in later years. We had fabulous parents and a wonderful, happy childhood.

My grandfather used to get the ferry over from Ireland to watch Everton, so I knew a bit about football and went to the odd game. My dad was a sporting man, too, steeped in cricket and football. He was an avid Burnley supporter but when they were playing away, he would go and watch Blackburn because Ewood Park was virtually next door. In fact, he would watch anyone he could but, because of my granddad, he had a particular soft spot for Everton. He loved going to Goodison and told us stories about the derby games in those old days. He said the Everton and Liverpool supporters would stand side by side and shake hands after the match and congratulate the winners; it's hard to imagine that now. He'd go and watch all the Home Internationals, too, with his Scottish friend Jock. One year, he would go to Hampden Park and watch England play up there, and the following year Jock would come to England and they'd go off to Wembley together. He loved his sport and couldn't get enough of it.

Martin loves cricket, too. He used to play for Lancashire schoolboys and could have had a career in the sport but he opted for football because he wasn't keen on 'hanging around in the dressing-room'. He still loves cricket, though, and during the summer he watches as much as he can. He and my father get on very well because their interest in sport is mutual.

It was 1971 when I met Martin and his wife at a party. I was about 22, also married, and my husband was a big Burnley fan. One of our neighbours was another Burnley player, Les Latcham, and that was how we were introduced. We all became very good friends and would go out for meals in a big group, maybe eight or ten of us on a Saturday night after a game. My first impression of Martin was that he was considerate, polite and quite shy. I think football brought him out of that to a certain degree, but he's still a very quiet man. He's entertaining when he's in company, but he likes his own space as well.

My then husband and I set up a studio designing and selling kitchens, bathrooms and bedrooms, and I did the designing. We were quite successful and ran it for 13 years but I think that contributed to our marriage breakdown because, when you live and work together, there's nowhere to run. We finally got divorced in 1985. Martin had been to Everton and back to Burnley by then and was player–manager of Bury by that time.

When we got together, I had no idea what I was letting myself in for but the concept of a footballing life didn't bother me at all. I'm a Catholic and Martin is Church of England and since we were both divorced, we didn't think we would be able to marry in a church. Because of my background, I didn't really want a registry-office wedding, and fortunately we found a little church on the outskirts of Burnley and the vicar agreed to it. I couldn't arrange it during the season so we married in June 1987. We had about 40 guests and it was a lovely day. Frank Casper, Martin's first-team coach at Bury, was there along with Terry Robinson, the chairman, but the rest of the guests were just family. We had the reception at the Dunkenhalgh Hotel in Accrington then flew off to St Lucia for three weeks. It was blissful. There was something in the press about it. I think there was a photo and a little write-up, but that didn't bother me at all.

Roy Vernon and his blushing bride, Norma, 17 February 1958

Roy and Norma Vernon with Mark, Neil and Roy Jnr

Maureen Harvey with her miniature Colin Harvey
– Joanna was born on 7 July 1970

Colin and Maureen Harvey,
Prestatyn, 21 January 1970

Colin and Maureen Harvey at home
with Joanna and Melanie

Annette and Alec Scott
christen their twins,
Alec and David,
Falkirk, 1962
(© Bill Miller)

Annette and Alec Scott acquaint themselves with the FA Cup, May 1966
(© Grade 'A' Photographic Service)

Maureen and Derek Temple marry in Dovecot,
Liverpool, Christmas Eve 1960

Maureen and Derek Temple with their sons,
Neil and Philip

Ted and Dolly Sagar marry at St Lawrence's Church in Walton, 8 May 1932 (© H.A. Smith)

Ted and Dolly Sagar on the Blue Anchor bowling green (© Provincial Press Agency)

Nancy Young assists Jean Parker with her broken ankle whilst Alex Parker, George Thompson, Alex Young and Alec Scott look on sympathetically, Torremolinos, May 1963

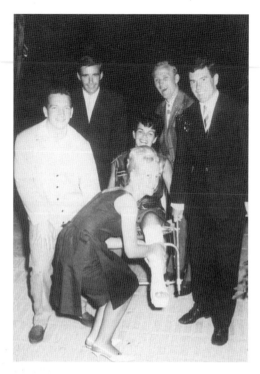

The Youngs, Parkers and Scotts relax in the bar at Las Tres Carabelas, Torremolinos, May 1963

'The girls were like beauty queens used to be, so glamorous in their one-piece swimsuits': Alex Young and Roy Vernon judge the Miss New Brighton beauty pageant (© Medley and Bird Ltd)

ABOVE: The wives leave Lime Street station for the 1966 FA Cup final at Wembley, the scent of victory in the air. Back row (left to right): Ann West, Pat Gabriel, Jeanette Brown, Pat Wilson, Margaret Pickering, Beryl Harris; front row (left to right): Pat Labone, Annette Scott, Nancy Young, Maureen Temple, Margie Rankin, Gwen Wright

INSET: Pat Gabriel and Norma Vernon toast the 1962–63 League champions

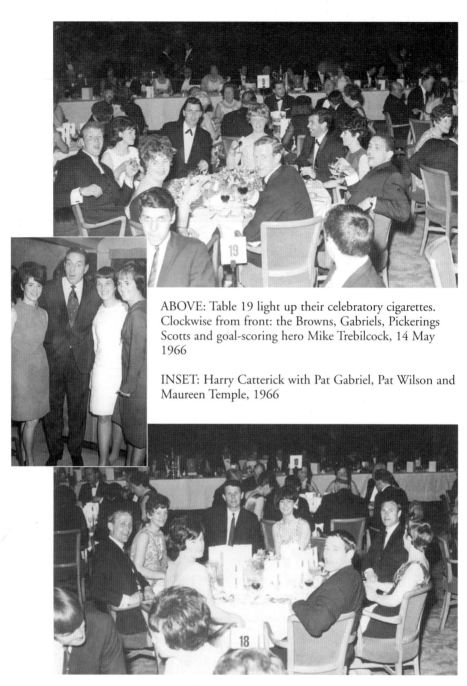

ABOVE: Table 19 light up their celebratory cigarettes. Clockwise from front: the Browns, Gabriels, Pickerings Scotts and goal-scoring hero Mike Trebilcock, 14 May 1966

INSET: Harry Catterick with Pat Gabriel, Pat Wilson and Maureen Temple, 1966

FA Cup winners: Alex and Nancy Young, Brian and Pat Labone, Ray and Pat Wilson, and Maureen and Derek Temple, 14 May 1966

We bought a house in Burnley and that was where we settled. We didn't have children together because we had a ready-made family. Martin has a son, Richard, and a daughter from his first marriage and I've got two girls, Helen and Sarah, and we all lived together. The funny thing is that Martin's daughter is called Helen, too, so when you called one you often got the other. There were some problems, of course, but everyone really did get on well and it was one big happy family.

I was friendly with other footballers' wives but, because Martin was the player–manager, I think I became a bit of a mother figure to the other girls. He had some super guys playing for him and I got to know most of the wives quite well – they were a good bunch. They were very supportive and loyal, and went to all the games, but maybe the most important role they played was to help keep their men's feet on the ground and that's vital – if a player is happy at home, then that will reflect on the pitch.

Bury are a small club with a great family atmosphere but they didn't have a tremendous amount of facilities and there was nowhere for these poor women to go on a match day. That was always a bone of contention with me. Their husbands were entertaining thousands of people, yet their wives and children were left to loiter in the corridors or outside in the rain. I thought it was so wrong. They spent hours waiting for their husbands to finish so they could go home, and there was nowhere for them to go. We told the chairman it wasn't good enough and they needed somewhere to come and belong. We managed to get a room organised for them in the end.

Martin would often tell us about his superstitions and he was adamant they worked. Apparently, when he was at Everton he would set off from home in his lucky suit or tie or whatever he'd worn the last time they'd won, listening to the Electric Light Orchestra on the tape deck in his car. As he got nearer to Goodison Park and there was a sea of royal blue, he would be driving past the fans with 'Mr Blue Sky' blasting out at full volume. He said that by the time he got to the ground, he was psyched up and ready for anything. As far as I know, footballers were pretty much all like that – they were so superstitious it used to make me laugh – but he really believed it worked, so who was I to argue? As soon as the team lost, it would all change again and he would soon be in pursuit of a new 'lucky tie'.

When he was there, Everton were going through one of their barren spells, although he did make it to Wembley for the League Cup final in 1977, a dour goalless draw with Aston Villa, but he made it nonetheless. He'll never forget seeing the fans on Wembley Way and said running out onto the pitch was the most fantastic feeling in the world. I can still remember the phone call I got when he got his England call-up; we were still only friends then but I was so proud of him. It was wonderful to know that he'd been asked to play for England. I don't think it can get any better than that because that's somebody saying he's the best in his position in the country and that has to be the greatest accolade you can get.

There was the odd Bury game I couldn't make but I always tried my utmost to be there. I'd just jump in the car and go, no matter where they were playing. I think he quite enjoyed it when I did that because, after the game, we would come home together in the car rather than him go on the coach, and he needed that little bit of time as player–manager to distance himself and think about what had happened on the pitch. When they lost, I was subjected to half an hour of horrendous ranting while all his frustrations came out, and if they won, he would wax lyrical on how wonderful his team had been. I think he needed somebody to bounce his thoughts off and I'd watched so much football that I did understand the game and I had a great interest in how it all panned out, although my perspective was very different from his.

We'd always stop off somewhere different on the way home and have dinner. We'd just find somewhere we liked the look of and have something to eat. He'd gather his thoughts and we would enjoy each other's company. It wouldn't matter where we were, though, there would always be somebody in the restaurant who would come over and say hello or ask him for his autograph. It was amazing. You would think you'd be in a place where nobody would have the vaguest idea who he was but they would just materialise – it never failed to astound me. I suppose he was quite recognisable by his hair, but it's a little thinner these days. We always reckon that Kevin Keegan copied him with that perm of his but Martin was the trailblazer, and his was natural.

Injuries were an occupational hazard. He broke his leg very early on when he played for Burnley and that kept him out for a while – he made a rug while he was convalescing from that; he could never be idle. Another time, he broke a wrist and he's had any number of head injuries and stitches. When he was very young he went to Germany and clashed heads with somebody and split his eyebrow open, and he's often come back with stud holes in his knees and shins.

Once, during a training session at Bury, he went up to head a ball and clashed heads with one of his players but, unfortunately, it was his face that caught the impact. He came home that night and I almost fainted when he walked through the door because he was wearing a mask and looked like the Phantom of the Opera. He'd smashed his nose and it had ended up on the side of his face. I can only imagine how painful it must have been. The consultant warned him it was going to really hurt so it must have been horrendous, but once they'd reset it and put it back more or less where it should have been, he was on the mend. He didn't really worry too much about getting hurt – it's wives who panic. He just picked himself up and carried on.

He didn't re-live games in his sleep and often he tells me that he doesn't even dream. I'm sure he does but he's not aware of it. He gets it all out of his system and then relaxes. The day after a match, his perspective would be very clear because he'd thought it through quietly and then he seemed to know what he had to do.

Pre-season was always a busy time but I was very lucky he didn't go away too often. He's been on the odd trip to Russia and the Isle of Man but you've got to get used to these things. I'm not too sure about the end-of-season tours, though. That was a different thing altogether and not something Martin particularly relished. If they'd done fairly well, they'd be away for a week, and it wasn't on the top of his list of favourite things to do. They call it bonding but Martin always used to say to me that when you've been with players through a season – in the dressing-room, training, travelling and working together – the last thing you need is to go on holiday with them.

He could also be transferred at the drop of a hat, but in a funny way it wasn't unsettling. I know we had children to think about but I always thought they were opportunities as opposed to ordeals. When you get involved with a professional footballer, you know it's always a possibility and you've got to accept it. He was manager at Bristol Rovers for a while in 1991 and we even had a short spell in Cyprus. We'd only gone there for a two-week holiday and got talking to someone in a bar and, within two weeks of getting home, we had the secretary from Apop FC, a Cypriot club, on the phone asking if he was interested in managing out there.

The chairman of the club was a very interesting guy. He was Greek Cypriot and invited us to come and meet him at the Grosvenor House Hotel in London and stay in his suite. It is amazing the sort of things that happen in football. Sometimes you'd have to pinch yourself. We were only in Cyprus for three or four months. The football there isn't the same as we know it in England. I can't really go into detail but let's say it was different. Nonetheless, it was a great experience. We had a lovely place out there, with lots of sunshine. The owner had yachts and a mansion, and everything he did was in a big way – it was quite an eye-opener and all a little bit surreal. We treated it as a lovely long holiday. We have lots of good memories from that, and a few ragged ones too, but nothing we regret. Our children didn't want to come with us so we didn't force them because they wouldn't have been happy, and we didn't know how long we were going to be there. The youngest would have been 17 then and was still being educated, so my mum stepped into the breach, God love her.

I think you need to have a broad perspective and take your chances, and we didn't want to get into our dotage and have any regrets. We always liked to have a go and if we didn't like it when we'd given it a try, we would come away none the worse. Nothing really daunted us.

Martin began as Bury's player–manager with about eight games left at the end of the 1983–84 season and the following year they got promoted to the old Third Division. That was a hell of a day. It's small fry compared to an England call-up, or being involved in the Premiership, but nonetheless it was just as important and I was so proud of him.

I was never expected to do anything other than be his wife and I can honestly say he's never expected me to do anything I didn't want to do. It was my decision if I wanted to work. I didn't have to but if I felt like I wanted to, that was fine. He never expected me to even go to a game. He would ask me if I'd like to go; he is always very considerate and never presumes anything.

There was nothing I hated about being a footballer's wife. I think I've been very lucky because he's a real family man. There were always women hanging around at games, but I never feared anything because he was very loyal and committed and still is. I can count the nights we've not been together and I trust him to the ends of the earth.

I wouldn't like to be a footballer's wife nowadays because I think the pressures are enormous. When Martin was in his heyday nothing was expected of us but look at the Victoria Beckhams of this world – they're followed around everywhere. I would really hate that. When Martin played, there was more of an element of innocence and everybody seemed to be happier because they could be themselves. Now, they're conscious of what they're wearing and where they're going and who with. It's too public and the thought of somebody rummaging through my bins or taking endless photos makes me feel quite angry. Martin would finish playing a match then we would have a drink and go home and that was it. Now they're on display all the time. Victoria Beckham is a good example because she's constantly in the news but nobody knows who she really is or what she thinks; they just judge her on her image and that's it. I really do feel quite sorry for her. It all sounds very shallow to me.

People still recognise Martin, particularly if he goes back to Everton. They've got one of his caps and an England shirt of his framed on the wall in the Legends Bar at Goodison and they always say there will be two tickets for us whenever we want them. We do go back. Sometimes he goes to do a match report for the *Lancashire Evening Telegraph* and sometimes it's just social but, whenever we're there, everybody wants to shake his hand. It's remarkable and ever so special. Suddenly, you'll hear somebody shout, 'Dobbo, it's great to see you.'

It's just wonderful to think that the fans hold him in such high regard. It's the same at Burnley, too. They've just started a Wall of Legends at Turf Moor and he was voted No. 2. They've got plaques built into a wall and they had the opening in February 2004. The former players had to walk around the pitch before the kick-off and there was a big dinner in the evening. The atmosphere was wonderful; there were 400 people at the meal and he got such a great round of applause, it made me feel so proud. It's a lovely feeling that he's done something special in his life. It's always nice to go back, see people and meet up with old friends. All the Old Boys get together and reminisce about the glory days and catch up with what they're all doing now. He still has fans writing to him wanting autographs and sending him photos to be signed. Some of them are avid collectors and it's nice that he's not been forgotten.

Martin's a frustrated writer and I think there's a book in him dying to get out. In the meantime, he writes a column for the local paper so he spends a lot of time on the computer. He can sit for hours writing an article and he's quite humorous in his work. They love him at the paper because he doesn't need a ghost writer; he does all the work himself and emails it to them for publication. He also scouts for Joe Royle at Ipswich Town and does some after-dinner speaking, so he's always quite busy. He's still quite a home bird and, as he's never been a pub person, he doesn't miss the usual lads' Saturday night out. When he was playing, he was always very concerned about his performance and wanted to give his best every game.

He's also a keen gardener and likes to be outside. We've got a big garden now and he's out there whenever he has time, but there never seems to be enough because he loves watching football so much. He might have played on a Saturday but if there was a game on the Sunday, he'd go and watch it. He just couldn't get enough and he's the same now. He'll watch any level and any age: children's games, friendlies and non-League. He was also the academy director at Bolton Wanderers for four years, when Colin Todd was the manager, a job that suited him nicely.

I like to garden, too, but I never seem to get much spare time and, now, as we've got four grandchildren, there are just not enough hours in the day. We've got two boys and two girls. The boys are Sarah's. Daniel is a keen footballer and always has a ball with him, while Thomas is only a toddler but he kicks it around too, because he sees Daniel and he wants to join in. Helen has two girls, Laura and Alice, and they are following in their granddad's footsteps, in a manner of speaking. They are both cheerleaders and help entertain the supporters before home games at Turf Moor – so the tradition lives on.

I work as a personal assistant to a chef in a restaurant called Chefs at Paragon. You know what chefs are supposed to be like temperamentally, but not this one. He's an excellent cook, too, but minor details and day-to-day things are not his forte, so I try to organise things for him. Martin said if I wanted to do the job that's fine and if not, that's also fine. I chose to do it, as I've nearly always worked, except when the children were younger. I really enjoy going to work and I leave Martin here, getting on with his writing.

My brothers and sister are still very close, although we're a bit far-flung now. John is a film editor and lives in London; Michael is still in Burnley and runs his own kitchen studio; Paul lives in Warrington and has just started his own electrical business; and Linda has been a teacher for years. We're all very lucky because, these days, families are not quite the same as they used to be. Yes, we have our differences occasionally, but on the whole we all get on and see each other as often as possible.

I suppose I did make some sacrifices for Martin's career, but that happens in any partnership and I think, if the truth be known, Martin really made more than me.

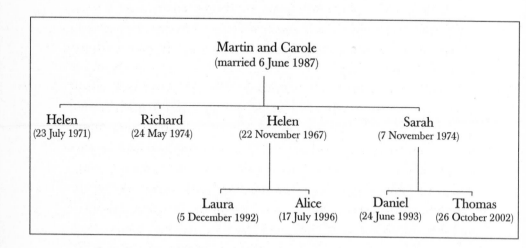

The Things We Do For Love

Janet Royle

Making his debut in a 2–0 defeat against Blackpool in 1966, Joe Royle became Everton's youngest player aged 16 years and 282 days. Royle was the leading scorer both in 1968–69 and 1969–70, and managed 119 in all before moving to Manchester City in December 1974 for £200,000. Subsequent moves to Bristol City and Norwich saw the centre-forward maintain his scoring touch – his last goal coming for the East Anglian side in a First Division game at Goodison. He managed Oldham with great success from 1982–94 and returned to Everton as manager in November 1994, guiding the club to safety and the FA Cup in his first season. He has been managing Ipswich Town since October 2003.

Born Janet Hughes, 25 April 1949, Everton, Liverpool

The house on Fowler Street was a huge three-storey Victorian terrace just off Breck Road and nearer to Anfield than Goodison Park. It belonged to my grandparents, who'd lived there throughout the war, and it was always full of people and cousins and noise. The cellar had been the bomb shelter during the Blitz and there was a big grid over the front step so you could escape if the house was hit. My mum was one of eight, so at one time there were eleven of us living there. It was great fun.

I'd stayed another year at school to learn shorthand, typing and bookkeeping, and could have stayed on and learned more, but I didn't want to go to night school again. I had other things on my mind; I really wanted to travel. My best friend Mo and I would talk about it all the time and we couldn't wait until we were 18 because we were going to join the Harrison Agency and then go to New York and become nannies. In the meantime, we had a holiday booked to Italy with another friend. We'd been paying it off for ages and hadn't even told our parents about it because we knew they wouldn't let us go.

By the time I was 17, I was already on my second job, working in the office at Ogden's Imperial Tobacco. I had a huge big ledger and would write off to the Liverpool Trade Protection Society to do a search on all the new customers, and a wonderful lady called Lily was teaching me my new trade. The tobacco leaves were hung out to dry a bit further down from the offices and the whole building and everything in it smelled. It wasn't a horrible smell – it was rich and unusual – but it was strong and it penetrated everything.

Lily became ill and was off work so all the girls from the office had gone to her house to visit, and that was where I first met Joe. She lived over the road from him, was good friends with his mum and had sons of the same age, so he was in and out of her house all the time. Joe was an only child so it was like his second home and every time I went to see Lily, he seemed to be there. He was 17, too, and just breaking into the team, although he had played one game a year earlier against Blackpool. It was the day Harry Catterick had left Alex Young out of the side and had caused a big commotion.

We were both going out with other people at that time. I'd met a guy who was really quite awful to me: he hardly ever turned up when he said he would and had gone away hitch-hiking around Europe to play his guitar. I didn't miss him very much.

Joe was much more attentive. One day he turned up at our house when we were on our way to the hospital to visit Lily to say she'd been sent home, to save us the journey. He'd just got a new car and was so proud of it. He'd borrowed the deposit from his gran and was paying it off. His wages were £12 a week, so he would give £3 to his mum, the car cost him a fiver and the rest was his. It was a dark blue Vauxhall Victor 101 and he asked me if I would like to go out for a run. We had a laugh and got on really well and I suppose that was where it all began because from that day on we started spending more time together.

On one of our first dates, we drove to Chester to have a look around the shops. He was still paying off the car and couldn't afford anything really good to eat so we had a meat pie and a cup of tea. He promised the next time we went, he'd treat me to something really special and he kept his word. We went into a little café and ordered prawn cocktail and ham salad. It was the first prawn cocktail I'd ever tasted and he said: 'You see? I told you I'd buy you something nice.'

Right from the start, he was lovely to me and we always had a great time. I remember he bought me a pair of earrings a couple of weeks after we started going out and I thought it was so kind. He was incredibly generous and thoughtful and, if ever he saw something he thought I would like, he would get it for me as a little surprise.

The holiday in Italy had cost £40 for two weeks' full-board. We took £20 each spending money and, before I left, Joe gave me another fiver towards my spends. We were so excited and just couldn't wait to go. We landed in Switzerland and travelled overnight on a coach into Italy. I didn't even go to bed; the first thing I did was go to the shops and spend the fiver on a lovely Italian-knit jumper for him. Mo couldn't believe it and neither could I. I hadn't expected to miss him so much and I was totally shocked when I realised that I couldn't possibly go abroad and leave him. I only ever went on holiday with the girls once more. The following year we got engaged.

I was worried he would be bored the first time he came to our house. My mum and dad were in the front room with the telly and my grandparents were in the back. They had a piano in there and sometimes they would have a singalong, then other times Gran would read. Granddad used to love horse racing and would get the *Timeform* every day and study it to within an inch of its life, but this particular night he was playing patience. Gran had just had her hair permed, so from then on Gran was 'Curly' and Granddad was 'Ace'. Joe and him got on great together because they talked about horses. Joe loved the horses – he still does – and they would sit for hours discussing form and jockeys and races. They got on like a house on fire.

After a while he asked if I would like to go to the match. He wanted me to go with his mum and dad, but I was shy because I'd never met them. I asked Mo to go and we took my little cousin Ronnie because it was his birthday. He was only about five but he was a big Evertonian. I paid for everyone and we sat up in the stand. Joe scored two goals that day. Walking down the road after the game all we could hear was, 'That Royle's too good for the reserves'; everybody was talking about him. Mo came with me to the next home game and we started going quite regularly.

Some days he would ring me at work to say he would meet me at lunchtime and we would go to Lau's, a Chinese restaurant in Kensington, where we would get a 2/6 (13p) 'businessman's lunch'. All the office staff at Ogden's wore these blue overalls and they reeked of tobacco. You could spot an Ogden's employee a mile away in those overalls, but you could always smell when someone worked there, even if they didn't have them on.

When we were courting, we would go out on a Saturday night to the Beachcomber, but, for a few years, on a Sunday we had a thing where we would go to the pictures and then the Berni Inn in Old Hall Street for a steak and an ice cream and coffee.

We used to love going house-hunting and were desperate to live in Formby but houses there were about £6,000 then. We eventually found a two-bedroom house in Ormskirk that cost £4,500 and it made such a big difference. We were painting and decorating it for ages and we couldn't wait to move in.

My biggest shock about being a footballer's wife was New Year. It had always been the biggest night of the year when I was growing up.

It was fantastic in Liverpool; there was a big, open square near Breck Road and everyone would congregate and you'd hear all the ships' horns going off on the Mersey – but footballers have to play the next day so New Year's Eve is an early night for them. If it was an away game and he'd gone away, I could go out, but when he was in, I felt a bit mean leaving him – even though he'd have gone to bed early and I'd just be sitting there on my own.

The date of the wedding had to be changed to June 1970 because Joe was on the reserves list for the World Cup in Mexico and we didn't know if he would get called up. Brian Labone, Alan Ball and Tommy Wright were away so their wives came to the ceremony instead. We had a white wedding at St Mary's in West Derby Village. Mo was a milliner and she'd designed all the hats, and she was my bridesmaid along with Marge, one of the girls I worked with, and my cousin Joy. We had our reception in the Grafton Ballroom, which was lovely. I've been back there since and it's lost a bit of its glamour but it was beautiful then.

We spent our honeymoon in Majorca; Rose and John Hurst ended up coming with us and stayed down the road in another hotel. We'd had a few little breaks together and had been saying that we must go away on a proper holiday. We met another couple there, Roy McFarland of Derby County and his wife Linda, so the six of us all went around together.

All three of our children were born in March, which means they were conceived in June – the close season. Lee was born on 21 March 1971 in Ormskirk Hospital, which turned out to be a really bad week for Evertonians. They were playing Panathinaikos in the European Cup quarter-final in Athens and it ended up 0–0, but it was enough to knock them out. Joe went away on the Tuesday and Lee was born the next day, the day of the game. They were coming back and going straight to a hotel because they had an FA Cup semi-final against Liverpool on the Saturday. He wasn't really supposed to come and see me but they were staying in a hotel in Lymm, Cheshire, and the kit was coming through to Goodison to be washed, so he hitched a lift on the coach so he could see the baby. The driver dropped him off at the hospital and then picked him up again on the way back. I didn't see him again until after they'd been beaten on the Saturday at Old Trafford.

Joe was always doing something in his spare time – he would never be idle. His friend had a bookie's shop, so sometimes he would go in there and help him – he knew how everything worked and how to calculate the odds. Another friend had a garage, so he might be there tinkering with cars. He would occasionally go to the auctions and buy a car to do it up and sell. A few of the players bought cars from him.

He had a terrible shoulder injury once. He'd gone up for the ball and the guy in front had bent over and Joe went right over the top of him and landed on his shoulder. It was awful to see him in such pain. Another time, he slipped some discs and we had a dreadful time then. Lee was only about nine months old. It was his first Christmas and the worst Christmas I ever had in my life. Joe'd had one disc done and had come out of hospital but he'd haemorrhaged and we didn't realise. We had to bring the bed downstairs and he went from being a 22-year-old fit, healthy footballer to being bedridden, in agony and unable to move. I remember Gordon West, Brian Labone and John Hurst came to see him and he was in a really bad way.

I've loved Morecambe and Wise since that day because on Christmas night Joe was in the next room and I sat down to watch the telly. It had been a terrible day and I thought I would never smile again. I ended up laughing my head off and I always loved them after that.

The doctor was with Joe all over Christmas. We took him back into hospital eventually and they did another disc while he was there. I didn't know if he was ever going to play again. He'd just made his debut for England when it happened, so that set him right back. He came out of it looking very ill; he lost an awful lot of weight but he made his recovery and got back in training.

I'd booked into Park House nursing home in Waterloo to have my second baby. It was a private hospital and, in theory, I was going in for a rest because the first time round in Ormskirk, a big, old-fashioned ward with 40 babies waking up during the night, all wanting feeding, I didn't get much sleep.

The pains started and I had to phone Joe at training but he didn't come until after they'd finished. On the way to the hospital, he got stopped for speeding, but when we explained what was happening, they gave us a police escort, taking us through red lights and seeing that we got there safely. By the time we finally arrived, I only had to wait ten minutes before Darren was born.

We stopped going out on a Saturday night when we had the kids and went out on a Sunday instead. He would be worn out and sore after a game, so he was just glad to get home and put his feet up. Living in Ormskirk made it a bit awkward too – if you drove into Liverpool, you couldn't have a drink and it was a nightmare trying to get a taxi.

Lee would come with us to the game and we'd drop Darren off at my mum's because she was only five minutes from the ground. We'd pick him up on the way home, get the kids packed off to bed and open a bottle of wine. We used to do these skillet meals and thought they were wonderful; you would mix the ready-mix packet with mincemeat and pasta and we thought they were really sophisticated and exotic. Joe would always go to bed early on a Saturday but he never really slept well.

I got used to him having injuries and cuts and bruises. The sheets would always be covered in blood from his feet or his legs or some other wound. He would shout out in his sleep; one night he asked me what position I played in. I don't think any footballers sleep very well because they're physically worn out after a game and they come out of the ground all hyped up, then they suddenly fall flat. For years, he would be up at five in the morning and taking the dog out running. As the dog got older, it used to see him coming and cower in the corner.

Our big night out became Sunday and I didn't cook a Sunday dinner for years. Joe's mum or mine would come up and babysit and we'd drive out in the country and eat in nice little restaurants with our friends John and Pat Kelly. We did that every week for about seven years. It was lovely because it was quieter and you got left alone, the service was better and you could easily get a taxi home.

The thing that was hard to cope with was the attention Joe got from other women. Certain women are attracted to success and they can't seem to help themselves but I didn't like it at all. Some of them were completely shameless in their attempts, although I don't know if men notice it as much as we do.

In May 1974, the team went off to Singapore, Kuala Lumpur and Hong Kong. Darren was about six weeks old so Lee would have been three. I went to stay with one of the other wives so I had to tell them at playgroup that Lee wouldn't be in. They took it for granted I was going to Kuala Lumpur because when I went back they asked if I'd had a nice time. I didn't know what they meant; I'd only been to Bebington on the Wirral!

I lost stones that week with all the running around; I never had a minute to sit down and used to live on boiled eggs and toast. The night before Joe went away, he'd taken me out to Tommy Smith's club – the Castle Gate in town. Joe had a Ford Capri at the time and we came out of the club to find it had been stolen. We were walking along to the police station to report it and one of our neighbours drove by and gave us a lift home. The next day, I drove him to Goodison, where they were leaving from for the airport. I was going to my mum's for Sunday dinner with the kids but on the way there the exhaust fell off my car, so I had two cars and couldn't use either of them all the time he was away. I would put the baby in the pram with the little one on the top and run down to playgroup then back again. They found the car a while later but it had been smashed up and was a write-off, and I got my exhaust fixed, eventually.

Everton would take them away an awful lot on a Friday night and we'd hardly see them at all over Christmas. On Christmas Day they would go to Alder Hey children's hospital in the morning to hand out presents to the kids then go straight into training before they could come home for dinner. They'd take them away on Christmas night regardless of whether they were playing at home or away. I was totally dedicated to the kids because I knew somebody had to be here for them and I felt it was my place. Joe was the provider and I kept it all running smoothly behind the scenes.

The transfer to Manchester City had been on the cards for a while but nothing had happened. Our boys had measles, they were terribly ill and it was coming up to Christmas. I'd put toys away in a shop in Ormskirk that I'd been paying off week by week. I was going to pick them up on Christmas Eve after Joe got back from training. He rang me and said he had to go over to Manchester City and all I could think about was the toys. I couldn't leave the boys because they were so ill, so Joe's mum and dad had to come over while I went to collect them from the shop or they'd have had no presents. He signed for City on Christmas Eve 1974 and they got hammered by Liverpool on Boxing Day.

We were still in our two-bedroom house at that time. My dad had died and Mum used to come and stay a lot so we desperately needed another room. It wasn't that far to Manchester so Joe could easily commute, but we started looking around. They'd built a cul-de-sac in the grounds of a big old house in Ormskirk so we bought a piece of land. Mum loaned us some money to put towards the deposit. The plot had been a man-made ornamental lake so we had to drain it first, then we started building. In the meantime, we sold our place and had to move in with Joe's parents in their two-bedroom flat. Joe and I, the two boys and our dog all squeezed into one room. We were there for about two months.

Man City won the League Cup in 1976 so we had to go to Wembley. All my clothes were in storage; Joe's mum used to work in the post office in Maghull and the lady had let us store all our things in the flat above. I remember clambering over all these boxes to dig out my fur coat to wear down to London – it wasn't quite as glamorous as it may have seemed. Joe met Willie Donachie around then and he's worked with him ever since. They're managing Ipswich Town now and they share a house down there.

The day I found out I was having Mark, Joe got transferred to Norwich and had to move down there straight away. I had to stay to sell the house and pack things up, so he would be in Norwich all week then drive back up after the match. He would stay for two nights and

177

then leave really early on Monday morning to go back for training. The things you do for love.

So I was seven months pregnant when I arrived in Norwich – I didn't know a single soul and, once again, the four of us and the dog were living in a hotel room because our house wasn't ready. They used to let me use the hotel laundry for the boys' clothes. That was a lonely time; I was on my own for ages. I left all the shopping for the baby until I arrived because I knew I would be on my own for hours and hours on end. I would be walking round Debenhams with my really big stomach and I often used to think the security people would be saying, 'Look, there's that woman again.' I spread it out so I would have something to do every day. Lee was ten and Darren was seven the month Mark was born.

The thirteen years we spent at Oldham were the best times of our lives. We lived up in the hills above the town and I always had to have a jeep because we would get snowed in. The club had no money and what Joe achieved there was unthinkable. Some years, the fans called it the 'pinch me' season.

When we got promoted, it was just brilliant. We were friends with the entire board of directors and we all became so close and such good friends; we still see them now. Everybody really appreciated what was happening and the whole town was alive and buzzing with the smell of success. It was wonderful. It wasn't a huge club and what they did was so unexpected.

I remember once going to pick up Mark from playgroup. They would cover the tables with newspapers when the kids were painting and when I got there they were laughing because there was a picture of Joe in there and Mark was completely oblivious. They were waiting for him to say something but he just thought everybody's dad was in the paper. I never think of Joe as a legend, he's just my husband and the boys' dad. I do know that we were very lucky to get the chance to do all this. Some people work really hard all their lives and they don't get any kind of recognition, so it's really nice to be acknowledged. At the same time, if the team are doing badly, you soon get to know about that, too.

All our boys have been good at football but not good enough. You've got to be really extraordinary now but I think, when you're a footballer's son, you've got to be even better than that. Darren still plays for Ashton United; he's played for a few clubs and I think the best he ever did was play for Altrincham, a Conference side. Lee played for school and pub teams. Mark played football and rugby at school and for a local pub team but Darren is the most dedicated. They all love their football and they're all Evertonians.

The only part of being a footballer's wife that I didn't especially like was the time we had to spend apart. It does make life interesting and when I think of the places I've lived, I realise I probably never would have even gone there. Bristol, Norwich and Oldham were just fantastic.

The worst times were when the kids were little and Joe would go away; it was difficult. Something always went wrong, like one would get ill or the car would break down. It was a drag that you could only ever go away in June, too. They still had Wakes Week in Oldham, when traditionally they would shut down the mills for two weeks in June, so we were OK then, but the summer holidays would start in July and Joe would go back to training literally the same week as the kids broke up for six weeks. So you had to do everything with them on your own and that was tough because I'd have loved him to be with us.

I didn't really trust anybody else to look after the children, other than my own or Joe's mum. I liked to know what they were up to and I really enjoyed being a mother. Sometimes, I was desperate to do things a little bit different but I think you turn around and realise everything has changed and you've become a wife and a mother instead of what you used to be. I found some photographs not long ago and I remembered that, once upon a time, I used to be a girl. I never resented it and my family were always there when I needed them, but it was a bit lonely at times.

I lost Mo to cancer the week before Princess Diana died. She was my dearest friend and we'd known each other since we were 11. Not a day goes by when I don't think about her and miss her.

I liked being a footballer's wife in the '60s and '70s. I think it was the best time. We felt we were so privileged because we had nice houses and lived in interesting places. I don't envy the attention they get now; it's so intrusive and the media are into every aspect of their lives.

The older you get, the more you value your friends and we've made some of the greatest friends you could wish for. They become more and more precious with time. It's so easy to make friends because everybody wants to be with you when you're doing well, but it's the ones that stick around when the party's over that matter to us.

We've always had the same values – we loved our home, the dogs, the family and the kids – and they're the things that have shaped who we are. There have been bad times, when Joe's career hasn't gone according to plan, and it teaches you that when things are going well, you should really enjoy it and we did just that – we're still having a fantastic time. I wouldn't have changed it for the world.

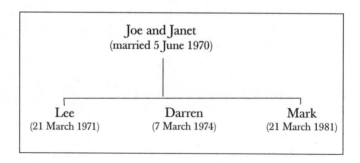

Joe and Janet
(married 5 June 1970)

| Lee | Darren | Mark |
| (21 March 1971) | (7 March 1974) | (21 March 1981) |

Our Lives Changed One Pancake Tuesday

Eileen Stevens

As an FA Cup winner with Bolton in 1958, Dennis Stevens joined Everton in a £35,000 deal in March 1962 and made his Everton debut at inside-forward against Sheffield United. In spite of an adverse reception from the home fans who held him responsible for the departure of Bobby Collins, he soon won them over and went on to score 22 goals in his 142 appearances. He played his final game in November 1965 and was sold to Oldham for £20,000 before finishing his playing career at Tranmere. He now lives in Bolton and is retired after a career in the rag trade, and spends a lot of time on the golf course.

Born Eileen Crewe, 12 September 1938,
Bolton, Lancashire

Like most girls from Bolton, Mum worked in a cotton mill, although she gave up work after she and Dad started a family and was with us all the time after that.

She had three daughters, all born within a year of each other: Edna, Marian and then me, the baby. We were and are very close, and still see each other most weeks. Mum had two boys before us girls were born, but they both died as babies. She vowed she wouldn't have more children after that, but then we came along. It was a hard life in those days, but we had a happy childhood and I have good memories of it.

I was very creative and qualified to go to the art college when I was 11, but I didn't take it up because Tonge Fold secondary modern was the school my sisters went to and I didn't want to be separated from them. I did take up art later in life, when our children started school, and I've pretty much been painting ever since.

I enjoy portraits and life drawing most of all. I started painting with oils and went on a number of art holidays and courses, where I did pastels and watercolours and even studied sculpture for about five years. In 2004, I won the Joe Lever trophy at my art club in Harwood and was thrilled to bits. I don't exhibit as much as I should but occasionally I have the odd show and sell my work. I should really devote more time to it, but there just doesn't seem to be enough hours in the day. It's a hobby really, but I enjoy it enormously.

My first job was as a receptionist at a photographer's shop, then I worked on the make-up and cosmetics counter in a chemist's for a couple of years. When I met Dennis, I'd only ever been to one football match with a group of girls. One of them had suggested we should go and watch Bolton, so I just went with the flow, but I'm very small and I was among the crowd so I couldn't see much and I hadn't a clue what was going on.

It was the week after my 17th birthday when Dennis and I met. I was with friends at the Palais de Dance in Bolton. He was an established player by then and one or two of the girls had already whispered that he was in there, but I didn't know who he was.

Dennis was the youngest of 12 children, born with a great love for football, but coming from such a big family there was never any spare cash for luxuries like football boots or match tickets. He was from Dudley originally and had a teacher named Mr Davies who believed in him and would take him to the big games at Aston Villa and

Wolves. The whole family chipped in to buy him his first pair of boots and we often wonder how different things might have been if it had not been for Mr Davies, his guardian angel.

He signed as an apprentice for Bolton when he was 15 and went into digs with an elderly couple called Mr and Mrs Nash. He was a scout for the club and they didn't have children of their own, so they took in the occasional lodger. Coming from such a huge family, Dennis was terribly homesick, so he soon packed up and went back home. His mother sent him to work on a farm so he would realise what the alternatives were for a working-class boy, and it wasn't long before he was safely back in his digs in Bolton and counting his lucky stars. He stayed there until he married me at 26 and he became the son the Nashes never had.

Eric Oldham, a teammate and good friend of Dennis's, who came from Newcastle, went out with my sister Marian. Dennis had already seen me around and asked Eric if we could get a foursome going, so that was how I got to go out with him. Eric finished at Bolton soon after and headed back to the Northeast to play for Gateshead, so he lost touch with Marian eventually, and they both married other people.

Dennis and I started dating and going out with a group of friends. We'd go to dinner dances, the pictures, visit family and get up to the usual things courting couples do. Sometimes we'd go off to the coast or the countryside for walks. He didn't have a car when I first met him, but he got one eventually and there was no stopping us then.

My dad was an insurance agent and a very keen Bolton supporter, so he was really impressed when we started courting. He supported Dennis throughout his career and even used to come over to Goodison with his friends to watch him play there.

We waited until the close season to get married and did so on 11 June 1960. His brother Derek was best man and my sisters and Dennis's niece were my bridesmaids. We married at St Stephen and All Martyrs in Bolton, which was my church when I was a girl. We went down to Bournemouth on honeymoon. One day, a guest in the hotel asked if there was anybody who played golf because he needed a partner, so Dennis volunteered and off they went. I went around the course with them because I'd never seen him play before, and that passed a pleasant afternoon. He played another round with the guy after that, too, but I honestly didn't mind. I went and spent the afternoon having my hair done and being pampered with a full beauty treatment.

By that time, we had a group of friends who were mainly footballers, so we would go along to the match and I would sit with the other girlfriends and wives. I was a friend of Nat Lofthouse's wife, Alma, and Ralph Gubbins's other half, Margaret. Alma has passed on but Margaret and I are still friends after all these years and we still go to see the Wanderers every other week.

Way back then, I remember going to Old Trafford when the floodlights were first in use. That was the first time I saw Duncan Edwards play. Duncan was one of Dennis's cousins. I was working at the chemist's at the time of the Munich air crash and I had gone over the road to buy a newspaper when I saw the headline. Dennis came to meet me after work and we couldn't believe it. Duncan didn't die straight away; he was a big, strong lad and died in hospital 15 days later. Dennis always says he was the perfect footballer, a player's player, who had so much respect from everyone. He was a lovely boy.

We've been down to Dudley and seen his grave there. If a grave can be lovely, then his is. An image of his face is etched on the headstone and some beautiful words. He was only 21 when he died and had the world at his feet. I believe his mother only died in 2003 and is buried nearby.

I needed a job that gave me Saturdays off so I could watch Dennis play, so I trained as a dental nurse and did that for about four years, only leaving when I was expecting my first son.

Dennis still has his payslips from back then and when we met he was on £20 a week plus a win bonus, but the average footballer was probably earning £10 a week. They got cash loyalty bonuses, too – after 5 years they gave him a lump sum of £750 and another £1,000 after 10 years' service. It was a lot back then but it was nothing like today; we'd have been millionaires if he'd been born later because he was a top-flight player for almost 20 years.

Our lives changed on Pancake Tuesday in 1962 when I found out I was pregnant and Dennis found out he was being transferred. It was all terribly exciting. At that stage, he had been at Bolton for 12 years and played almost 300 games. He normally played at inside-right but this particular week he'd been playing out of position at centre-forward, standing in for Nat Lofthouse. He had a disappointing game, was booed off the pitch and came home that night vowing that that was it and he wouldn't play for Bolton ever again. The word got round that he was upset by the reception he got from the crowd and the next thing he was approached by Everton, who offered Bolton £35,000 for him.

We both went over and discussed everything with the manager Harry Catterick and Dennis signed the forms that morning. It was very sudden but it wasn't totally unexpected. Once you realise things are not going as well as they might be, there's always the possibility of a move.

By this time, he was 29 so he was heading towards the end of his career anyway. We arrived near the end of the season and he made his debut away against Sheffield United, where they drew 1–1. A couple of days later, there was a night match against Chelsea at Goodison – Everton won 4–0 and Alex Young scored two. That was when we realised Alex's status as a hero. He was brilliant that night and the fans cheered him off the pitch. They just loved him. Then, in the first full season Dennis played, Everton won the League.

We moved into an Everton club house in Nantwich Close, Birkenhead. Not many of the players lived on the Wirral but we went over there because Tommy Neil, a former Bolton player, lived over there with his wife, Audrey. Dennis was his best man and they were in digs together with Mr and Mrs Nash. They suggested we could live in

Birkenhead so we would be near them and I would have company once I had the baby, and at least we would know somebody.

We lived round the corner from them and they introduced us to a few people and several neighbours, so we weren't complete strangers. Gary was born in Arrowe Park hospital on 17 October 1962 at 6.30 in the morning. In those days, fathers weren't allowed to come in until visiting time so we had to wait all day for him to come and see us. We were both absolutely delighted with our baby.

Most of my time was taken up with looking after Gary and I just managed to get to the home matches every other week, thanks to my neighbour, Ann. She would look after him and he says he can still remember it now; he was only about three at the time so his memory goes back a long way. It was an exciting time to be an Evertonian – there were huge crowds every week and they were top of the League and fabulous to watch.

Dennis used to relate all kinds of stories of players laying their kit out in a certain way and wearing lucky socks, but I don't think he was superstitious at all, he just got on with it. As a young woman, I didn't realise how important the match was. I realise now but then, I suppose, I was more concerned with my baby and I didn't take that much interest. When Dennis was leaving the house, I'd ask who he was playing that day. We nearly always had a tiff over something-and-nothing on a Saturday before the match and, looking back, I realise it was tension. He would sit very quietly in the chair, deep in thought, and he would be focusing his mind and going over what might happen and what the tactics would be. I would still be stinging about our row when the game had finished but he'd forgotten all about it, especially if they'd won. In fact, he wouldn't even know what had been said in the first place.

Before he went to a game, he would eat something very light, perhaps poached eggs on toast or just a piece of toast. We never went out the night before a match; in fact, from Wednesdays onwards we hardly ever went out because it was the build-up to the game. He was very serious about his football and incredibly dedicated. I suppose that's why his career lasted as long as it did.

I didn't really know much about football. It's only since we've been watching Bolton play over the last few years that I feel I've got to learn more about the game. I don't suppose I watched them play then, I just watched Dennis. If you go to a match and you don't know anybody involved, you tend to watch the whole thing and the opposition as well. It was a bit nerve-racking being there but it wasn't strange to see him play because that was all I knew. I'd been watching him ever since we met.

He's always been a devoted family man who spends time at home pottering around the house and doing a bit of decorating. He likes to spend time in the garden, too. He also spent a lot of time with the children and me, and is still a very keen golfer. He liked to organise charity matches and dinners as well, and he did that for a number of years, getting the players together and raising money for various causes.

I think more things happened in our short time at Everton than they ever did at Bolton. We got lovely hampers and special treats at Christmas and there was always a present for the wife – it was so nice to be thought of. The club was very generous and I don't remember anything like that happening at Bolton. I remember one time John Moores had told the players that if they won a particular game they would get a brace of pheasant each. Sure enough, they were delivered to the house and I hung ours in the garage. They still had their feathers and I didn't really know what to do with them, so in the end my mum plucked them and did whatever needed doing and my sister poured a bottle of Chianti over the top and roasted them. They were delicious.

I kept a scrapbook and clippings from the papers of all his achievements, and I've still got it somewhere. I also have a photograph of when he was playing for Bolton against Chelsea and Roy Bentley's boot was too high and caught Dennis in the ear. It ended up hanging off and needed stitching inside and out; it was pretty gruesome. He had lots of scrapes and knocks and bruises but that's the one that sticks in my mind the most.

He re-lives matches more in his sleep now than he did when he was playing. Sometimes he shouts out instructions and sometimes he kicks. He seems to have perfected the art of going back in time.

When Everton won the League it was amazing. We were at the peak of everything: we'd just had the baby and we were both thrilled to bits with him and, after spending so long with Bolton, suddenly Dennis had a winner's medal. I think that was the highest point of his career. I could kick myself for missing the last match, though, as I'd been to every home game of the season. We'd been told we were being taken away to Spain in celebration of winning the League the following week so I'd spent the afternoon in Liverpool looking around for something to wear and missed the best match of the year. It was against Fulham and Roy Vernon scored a hat-trick. They did a lap of honour and collected their medals – the fact that I missed it still fills me with regret 40-odd years later.

Dennis went away quite often pre-season; when he was with Bolton they went off to South Africa just before we were married and after we got to Everton he was off in Australia for about six weeks. He was happy for the first ten days or so and enjoying it, then the tone of his letters changed and he wanted to return. He's a real home bird and family man, and he wanted to get back to us. I passed the time by visiting my family in the Isle of Man for two weeks and also went to Dudley to see his family and stayed with my mum for a while. When you're young, six weeks seems like such a long time. Gary was only small then, so it made it seem even longer. I couldn't wait for him to get back.

I was expecting Julian when we left Everton in December 1965 and he was born the following April, after Dennis had been transferred to Oldham for £20,000. Gordon Hurst was the manager who signed him but he left fairly soon after and Ken Bates came in as chairman. Dennis didn't click with the new manager, Jimmy McIlroy, and only stayed for one season then went to Tranmere. So, really, he went back to where we'd just come from.

We decided that, as his career was coming to an end, we would buy a house in Bolton and Dennis would commute, so that's what we did and we've been in the same house ever since. Julian was born three weeks after we moved. The arrival didn't interrupt any games because he was thoughtful enough to be born on a midweek evening. He's married to Ruth now and they have two children, Olivia, who's a wonderful dancer, and Lloyd, who's just mad about football. He's only a toddler but all he ever thinks about is kicking a ball.

Dennis had been at Tranmere only a season or so when he slipped a disc. He was playing at the time and they plied him with painkillers while the match went on, but that finished him off, really.

It was by chance that he ended up working as a gents' outfitter. We went to a party and some people came along and one of them was in the rag trade. A new shopping precinct was opening close to where we lived and we were looking for any kind of business at the time that we could run together, maybe a newsagent's or something.

This man said he wanted to open a men's outfitters. Dennis had been offered a job at an engineering company but it all fell through and he made his decision right there.

He'd always had an interest in fashion but he had to learn from scratch. He found it challenging and that spurred him on. We had our shop for about 25 years in the end; it was called Dennis Stevens Menswear. We were originally in a precinct but we built our own shop opposite. We sold it in 1993, when he was 59, and retired. A young man called John Francis took over; he'd been coming into the shop for years asking if he could buy it. A couple of years before selling up, we started to do dress hire and John continued with that – he's still got the shop and his whole family are employed there. He's done very well for himself and we still pop in and say hello to them.

Being a footballer's wife was wonderful. I considered myself very lucky because he went off for training between 10 and 12 and was home again with me and the boys by 1 p.m., so he was always around helping with the children. I thought I was so lucky. I didn't have to go out to work or worry about where the next penny might come from, and always felt that we had a very relaxed and happy time.

There was nothing about the life that I didn't like. People would phone and knock on the door, and it still happens. That never bothered me at all because you're in the limelight and it's just part of the job. It's very flattering to be remembered after all this time and to know that people are interested in you.

I don't know whether I would like to be a current footballer's wife, though. If it's anything like the TV series then I don't think I could cope because it was certainly nothing like that in our day. I don't really know what you'd do for fun if you earned £60,000 a week, but I imagine it depends on your personality in the first place. If you're going to go off the rails, then I suppose you will but that kind of money might make it easier. Whatever they want, they can just go and get, and I'm not sure it's a good thing to never want for something.

I feel sorry for Posh and Becks; I think they're a nice couple. They've encouraged a lot of publicity but I suspect a lot of it is tongue in cheek and they're having the last laugh. I don't know whether the adultery accusations are true but I can't stand these women who kiss and tell. They don't think twice about ruining somebody's life and there are children involved, so it's not right.

There's a real love of sport that runs right through our family and it makes me so proud. Both my sons played amateur football and Julian still plays in a team. Gary is married to Andrea and they have their own family so he's given up playing, but he still trains and manages a team of 12 to 14 year olds called Eagley Juniors.

Elliot, my eldest grandson, plays football for his school and for Eagley Juniors on a Sunday morning, and he's keen on skateboarding, too. Seb, his brother, is a rugby man and even Holly plays football at school and hopes to be chosen for the girls' team when she's old enough. Freddie is still a baby and he's so adorable; he's got lovely curly hair and he's such good fun.

I don't think I made any sacrifices for Dennis or his career. We always thought we should have our own freedom and pastimes and that's what we did. He would have his golf and go on the odd holiday and I was always very interested in the arty side of things, so we've teamed up well together.

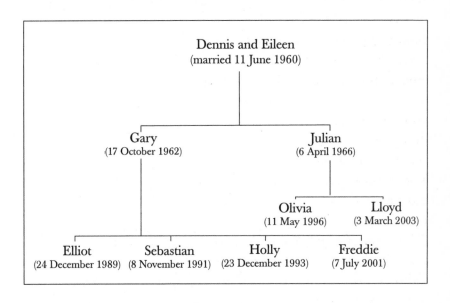

Nobody Loved Football More Than Tony

Marina Kay

Tony Kay began his career at Sheffield Wednesday, where he played eight seasons and made an impression on the future Everton manager, Harry Catterick, then in charge at Hillsborough. He joined Everton in a £55,000 deal in December 1962 and won a Championship medal five months later, but only lasted another season, playing his last match as a professional against Wolves on 11 April 1964, the day before the *Sunday People* printed its 'bribes' exclusive. In April 1965, along with former teammates David 'Bronco' Layne and Peter Swan, Kay was found guilty on charges of 'conspiracy to defraud' for his part in a betting scandal while he was a player with Wednesday. All three were jailed for four months, fined £150 and banned from professional football for life. Kay won one England cap and continued to play amateur football until he was 61. He now works as a groundsman in south London.

Born Marina Platts, 29 July 1936, Southy Green, Sheffield

Sheffield was one of Hitler's main targets during the war because of its steel industry and I can still remember the sky being completely lit up

192

by the air raids during the Blitz. My dad was called up in 1940, when I was four and my brother Geoff was a two-year-old toddler.

Our street in Southy Green eventually got hit so we had to go and stay with my grandparents at the Sheffield United side of town. Mum's role in the war effort was to work as a tram conductress, so Geoff and I went everywhere together and would play in the streets with our friends until it went dark. I never left the house without him, he was great company. He was thoughtful and more reserved than me, and our childhood was full of laughter and adventures.

I loved my nan and granddad to bits. Granddad was an old rascal and worked as a bookie's runner. Bookmaking was illegal then and I remember him standing me on the street corner and telling me to keep an eye out while he took bets. When my mum found out, she wasn't too pleased.

I was eight years old when a man wearing an army uniform knocked at the door. I went and told my mum there was a soldier outside looking for her. She came out of the kitchen and, as soon as I saw her face, I realised it was my dad. Straight away, I could see why she'd fallen in love with him. He was so handsome; he had black hair, big blue eyes and the most beautiful smile.

Our bombed-out house was rebuilt when the war ended and the four of us went back to live there, and that was where I stayed until I got married. If I'd stayed with my grandparents, I probably wouldn't have met Tony because he was from the Sheffield Wednesday side of town.

I adored my dad and we grew very close, but he'd contracted tuberculosis in the Far East and became ill almost as soon as he got home. He was in and out of hospital most of the time so we never went anywhere with him because he was too sick, but I would sit with him for hours and hours, talking and getting to know him. Sometimes he could hardly breathe and would just sit in his chair and then he'd be back in hospital again. I didn't have him for long – one time he caught pneumonia in hospital and he was too weak to fight it. He was 32 when I lost him and I'd only known him for six years.

Tony lived at the bottom of the hill in Southy Green and I lived at the top. We went to Shirecliffe to play their school at netball once and he stopped to watch the game but he was with his pals and they were all jeering and wolf-whistling and trying to put us off. He had the reddest hair I'd ever seen.

My best friend Marge was in the Woodcraft Folk and she knew Tony from there. Woodcraft was a bit like Boy Scouts but without the discipline. They would go tracking animals, studying nature and learning about the countryside. Tony loves that sort of thing and he loves to be out in the fresh air. Marge introduced us when I was 15; I'd finished school by then and was at commercial college learning shorthand and typing. Tony was a plasterer working on a slum-clearance housing project called the Manor Estate. He'd been an electrician before that but he got the push for acting daft. I liked him and he made me laugh.

We started courting and would go out with a crowd of friends from school to the dance at the City Hall or to Glossop Road baths. On a Saturday night, they would cover the swimming pool with boards and it became a dance floor; it was a bit springy, but it did the trick. Everyone was jiving and rock 'n' rolling to Bill Haley and I loved it. Tony didn't like rock 'n' roll much so I'd dance with somebody else and save the waltzes, foxtrots and quicksteps for him. The Big Band sound was his kind of music and he would whirl me around the bouncy dance floor.

I didn't know anything about football and I still don't, really. Tony was quite happy with that; his dad was the one who followed Sheffield Wednesday. My mum remarried a few years after my dad died; Peter was an upholsterer and joiner by trade and he wasn't into football either; he liked motorcars and motorbikes. I didn't get on with him at first and I resented him but, as the years went by, we got on a bit better.

Tony signed full time as a professional for Sheffield Wednesday when he was seventeen, but he only started to play regularly in the first team about four years later. He didn't have a car until after we married so, in our free time, we'd get the bus to Nottingham or Derbyshire and go and have a look around. We tried to get out of town if we could and would wander off into the countryside, just the two of us.

I remember he had a suit and I had a dress made in matching fabric: it was dark-blue check and we thought we were the bee's knees. We had a fantastic time in our teens but we used to argue. His parents and mine were friends and they used to go to the same social club, so they'd know when we'd fallen out and would engineer ways we could bump into each other. Eventually, he'd come round to our house and my mum, or 'The Dragon' as he used to call her, would shout 'Stanley Matthews is here' and we'd get back together again.

There were no restaurants or places for teenagers to go to in Sheffield and everything used to close at ten o'clock, so, now and again, a group of us would book a coach to take us over to Manchester or Nottingham for a night out, or else we'd shoot over to Derbyshire, which was only fifteen minutes away, where everything stayed open till eleven. Marge met Jim, her future husband, when she was seventeen and they're still together and happy to this day. Once she got married, she didn't really come out with the group any more. We had some other friends called John and Nina Wragg; she was a very excitable Italian and started to teach me to drive in her Triumph Herald. I enjoyed it and got right up to taking my test, but when we moved to Liverpool the traffic was a lot heavier and faster, so I never carried it on.

My brother Geoff went to do his national service in the army and was posted to Aden in southern Yemen while Tony went into the RAF because he was promised a local posting so he could continue to play football at the weekends. Initially, he did his square-bashing at Padgate in Warrington and was supposed to be there for six weeks, but he broke a bone in his foot playing for Sheffield Wednesday reserves and was sent to the casualty wing with his leg in plaster. He decided he'd recover more quickly in the comfort of his own home, so he picked up his wages, altered his sick note from three days to eight, and headed back to Sheffield. Unfortunately, Wednesday sent a telegram requesting the RAF release him for a game and that was when they realised he wasn't there. When he got back, they put him in the jail for three weeks for going AWOL.

He was more mischievous than bad and he never got into serious trouble; he just got bored really easily. Another time they charged him with 'dumb insolence' and made him peel a mountain of spuds as his punishment for giving the drill instructor one of his withering looks.

Life went on and, while he was in the RAF, I was working as a secretary for British Steel and still going out dancing at the weekends with my friends. We would write to each other two or three times a week and he would send me pictures of my heart-throbs – Burt Lancaster and Rory Calhoun – which he'd cut out of magazines, to keep me going till he got home at the weekends. We even had gold bracelets made: mine said 'Tony and Marina' and his said 'Marina and Tony', and I wore mine all the time. I missed him madly while he was away, but I didn't tell him.

We got engaged on my 21st birthday and the only advice we got was from the local landlord, Ted Catlin, who was also the Sheffield Wednesday scout, and he told us we weren't allowed to sleep together the night before a game.

Tony is ten months younger than me so he had to get permission from his parents, but we married in St Cecilia's church at Parsons Cross in Sheffield on 28 September 1957. He had a match in the afternoon so we had to have our wedding at 10.30 in the morning. The following day, he went to Doncaster with Peter Swan – I suppose that was my honeymoon.

We moved in with Tony's parents, Jenny and Mac, after the wedding. Tony was always away and I was pregnant so it was just perfect and it meant that I wasn't on my own. I couldn't have wished for better in-laws. Jenny was a great ally and we got along famously; she was the only person who called him Anthony and he was the apple of her eye. Mac was wonderful, too. Warm, clever, funny and gifted with a beautiful voice; he was always bursting into song. Tony and him would have contests and try to out-sing each other.

Nobody was more dedicated to football than Tony. We always say that when he pops his clogs, we'll put his ashes in a leather case-ball and kick him about. His first love was actually rugby but he wasn't tall enough. He was great at cricket as well – in fact, he was selected for trials for Yorkshire, and I've washed enough of those whites to last me a lifetime. He was as fit as a fiddle; he used to race the bus up the hill while he was holding his breath and he trained hard all the time. Somebody had told him to mix sherry with a raw egg because it was supposed to give you a big boost of energy. It sounds ridiculous but he swore by it and drank it before a game. He said they gave it to greyhounds and it worked well enough for them.

Ricky was born two weeks overdue in March 1958. Jenny was cooking the tea when I got the first twinges; she went to phone an ambulance, but I refused to go until I'd eaten. It was just as well because I had a long night ahead of me and ended up having a Caesarean. The only thing I can really remember is the ambulance with bells ringing and flashing lights, but he was born beautiful and perfectly healthy.

Albert Quixall was a Wednesday player and the first footballer to take ballet lessons. His wife had a dancing school and he used to do the publicity shots with her. He was transferred to Manchester United when they tried to rebuild the team after the Munich air disaster, so after Ricky was born we moved into his old club house.

Tony went into business with Peter, my stepdad, and they called themselves Burniston and Kay Property Developers. One time, he was up a ladder fixing a sign when Eric Taylor, the Wednesday manager, drove past and saw him. He'd already told him off about having a kick about in the park with the local lads but to see him dangling off a ladder was too much. He reminded him that he was a valuable player and wasn't insured to do any dangerous jobs, so he had to take a back seat in the business. Peter took over the day-to-day running of it and Tony would lend a hand when he could. The business did quite well and he carried it on when we moved to Liverpool.

We had to move to a bigger house when I fell pregnant again, so we bought Jimmy McAnearney's place. Russell was born in April 1960 and, before I knew where I was, my little girl Toni was born in July 1961. Tony came to the hospital with a suitcase full of little dresses, demanding to see his daughter. All the boys were born bald but she had a real thatch of red hair; it was like a comedy wig, some two year olds don't have as much hair as she did.

She could be a bit volatile at times; we used to say that when that midwife smacked her, she didn't shut up for 13 years. They say women are supposed to bloom in pregnancy, but I looked bloody awful. I felt fine but I was really pasty-faced and people were always asking me if I was ill. That bloom just wasn't there and my hair was terrible, but the kids were all beautiful.

I never thought we would leave Sheffield; in fact, it was only days before that I'd been talking to some of the Wednesday wives and had said we would be there for life. A week later, he was transferred to Everton and had to go straight away. Yet again, I was pregnant and I decided not to move until after the baby was born, but I knew I would be going eventually. I wasn't scared of moving because I knew Tony would be there, but I was scared of leaving my friends and family. I'd never been away from Sheffield apart from on holiday, so it was quite daunting. Jenny was the most brilliant mother-in-law you could hope for and I knew how badly I was going to miss her.

I was heavily pregnant in 1963 when the team went to Torremolinos in celebration of winning the League, so I couldn't travel. The club gave me a beautiful cocktail watch instead and I still have it. It's engraved on the back with ''62–63 Champions'.

Jamie was born on 28 May 1963. Alf Ramsey had given Tony his England call-up and he flew with Brian Labone from Torremolinos to Bratislava for a close-season tour. He was in the squad against Czechoslovakia and East Germany and made his debut against Switzerland when Jamie was a week old. He scored from the halfway line that day and England went on to win the game 8–1. I saw it on the television and almost burst with pride. I got a dozen red roses from Frank Clough, a journalist on the *Daily Mirror*. I was twenty-six and had four kids all under five. My dancing days were over and I felt like I'd been washing nappies forever.

Before I went over to Liverpool, and to make up for missing

Torremolinos, Tony said I could go away on holiday and that Jenny and my mum would look after the kids between them. I went to Majorca with my sister-in-law Joyce and we had a fabulous time.

Joyce is five years older than Tony and she absolutely idolised him. She had the same red hair and a fantastic sense of humour and worked in the Batchelors food factory. Some days she'd bring home Victoria plums the size of coconuts. Her uniform was a green overall and a white turban; she looked quite exotic and one year she won the Miss Batchelors beauty pageant. As Tony and I started courting, she married Dennis and moved round the corner. They called her first daughter Denise Marina, after me. We're still very close to this day and she's still great company.

Everton's chairman, John Moores, sent a chauffeur-driven car to take us to Liverpool when Jamie was about four months old. The first house they showed us was in Aintree and it was lovely, but it wasn't big enough for the six of us so they offered us another in Maghull, which was perfect because it had an extension over the garage. Part could be used as a playroom and the rest as a bedroom, and that was where we settled.

I needed to get somebody to help me with the kids because Jenny wasn't there any more, so we got a woman in and I decided I would go back to work part time as a shorthand typist at a local agency, just for a week out of every month. I loved it, it kept my hand in, and it got me out of the house and into adult company for a few hours; but then the papers got hold of it and printed a headline '£100-A-WEEK WIFE WANTS A JOB'. I only worked two or three hours at a stretch but they thought it was outrageous because Tony was the record signing in the country and was earning £60 a game. The big money caused a sensation at the time, but the media seemed to have forgotten the players had been on strike a couple of years earlier when they were only earning thirty bob a week for entertaining tens of thousands of people.

I met some great people in Maghull and I loved living there. The club was good to us, too; they would send us groceries every week and it was nice to be remembered. When you move to another city, you have to start all over again. I got to know my neighbours, who were very kind to us, but it was so lonely when the kids had gone to bed and the house was really empty and quiet.

Jenny used to come to Liverpool a lot; she'd phone from the bus station and say she was on her way or she'd ring my mum and the two of them would come over in her car and stay for a few days. We were great friends and it made it much easier to cope with things.

Tony and I still argued from time to time and one night I threw all his clothes out of the window. When I woke up there was a white rabbit in the bathroom that he'd found in somebody's garden on his way home from a nightclub. He often used to bring it home with him after that.

My closest friends were Norma Vernon and Gordon Brown's wife, Brenda. Gordon was what they called a spiv, a wheeler and dealer, and a mad Evertonian, and he took a real shine to Tony. The Browns helped us a lot; they were older than us and took us under their wing. Gordon died a few years ago and there was a massive turn-out for his funeral; I couldn't make it but Tony went and I sent a wreath from us all.

Most of the players lived in Maghull and a bunch of us used to meet up every now and again: Jeannie Parker, Alex's wife, Pat Gabriel, Norma Vernon and Rowdy Ron Yeats's wife, Margaret, but we all had young children so we didn't get together that often.

It was quite a lonely life because the men were always away. Christmas was the worst because there were lots of games, they still had to train every day and they couldn't eat too much or drink. In the summer, you wanted to go away with your kids but the men would be on tour or at a training camp somewhere, so holiday time was always a bit lonely, too. If we could find a babysitter, I'd go out to special occasions, but I didn't go to a match unless it was a big game because he didn't really like me to watch him play.

The thing that wound me up about being a footballer's wife was when I went out for an evening with Tony – and those evenings were so few and far between – and people would come and pester. It got right on my nerves. If they just came over to say hello or ask for an autograph, then that was fine, but they would pull up a chair and want to discuss the match in detail, and I knew that would be it for the rest of the night.

Then there would be the women coming over and trying to edge me out of the conversation. I've known girls come and stand right in front of me with their back to my face. It's annoying and you can't really do anything, although I lost my temper on a couple of occasions. Once, I remember, was after a party and we were getting in the car to go home. This woman came up screaming at me for some reason or another and stuck her hand through the window and tried to pull my hair – so I wound the window up and trapped her in it.

The night before the match-fixing story broke we were in the Royal Tiger in Liverpool. Gordon Brown had got the nod from somebody at the *Sunday People* that they would be running the story the next day and it was as if the bottom had fallen out of the world. We were trying to avoid the reporters, but they were everywhere, so we darted off in the car but there was a crossed wire somewhere in the dashboard and every time we turned a corner, the horn blew. We were trying to get away but telling them where to look at the same time. We didn't stand a chance.

As if it wasn't bad enough, the story was reported wrongly. The headline was 'Football's Shame' and it said Tony had thrown a match against Ipswich, when in fact he'd been voted man of the match that day. His crime was to bet against his team, which was more stupid than sinister but it had happened so long ago, he'd forgotten about it by then. Literally overnight, my life changed and it became a waking nightmare. It was terrible and it kept getting worse. One minute I had people to talk to and the next they were avoiding me. I don't think it was because they all necessarily believed what they were hearing; more that they were embarrassed and just didn't know what to say. I felt very isolated and alone. Jimmy Tarbuck rang and invited me and the kids to go and watch him in pantomime with Frankie Vaughan. They sent a car for us and off we went. The kids were thrilled to bits and they went backstage afterwards and met the cast. I was so grateful.

I never thought Tony would go to prison, but I think he knew. The trial was at the Nottingham Assizes and, on the last day, I was at home with the kids. I asked if he was taking the car and he said he would leave it behind. I knew then that he wasn't coming back.

It was an open prison called Thorp Arch in Wetherby, near Leeds. Gordon Brown used to drive me there to visit. Peter Swan and Bronco Layne were in there, too. There was a photo in the *Daily Express* of me standing at the gates with Tony's football boots. I've never seen that picture since; they were supposed to send me a copy but, with the move back to Sheffield and everything, I never got it.

The prison governor was very kind; he rang me a few times to say Tony was depressed and sad, and he let me talk to him. Tony's job was to make camouflage nets for the armed forces, but the nylon made his eyes really sore so he was put on gardening duties instead. I think he quite liked it because he was outside in the fresh air. I visited once and they didn't know where he was, but they found him eventually in the middle of a field. He wasn't trying to escape or anything, he was just meandering.

He didn't look well, so I decided to cook him a steak next time and take it with me. I wanted to keep it warm so I rolled it up and put it in a thermos flask but when I got there we couldn't get it out again. We didn't know whether to laugh or cry.

Everton were all right with me. They said we could buy the house, which we started to do, and then they backed off and kept their distance. They weren't nasty or anything like that, but they stopped sending the weekly groceries.

Tony, Peter and Bronco were sentenced for four months and when they were due for release there were dozens and dozens of reporters hanging around outside the gates and right around the prison walls. The governor had been in the army, so he came up with a tactical escape plan. He decided they would be let out in the middle of the night and they were smuggled out over some sports fields at the back of the prison and bundled into cars. Peter Swan and Bronco Layne went off towards Sheffield and we never saw them again. We sped away to Liverpool with Gordon at the wheel. We cuddled each other all the way home; I couldn't let go of him.

He'd started a waste-paper business before he got sent to prison and I kept that going. Tony took it over again when he came out, but the football wasn't there and he couldn't handle it. He still went training every day but the trouble was that the day the ban came he went into 'self-destruct' mode; he pushed the button and he wouldn't let go. He couldn't handle the concept of living without football – it was more than he could bear – and he started drinking a lot. He just couldn't cope with the void in his life. Nobody loved football more than Tony and I honestly believe that.

Jenny was diagnosed with cancer and I went back to Sheffield to see what was going on and she died while I was there. I had to tell Tony and I didn't know what to say because he loved his mum more than anyone else in the world.

He'd been to see her with the rest of his family the night before, when she'd come out of the operating theatre. She said she was feeling fine, so they all went home. For some reason, Tony went back alone and asked if she was really feeling all right. She told him everything was fine and there was no more pain and she died shortly after he left. She was 52 when we buried her and she'd died in the hospital she'd been working at for years.

Mac went to pieces. He'd been a bit of a lad in his day and had entered a boxing match to win the money to buy her a wedding ring. He loved her to bits and his heart was broken. He recovered eventually and, years later, he remarried, but it was never the same. His new wife was fine. She looked after him and they had each other for company but she and Tony didn't see eye to eye and it was a mutual dislike. As soon as Mac died, she went off to live with her family in America.

Tony left England for Spain in 1967. I was still living in Maghull and had put my secretarial skills to use working for an agency, but I had to try and fit it in around school hours. I tried to keep the house on. They turned the gas off, they turned the electricity off, but it was when they started digging up the drive to cut off the water I realised I would have to surrender. I left Maghull in 1969 and went back to Sheffield; Geoff drove over and picked us up. We always joked that we went there by chauffeur-driven car and came back in a rent-a-van with four kids, two goldfish in a bowl on my knee, a pregnant cat, no job and no home but, as they say in Yorkshire, 'Ne'er mind, eh? Summat'll turn up.'

My mum had settled in the same area as my grandmother, the Sheffield United side of town, so that was where we went too. I got a bit of flak, but nothing I couldn't cope with. There was a bit of name-calling and people talking in stage whispers; one fella used to stand behind me singing made-up songs – one day I'd had enough so I rounded on him and gave him a crack.

Geoff moved over to Spain in 1985. He bought a steak bar in Nerja, near Malaga, and soon settled into the way of life. He sold it a few years later and invested in a beach bar. It suited him down to the ground. He became known as 'Geoff the Beach' and that was where he stayed until he became ill in 1996. He had tests but nobody seemed to know what was wrong, so I told him to come home and we'd get him checked out properly. He was diagnosed with cancer and died in Sheffield in 1997; it was the most awful shock.

The only time I really resented Tony was when Russell came home one day sobbing. I asked what was wrong and he told me his friend had gone to town with his dad but he couldn't go because he didn't have a dad. It was times like that I hated him. I took all the kids over to Spain to see him a couple of times but my middle two are so fair-skinned, they just couldn't handle the heat. We could never have settled there.

None of my sons plays football. They played at school but not to any great standard. Imagine having Tony Kay as your dad. He was a hard act to follow. Ashley, one of my grandsons, is a really good footballer but I don't think he's interested in following it as a career. His brother Gavin played ice hockey for the Northern Counties but he prefers roller hockey now, he's good at that, too.

I never felt as if I made any sacrifices for Tony because we were teenagers together and we'd done most of the stuff we wanted to do by the time the children came. We had a great time, it was fantastic, but I'm glad I'm not a footballer's wife now. I don't envy them at all; they've got nothing I want. I'm quite happy being a mother, a nan and a great-grandma. I'm not answerable to anybody, I can do whatever I please and I don't have to compromise or fight anybody for the TV remote control because it's mine. No shirts, no cricket whites or stinking socks, no lying awake at night waiting to hear the car pull up and wondering where he's been.

We're still in touch and I see him from time to time and we all think the world of him. He's a legend around these parts. People still talk about Tony Kay in Sheffield. He was the local hero.

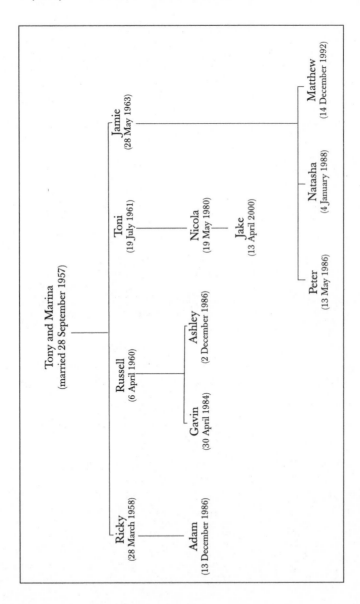

Football Makes You Quite Tough

Irene Lee

A former Aston Villa and Shrewsbury defender, Gordon Lee went into management and was headhunted from Newcastle – whom he led to the 1976 League Cup final – to become Everton manager in January 1977, replacing Billy Bingham. A workaholic, Lee gained total respect from the players but, another League Cup final and an FA Cup semi-final apart, his best wasn't good enough and he was dismissed in May 1981. He went on to manage at Preston and Leicester, and now lives on the Fylde coast, is a fanatical golfer and spends the rest of his spare time looking after his grandchildren.

Born Irene Walkeden, 12 March 1936, Cannock Chase, Midlands

Dad was a coal miner and, like most women in those days, Mum stayed at home to look after us, but sometimes she made leather handbags in the front room to earn a bit of extra money. She was very enterprising and, during the Second World War, she used to take in washing and clean a cornershop so she could get extra rations under the counter. We didn't have many luxuries, but I can remember my childhood as being perfectly happy and I don't recall any raised voices or arguing.

My brother Jack was ten years older than me and had been injured during the war. When he was demobbed, he went to work in a die-cast factory and my other brother, Roy, worked down the pit alongside Dad.

School was in a little village called Great Wyrley. It's still there and, although I didn't really like it, I stayed on to attend night classes and learned shorthand and typing. I left at 15 and got a job in a local firm operating the switchboard and doing a bit of typing and general office duties.

I was in my teens when there was a roof-fall at the pit. Dad was buried alive and had to be dug out. He was conscious all the time and told the rescuers not to move him because he knew he'd broken his back and, if they did, he would be paralysed. Roy was part of the team that dug him out and they both vowed never to go underground again.

Nobody really expected him to live for long afterwards because it had been such a shock to his system, but he recovered eventually and could still get around, although he was pensioned off at 52. He defied them all and lived for another 20 years, and did occasional light work for a local farmer to keep himself busy.

Gordon was from a little village called Hednesford but when we met he was based in Stafford doing his national service with the RAF. Everybody used to go to the civic dance hall on a Saturday night because, apart from going to the pictures, there was nothing else for teenagers to do. He's not the best dancer, but who was I to tell him?

Aston Villa had already signed him as a schoolboy but he couldn't get out of the RAF, so he was stationed nearby Hednesford, which meant he could play for the local team at the weekends. I didn't know anything about football and it didn't really interest me, but when my dad had recovered enough, he would take me to watch Gordon play. Dad enjoyed football but he hadn't really gone and watched games because he'd always worked shifts.

As soon as Gordon finished with the RAF we got engaged, then married soon after in September 1955. We had a white wedding at St Luke's in Cannock; my sister, Pat, and my sister-in-law, Lillian, were my bridesmaids, and Derek, one of Gordon's four brothers, was best man. Gordon was 21 and I was 19.

For our honeymoon, we went on the train to Margate, which was considered a long way from the Midlands then, but we had to return a day early because Aston Villa's third team wanted Gordon to play on the Saturday. I didn't mind coming back because I knew how important it was to him.

After we married, we moved into a little two-up two-down in Heath Heyes near Hednesford. By the time we'd had a bit of work done and had a bathroom built, Gordon was playing regularly for Villa and earning £10 a week plus a bonus. In the reserves, the bonus was £1 for a win and 10 bob (50p) for a draw, and it went up to £4 for a win and £2 for a draw when he got into the first team. I remember that vividly because, at the time, I was earning more than him as a secretary.

By tradition, his family were Wolves fans but they were loyal to Gordon and followed his career, so I would go to the game with another of his brothers, Dennis. Initially, I felt as if I should just go to show my support but the more I went, the more I learned about the game and I really got to like it in the end.

Villa were quite good then. Joe Mercer was the manager and Gordon was one of the 'Mercer Minors'. They called him the 'Utility Man' because he could play anywhere, but he shone brightest when playing in defence. These were the days before you were allowed a substitute, so if you had a team member who could play in any position, he became a great asset and the manager knew he could always switch him.

Footballers were tough in those days. I remember one time Gordon coming home with a really bad elbow injury and having to go to hospital, but the injury that really sticks in my mind is when he was playing for the local team. He rang the doorbell and when I opened the door, blood was pouring down his face. He'd cut his head but they hadn't done anything to stop the bleeding and he just shrugged and said it would be OK. I can still see him now, standing there covered in blood, but he was so casual about it.

We had our children in the close season so they didn't interfere with football. Our first was born on 19 May 1961, when Gordon was on tour in Russia. Nikita Khrushchev was the Premier and the Iron Curtain still existed then. He played against Spartak Moscow, Moscow Dynamo and Tbilisi, and they were there for about a week. He was due back the same day as the baby was due and Gary arrived about an hour before he got home.

When Gary was four, we went to live in a big semi-detached house in Great Barnett, which was much nearer the ground, and that's where our daughter, Christine, was born on 18 May 1965. You didn't have your children in hospital if you were fit and healthy in those days, so they were both born at home.

We were at Villa for 11 years and Gordon was more or less at the end of his playing career when we moved to Shrewsbury in 1966. He was hired as player–manager but he only played a couple of games.

People say nobody knows more about football than Gordon Lee and I think they're probably right. He doesn't know much about anything else, but he has an encyclopedic knowledge of players from any division, including their characteristics, statistics, strengths and weaknesses, and all kinds of other trivia.

He was incredibly superstitious. He wouldn't change anything in his routine – right down to the oil in his car – and if they'd won, he asked me what he was wearing the previous week so he could wear the same again, and that went right down to his socks.

It was quite hard to be a footballer's wife – even more so when you were a manager's wife – and although I didn't have much spare time when the children were young, it was very lonely. Gordon and I didn't spend much time together: he'd get home really late on a Saturday night and have the Sunday off but he didn't have a chance to get involved with anything. He'd sometimes take the children out and then it was time to go back to work again. To make matters worse, he was an absolute workaholic. I'm very independent, though, and I can cope on my own, so it wasn't too bad. If you're not self-contained, it would be impossible and I just had to get on with it.

In 1970, I had another daughter, Sharon. She was born in hospital in Stoke-on-Trent, so we must have been at Port Vale then. We liked it there, too. Gordon took them up to the old Third Division within a year.

The thought that we could be moving at a minute's notice didn't bother me at all; in fact, I liked that aspect of our lives more than you would imagine because every time we moved, it would be to something better. The house would be better and his job would be more of a challenge and he really thrived on that.

The kids weren't always happy about uprooting, though. We were living in Trentham when he got the Blackburn job in January 1974 and we bought a house in Lytham, up near Blackpool. Gary had passed his 11-Plus so he went to Kirkham Grammar School. He wasn't very happy about it because it was a rugby school and he loved his football but it worked out fine for him and he did really well. I remember Christine's tears because she didn't want to leave her friends and she sat in the back of the car with a goldfish in a bowl, crying all the way there. Once they got settled they were OK and Lytham is a nice place to live. It must be, because Christine's still here 30 years down the line.

With having the children, I never really seemed to get to the games, so I didn't get friendly with any of the other wives. If you move away from your family and your friends, then you've sacrificed your babysitters and have to look after the kids on your own. I wouldn't have left them with anyone unless I really knew and trusted them. By the time Gordon took over at Everton, and Sharon was of an age where she could come along, we'd all travel to every match – before that we were pretty much stuck at home. We didn't go with Gordon, though, because he had to be there much earlier to sort the team out and everything, and couldn't have us tagging along, so I would drive there later on. It wasn't really very far, about a three-hour round trip, and we all looked forward to it as the highlight of the week.

Blackburn won the League in 1975, and promotion to the Second Division, and that was when Gordon was headhunted by Newcastle. I can remember when he made his decision to go to the Northeast and all the players came to our house to try and talk him out of it. Sharon was five then and they were saying to her, 'Tell your daddy you don't want to go.'

We sold our house and all moved over to Newcastle. We went to all the home games and they made it to Wembley for the League Cup final against Manchester City in 1976. Unfortunately, there was a terrible flu bug going round at the time and a lot of the first team were unable to play. They were beaten 2–1 and we were absolutely heartbroken. Gordon was very well thought of there: the fans used to sing 'Gordon Lee's black-and-white army'. I've still got a photo of Sharon and Christine all dressed up in black and white. We were at Newcastle for two seasons and then, in the January of 1977, the call came in from Everton and we moved back to Lytham.

The people at Everton were really good to me, from the directors and their wives to the ground staff. We would go to all the matches and were invited to the chairman's house from time to time, and everyone was really kind. The secretary, Jim Greenwood, and his wife Mary became friends of ours, too. They lived in Southport and we'd go and see them occasionally. John Moores was there then, too. We went to Prague for a Uefa Cup game against Dukla and he came on the coach with us. He was everything you've heard about him and more besides – a genuinely lovely man.

I probably shouldn't say that Gordon had a favourite player but he did and it was Micky Lyons. They got on famously and he really liked Martin Dobson and Bob Latchford, too. I haven't got a bad word to say about anybody at Everton. They were the best years of our lives.

Because we lived so far away from Liverpool, we never went out socially with the players and their wives. It was a bit different being the manager's wife anyway, because the players' wives didn't really know how to behave in front of me. Some of them treated me just the same but others were very peculiar. I think some of the other managers' wives were a bit strange, too, thinking they were more important, so it caused some uncomfortable feelings, but I'd been a player's wife, so I knew what it was all about.

I don't think the club expected anything of any of the wives. Maybe some would push themselves forward, but that wasn't my scene at all. They don't particularly want you there, so if you're hanging around, all you're doing is getting in the way, really.

People were always knocking at the door or ringing up looking for favours, autographs and tickets. The phone never stopped ringing. In fact, to this day, people still phone him asking for tickets. You won't hear from them for ages then all of a sudden you'll get a call and they'll finish off the conversation asking if he can get them tickets for Wembley or the last match of the season.

I've had a few proud moments, and got to go to Wembley again with Everton in 1977 for the League Cup final, coincidentally against Aston Villa. It ended up 0–0, so it was replayed, which ended up 1–1; we lost 3–2 in the second replay at Old Trafford. I think football makes you quite tough in some respects, but that time I came home and watched it again on the television and cried because it was so sad.

That was a bad year for Gordon and an even bigger disappointment was when Everton played Liverpool in the FA Cup semi-final and Clive Thomas disallowed a perfectly good goal from Bryan Hamilton, which forced a replay. He was absolutely wretched. I travelled on the team coach that day and left the ground early because I was so upset. Gordon still says that it was the most devastating day of his managerial life.

Getting sacked is an occupational hazard of being a manager and you pretty much know that one day you're going to leave under unpleasant circumstances. Not many managers leave when they're winning, unless they've been headhunted, which he was a few times, but not with Everton. He left in May 1981, then went to Preston a few months later for a couple of seasons. He finished off his managerial career at Leicester in 1991.

I suppose he's got very divided loyalties when it comes down to who he should support, but if somebody asked him outright, he would say Everton, and so would I. He had all his success there, we spent the best years of our lives there and we've never moved from the Northwest. He's still mad about football – he knows absolutely everything that's going on and he's always got his head in a newspaper – but he's passionate about golf now as well. I was a football widow then and I'm a golf widow now.

Everything Gordon does, he does well. There's no middle ground with him, whether it's painting, managing, gardening or golfing. Whatever it is, it's done to perfection. Wherever he went, the players had the utmost respect for him because there was nothing he didn't know about the game and he studied it in the most minute detail. I can't recall anybody saying a bad word about him and that's quite right because he's a good man.

Life is great now. He's a member of a celebrity golf team who raise a lot of money for charity and I sometimes go with him for the day. We were at a tournament recently and Duncan McKenzie was there. I don't know if they didn't like each other, but Gordon sold him to Chelsea in 1978. I think there was a clash of personalities back then but it was nothing nasty and they get on all right now.

Apart from our couple of years in the north-east, we've lived in Lytham for 30 years now. My kids, especially Sharon, are Lancastrians, not Midlanders. Christine and I are practically neighbours, so we get to see our grandchildren all the time and play a part in their lives. We live down a lane that used to have fields at the back, with cows hanging over the fence at the bottom of the garden; now they've built an estate there. It's a nice one with big posh houses, but it's not as nice as the fields used to be. Christine lives on that estate.

We've got five grandchildren altogether – four boys and one girl – so hopefully one of them will have some football talent. It would be lovely if we had another player in the family. They're all very keen, too, so we'll just have to keep our fingers crossed.

I sacrificed my career for Gordon's but I've enjoyed it and he's made sacrifices for me. That's what being in a relationship is all about. If I was young again and had the chance to be a footballer's wife, I would take it. I wouldn't change my life at all and I don't regret anything. It was hard work a lot of the time, and I used to get angry and fed up, but I wouldn't alter it. I think the worst part was the loneliness and the isolation, and I seemed to be constantly running around after the children because they all went to different schools at different times.

But that didn't last forever; they soon grew up and, when Gordon was around, he always did as much as he could. We've been together for almost 50 years now and we're still going strong.

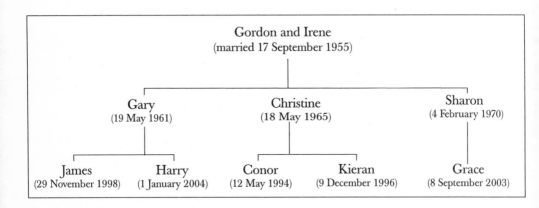

214

What Were The Chances Of That?

Maureen Temple

A schoolboy signing, Derek Temple made his senior debut against Newcastle in March 1957 and scored 82 goals in his Everton career, including the winner in the 1966 FA Cup final. He played his last game for Everton in September 1967, before being transferred to Preston North End for £35,000. When he retired, Temple began working for an industrial cleaning company, where he is still employed. He won one England cap and now lives in Ormskirk.

Born Maureen Molyneux, 31 August 1941, Dovecot, Liverpool

My first recollection of my dad is when I was four years old and we were living with my grandma in Aldwark Road, Dovecot. I was playing in the garden when one of the neighbours told me to go and tell my mum that Daddy was coming home. It was during the war and he was stationed in Egypt, so Mum took no notice of me. The very next minute, he walked through the door wearing his army uniform.

Mum comes from a big family, with five sisters and a brother, and we all lived together at that time, so if one person left, you didn't really notice. I have an elder sister, Pat, and I'm three and a half years older than my brother Keith, so my dad must have seen me when I was a baby but I don't remember it. I do remember my mum saying that every time he was home on leave she became pregnant, though. Keith's name is Ian Keith really, but when my dad got home he said he didn't like Ian very much and we dropped it and called him Keith from then on.

We had a normal and completely happy childhood. When you're from a large family, things happen and you just take it in your stride. I can remember a lot of people always being around but I don't recall any major upsets. They say the second child is in a hurry to catch up but I wasn't in a hurry to do anything. I was quite happy to stay in whatever situation I found myself. I wasn't the discontented kind, never thought about anything that didn't affect me and was quite content with my lot. There's so much to be scared about in society now, but we were protected from all the horrible things in life then. It was all so innocent and I was quite grown up before I realised there were things that I knew nothing about.

I went to Dovecot secondary modern and was in the 'A' stream at school. I passed my O levels and went to college, where I learned make-up and manicure. Derek went to the same school as me – he lived a couple of roads away, and we were practically neighbours. I didn't know him at school because he's three years older but I met him through my sister Pat. He was part of her group of friends and I do remember him from being quite young because, one day when I was walking home from school, there was an ambulance dropping a boy off at his house who'd broken a wrist playing football. It stuck in my mind because to see an ambulance was a rare occurrence in those days. It was only years later that I found out it was him.

Looks count for a lot when you're 14. I thought Derek was a really good-looking boy and, when I started talking to him, I realised he was a nice person too. We went out in a group and to parties together but only started dating about a year later. My mum and dad thought he was the most wonderful thing on two legs and, if we ever had a tiff, they always took his side and I used to get quite put out about it.

The only thing I knew about football was that my brother played it at school. In fact, when I met Derek, I don't think I even knew he was a footballer. I was the little sister in a big group and I didn't ask those kinds of questions. I knew he went to work but that was all. I really became aware of it when he played for Everton reserves. He'd worked his way up through the Liverpool schoolboys, Everton youth, England schoolboys and England youth. He made his first-team debut in the spring of 1957, when he played alongside Dave Hickson, but his career was interrupted by national service. I suppose he was lucky because it was delayed by 12 months but they caught up with him in the end and he had to go.

In those days, you did everything your mum and dad said because they were older and wiser. They told us not to get engaged because there were two years ahead where we would be apart and we might change our minds, so we took their advice. I missed him terribly when he was away and that was something that never got any easier with time. Even after we'd been together for years and he went to play a match or was away for a couple of days training, it was upsetting.

When he was first in the army, he was posted at Harrington Barracks in Formby for his basic training and he would come home as often as possible. Then he was sent out to Kenya and I didn't see him for ten whole months and that was very hard. It was an awfully long time to be apart and we wrote to each other all the time.

I would catch the tram to Binns Road in Edge Lane, where I started working in the Meccano factory. The job I had involved the forerunners of computers – little punch cards and a tiny keyboard. Now they have microchips but then, if you pressed the key, the corresponding hole came up on the card and it stored the data and personal details about the customers, then it went to another machine that was more sophisticated and read the information.

Derek finally came back in December 1959. We'd spent enough time apart to know that we definitely wanted to be together, so we just carried on where we left off and got engaged in the January.

My dad would take me to watch the home games because I couldn't drive and I never went anywhere on my own. I loved watching him play, although it made me nervous. He started off as a centre-forward but ended up on the left wing; that was Mr Catterick's decision. He was the leading goalscorer with Liverpool schoolboys for years – in fact, it was only quite recently that his record of 70 goals in a season was broken. He loved to hit a volley into the net and to see him score was the best feeling in the world, especially if it was a skilful goal.

There were nightclubs in Liverpool but we never went to them. I was more into the ballroom dancing side of life. We would usually go to the Grafton. Derek wasn't much of a dancer and had no sense of rhythm, which seems odd when he can kick a ball and play football so well. We shuffled around the dance floor and, if the truth be told, we're still doing that to this day.

Our wedding was arranged for May 1961 but Everton were going off on a tour of America, so we had to reorganise everything and we married on Christmas Eve 1960 in the Church of the Holy Spirit in Dovecot. It should have been at three o'clock in the afternoon but the wedding in front of ours was delayed. I don't know why it was late but that was the one and only time in his life Derek had been on time and they had to take him round the block about half a dozen times.

We didn't get out of the church until about half past four and by that time it was pitch black, with snow, sleet and freezing fog, and not very suitable for taking photos. Brian Labone and another centre-half, David Gorrie, were there and Derek's brother Albert was best man. Although it was a Saturday, there was no match that day, but there was one on the Boxing Day, so we didn't go away on a honeymoon. My grandma had gone to stay with her daughter for Christmas so we stayed at her house over the holiday period and when the football season finished, we went to Jersey for a fortnight in June.

We flew to the Channel Islands from Liverpool and, although Derek had travelled extensively, it was the first time I'd ever been on a plane. It was one of the little island-hoppers with the nose pointing up and tiny propellers. The weather was really bad and the plane was bouncing around like mad, but, in my naivety, I thought that was what planes did and it was only when we landed that Derek mentioned the turbulence and I realised it wasn't supposed to be like that. It didn't put me off, though, and I still like flying.

My brother and sister were still at home so there was no room for us there, so we went and stayed in Kensington with my Auntie Joyce and Uncle Arthur while we were waiting for our house to be built in Ormskirk. I still saw my parents every day. We never lived in a club house; we moved straight out to Ormskirk and we live in the same house to this day.

Our first baby was due when Derek was on a pre-season tour in Australia. They were away for five or six weeks, so my mum came to stay with me for a few days during the week, then we'd go and stay with my dad for a change of scene because by that time my brother and sister were married and he was more or less on his own. Derek was safely home by the time Neil was born in Ormskirk hospital on 17 July 1964, a couple of weeks overdue.

We would drop off Neil with my parents on a match day and go to the game. I always went to Goodison with Derek but he had to go in at least an hour before the kick-off and there was nowhere for us wives to wait, so I would sit in the car, or, if there was another wife waiting, I'd sit in her car and we'd chat until it was time to go in.

He would be disappointed in defeat but he didn't bring it home with him, it just spurred him on to be better the next week. I don't remember him getting uptight before the match either. There must have been a certain amount of nervous tension there but that's all part of the game.

He had a couple of bad ankle injuries, one of which damaged his cartilage, but as he couldn't train he didn't realise about his knee until he went back into training and he just kept breaking down. They took him into Gateacre Grange nursing home for an exploratory operation and discovered a big tear in his cartilage, so he had to have it removed. He missed out on the 1963 Championship because of that and it put him out of the game for quite a while. Another time, he was playing against Leeds and he was carried off

the pitch. It shocked me and I had to go and have a word with Harry
Catterick to find out what it was. They told me he was OK and he'd
just been winded and knocked about a bit, and he came back on in
the second half. I was so angry because he was such a clean player –
he only ever had one booking in his entire career and he didn't do
anything to deserve such a tackle.

In the early days, I was friendly with Pat and Brian Labone, and
Beryl and Brian Harris. Then Annette and Alec Scott, Dennis and
Eileen Stevens, and Ann and Gordon West came along, and they were
the main circle we socialised with, but it's such a transient life and
these people move on. Derek and I were the only constant as people
moved on and the group got smaller. We lost touch with most of them
but we still see Dennis and Eileen regularly and we're all dear friends,
and we're still in touch with Brian Labone and Annette Scott.

Derek already had three caps for England schoolboys and the
Under-20 team when I met him, and he won his only full cap in 1965
against West Germany in Nuremberg. He still has a West Germany
shirt among his souvenirs and keepsakes.

We would go out on a Saturday after the match but not into
Liverpool. We'd start off in a little restaurant in Ormskirk called the
Wincot. It's not there now – there is a housing estate on top of it – but
we would start there then head out towards the Sands and Toad Hall
in Ainsdale or to the Kingsway in Southport. Other players would go
to Liverpool but we never did that. We'd drop the children off at my
mum's on Friday night or Saturday morning and pick them up again
on Sunday night. Mum was wonderful like that, she always wanted us
to go out and enjoy ourselves.

Everton didn't really bother with the wives and I can't remember
having much to do with the club, really. It was only the men that
mattered because they were the ones playing football and they were
important, until somebody else took their place. There was no
sentiment. Once you were gone, that was it. Over a period of time, a
different set of fans would come in and people would be forgotten.
When I think of Everton, I think of the Everton I knew, I don't think

of it as it is today and I honestly don't think I would be able to name one of the current players.

When we made it to the FA Cup final in 1966, the players went down to London on the Thursday. Derek and I were at home in bed on the Wednesday night with the baby in the next room and the phone rang. The caller said he was Derek's mum's doctor and she was going blind and calling out for Derek. Of course, I panicked, but Derek is a bit more streetwise and I could hear him questioning this person. When he put the phone down he told me he didn't recognise his name, so he rang a neighbour who went round to check up on his mum and there was nothing wrong with her. I think this man must have been trying to get us out of the house, knowing that we had Cup final tickets here, so they could come in and steal them.

Derek left for London the next morning and I had to have the police coming round every hour, checking to make sure I was all right. Looking back, it was quite frightening and very sinister because I was alone with an 18-month-old baby, but we were fine.

We caught the train from Lime Street but the rest of the day is a blur. What I do remember with great clarity is the day before, because that was when I realised Ann West and I had the same dress for the evening do. Ann's was turquoise and she'd bought it in Lytham St Anne's and mine was in pink from a shop in Southport. I rushed out and bought another one that day. It was navy chiffon with a flower at the waist and, lo and behold, it was the same as Annette Scott's. What were the chances of that?

We were so nervous before we headed for Wembley that none of us could eat. I don't suppose anyone could have been aware of how nerve-racking it was because there was so much riding on it for our husbands.

Derek had scored in every round except the semi-final, when he crossed the ball to Colin Harvey, who scored. In the final itself, we drew level at 2–2 after being two down and there were about ten minutes left of the game when Derek got the ball a long way from goal. It was like it happened in slow motion. He had plenty of time to make a mistake and I could barely watch. All I kept saying was, 'You can't miss, you can't miss,' and I was holding on to Annette Scott so tightly that I pulled her off her seat. I was so scared he'd miss because I could imagine how awful he would have felt for the rest of his life. He had the ball for such a long time, anything could have happened – he could have lost his concentration or fallen over or thought for too long, but he didn't.

If you ask him now what was going through his mind, he doesn't remember; he was too busy thinking about where the goalkeeper was and keeping the ball under control. We all leapt out of our seats when the ball hit the back of the net and were begging the referee to blow the whistle before we had some kind of breakdown. It's nerve-racking for wives to watch such an important game. The fans want them to win because it's their team but the wives want them to do well because they know what it means on a personal level. I imagine that goal was one of the proudest moments of his career, alongside playing for England. It seems such a shame that the twin towers aren't there any more. Wembley had so much history.

After the reception, we were going back to the hotel with Pat and Ray Wilson. There was a brass plate on the doorstep and, as I turned around to talk to them, my foot slipped on the metal and I ended up on my bottom in front of the great West Indies cricketer Gary Sobers, who must have been staying there, too. I don't drink and I was so embarrassed. I felt like protesting my innocence. I fell quite gracefully, but they were all howling with laughter. I don't think Gary Sobers spread any rumours about me but I never wanted to wear stilettos after that. It was a truly unforgettable weekend all round.

Our second son, Philip, was born on 18 July 1968 at Park House nursing home in Waterloo, four years and a day after his brother. With two boys and Derek in the house, it was like having an army because they were all very sporty. I enjoyed sport too, so we all played tennis and badminton together. In his spare time, Derek ran an amateur club for children called West End and they were always off playing somewhere. The only drawback was I had to wash the dirty kit.

Our lives were pretty full; there was a lot of spare time when he was playing football but when he went into the real world it all came to an abrupt end. Working nine to five, five days a week, is quite an eye-opener and it took some getting used to, more so for him than for me because they're so protected in football. Everything is done; they don't even need to keep their own passports up to date or book hotels and restaurants, so when players come out, it's a different world. It didn't make any difference to me; the only thing I noticed was that he wasn't around as much and he didn't take the boys out as often as he used to.

Derek finally finished after a couple of seasons at Preston and two seasons part time at non-League Wigan Athletic – he was ready then, because it was physically demanding and it took so much out of him.

As he got older, it became more difficult. He never lost his love for the game; but pre-season training was really intense. Towards the end, he would regularly come home, have a cup of tea and the next thing he would be fast asleep. A lot of the players would lose their fitness over the summer and the coach, Tommy Eggleston, was very keen on getting them back into shape and would take them to Ainsdale beach and have them up and down the sand hills.

As far as carrying on the footballing tradition, my boys played a bit but neither of them was interested enough to pursue it. Neil could have taken up tennis but he wasn't bothered. He was very shy, like Derek, and he didn't want to be projected as the centre of attention, which I don't think he could have coped with. Philip plays the occasional game of golf and squash but he's busy with his life and he's got a young family too, so he's taking them off here and there and never seems to have any spare time. His wife is a tennis coach, so they're quite a sporty family. They're both Evertonians and Neil is really keen, he's been down to Wembley with Derek a couple of times. He has two stepsons and he's converted them to the cause but his little boy isn't really into sport yet.

We still have people coming to us for autographs and photographs. Over the years, we've given away an awful lot and people still ask for them now, but what we've got left I want for the boys and our grandchildren. It's still nice to be remembered, though, even after all this time.

Philip's children go to Greatby Hill school in Ormskirk and when older people hear the name 'Temple' they sometimes ask if they're related to Derek. They come home now and again and say, 'Do you know what, Granddad, my teacher told me you used to be famous.' When I think back, it feels as if that was somebody else's life, it all happened so long ago.

When Derek was a teenager, he attended Anfield Commercial College doing business studies but he was taking time off to go and play football matches so the principal asked him to leave because he was taking the place from somebody who would be there all the time, so he gave up his academic training. What he'd already learned stood him in good stead in later life when he went out into the real world, though. He worked in double glazing for a while and then insurance; it was all on the administrative side of things, so he was always academically minded. He works for an industrial cleaning company now: when people want the outside of buildings cleaned, he advises them on the chemicals they need and he really enjoys it. I didn't work while I was bringing up the boys but when they started getting independent I thought I would resume my career. The last job I had before I retired was as an audio typist at a recruitment agency, raising and chasing up invoices.

Derek still loves football, will watch five year olds playing in the park, can't walk past a kid kicking a ball and, if it comes his way, he'll kick it back to them. He shouldn't really, because he's got an artificial knee, but he can't help himself. He'll watch any game on television, too. If we're out, he'll even set the video so he doesn't miss a minute of it – he'll watch foreign teams, lower leagues, absolutely anything, regardless of the standard.

Derek was due to retire last November but he stayed on. When he finally does retire, I'd like him to take up golf again and I might even have a little dabble myself. We both like gardening and going for long walks in the Lakes or in Wales. When he was suffering with his knees, he couldn't walk anywhere for a couple of years. It was really difficult while the doctors performed keyhole surgery, scraping and washing out his kneecap. When they finally operated in May 2001, they replaced it and it took 12 months before he was right again. Even when the crutches had gone, he had a walking stick for a long time.

There was nothing I hated about being a footballer's wife, but I found it a bit intrusive at times. I wouldn't like to be a footballer's wife now because it's all getting a bit silly. I think there would be more of a conflict of interest with us, if Derek's career were happening now.

I don't think I made any sacrifices for Derek's career; I was just happy the way things were going along. I passed my college exams and it was Derek who encouraged me to follow my own interests. There was never any conflict and I don't remember giving up anything for him; but if I did, I did so willingly.

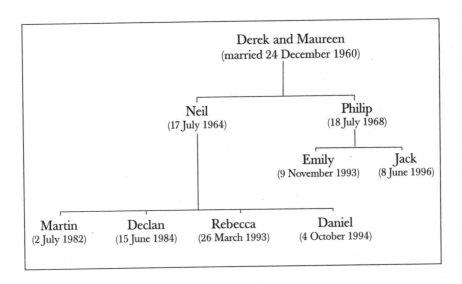

You Make Your Own Luck

Dolly Sagar

Ted Sagar's Everton career lasted an unbelievable 24 years and 2 months. Snaffled from under the noses of Hull, who had already given him a trial, the former miner arrived on Merseyside in March 1929. He played in the 1933 FA Cup final, the first time players wore numbers on their shirts, and became the first-ever Wembley keeper to wear the number 1. Sagar went on to win four England caps but his career was interrupted by the Second World War, when he was sent abroad on active duty. He returned as good as new and with the added bonus of a wartime Northern Ireland cap. His final game, his 495th, was in November 1952 against Plymouth Argyle. He retired and went into the licensed trade but sadly passed away in October 1986.

Born Dolly Evans, 6 June 1909, Walton, Liverpool

We were brought up in Chirkdale Street in Kirkdale. My dad was a lovely man and worked as a clerk for the railways. He was good with figures and very trustworthy, so on match days he would earn a bit of extra money working on the gate at Goodison Park. When I was a little girl we'd sometimes go with him; we could just fit under the turnstiles, so Dad would let us in and we'd sit on a little seat at the edge of the ground. I loved going to the game, but I never guessed I would end up married to a footballer.

Our childhood was quite sad. We were four girls and one boy, I was the second youngest, and my poor mother died when I was five and left us all behind. My auntie moved in to keep house for us while we were very young and, when I was about 12, my dad remarried. His new wife was also widowed and she worked in the railway office, too, but we didn't like her very much. She was crafty and thought she could manipulate everyone but we were all working and independent by then, so we all stuck up for ourselves.

My school was in Arnot Street in Walton. I loved it and stayed on until I was 14, then I got a job at Saunders, a pharmaceutical factory in Liverpool's city centre, where they did the labelling and bottling. I used to fill tins and jars with ointment and label up the bottles of medicine and I got paid 11/6 (57p) a week. I was on piecework, so the faster I worked, the more money I could earn. It was hard graft; I started at 8 a.m. and finished at 5.30 in the evening. I didn't especially like the job but it was clean work and you didn't question things in those days, you just stuck it out. I stayed there until I got married at 22.

Ted was one of six children born into a mining family in Campsall, South Yorkshire. Two of his young sisters died the same week his dad got killed in the Battle of the Somme. He was only 32. Ted became the breadwinner and worked permanent nights in the pit so that he could earn enough money to keep his family, otherwise they'd get their house taken from them.

One Sunday afternoon, he was playing in goal for Thorne Colliery and a man came over to him and asked how long he'd been a footballer. Ted explained he only had a game on a Sunday afternoon with the boys when he'd finished his shift. The man was a scout from Hull City and told him he was very interested and thought he would make a good player.

He said he'd been watching for the last few weeks but he hadn't said anything in case he built his hopes up, but that he was very pleased with him and would mention him to the club. A man came over the next week and he played his best. He went for a trial with them but, before they had the chance to offer him a contract, Everton came over and said they liked his style of play. He was just what they were looking for, so they signed him up.

It was March 1929 when he came to Everton and we were both nineteen. Everton signed three or four new players around that time and they all moved into digs above the sweet shop on the corner across the road from Goodison Park. Johnny Wilkinson was one of them and Tommy Robson was another. They were all good-looking boys but they didn't know anybody or have anywhere to go because they weren't locals.

I'd had a few years flirting with boys in Stanley Park and I'd had a boyfriend but we had a tiff and he fell out with me. These two girls I knew met up with the new players and told them the teenagers congregated in Stanley Park and there would be plenty of people for them to meet up with there. Ted was introduced to my sister, Flo. She already had a boyfriend and he asked her if she had a sister at home who would meet him that night and she immediately thought of me, so we met on a blind date. I thought he was lovely when I first saw him; he was blond and tall and had the biggest hands you've ever seen. I was thrilled to bits and I fell for him right away.

Ted was such a gentleman; he would take me out to the pictures but not to the Walton picture house like everybody else – we'd go into town. He would go into Liverpool after training and would wait for me to finish work and meet me every night, and sometimes he'd buy me a box of chocolates. I fell in love with him straight away. I thought he was gorgeous and all the girls from work were jealous of me.

He only had one suit and it was really cheap – he hadn't got anything smart to come to Everton in, so his mother had bought it for him. It was brown with a stripe and I didn't like it one little bit. I took him to Burtons and told him they would rig him out properly. He listened to what I said because he'd never worn a suit before, so he didn't really know what was good and what wasn't. His mother bought him some spats, too. They were so old-fashioned. He asked if he should wear them and I told him he could but not when he was with me.

My dad was made up when I told him I was going out with a footballer and so were the club – they liked it if their players were courting because they were more settled and they didn't go out drinking and getting into trouble. Dad thought Ted was a nice lad and he said he could come and lodge with us in Chirkdale Street. My dad was very well-in with the management and he told them he would keep an eye on Ted and make sure he wasn't going off the rails. Dad was like a father to him and, for his mother's sake, that was a great relief because she was terribly worried about him being so far away from home.

Ted liked a drink but he wasn't a big drinker. With him lodging at ours, my dad would take him out for a pint. He was very much a father figure to him and he would never let him drink too much. He wanted Ted to meet the fans in the pub sometimes because they would make a fuss of him and he really enjoyed that. He'd had a lonely life when he was a miner and it made his heart sing when he was surrounded by Evertonians because they really liked him and enjoyed his company. He was a kind man and easy to get along with. My dad never let him get drunk and he never dreamed of going out on a Friday night before a match. He took his football very seriously.

When the close season arrived, he went home for a while but he came back quite quickly and asked if he could come and stay at our house again. He said he didn't want to be away from me for that long. My dad asked if he minded sleeping in the attic, because we didn't have a big house, and he said he would sleep anywhere so we could be together.

It was a real love match. I couldn't believe my luck and I remember he kept saying he was going to ask my dad for permission to marry me. Eventually, he asked if we could get engaged and my dad said 'Certainly'. He was a nice boy and just the sort of person any father would want his daughter to get involved with.

Somebody told me it was unlucky to marry in May but we didn't take any notice; we both believed that you make your own luck. Our wedding was on 8 May 1932 at St Lawrence's in Walton – it was a Sunday because he was playing on the Saturday. We went to see the vicar and explained our case and asked if he could make it late in the afternoon but he said he had to fit it around the Sunday services, so it had to be in the morning. I said that was fine because I thought everyone would be having their Sunday lunch, but it must have got round the ground the day before because half of Liverpool turned up to wish us well. There would have been a few burnt roast dinners that day; their mothers must have been going mad.

The vicar said he'd never had so many men in the church at once and there was a policeman there to control the crowds. I was a local girl so I was well known too, and it made me laugh to see them all packed in there. They were shouting 'Come on, Teddy' when we walked down the aisle and it was a great day. We couldn't have a honeymoon because the season wasn't over but later on we sailed to the Isle of Man from the Pier Head in Liverpool. We went on to win the League in 1932, so when we married, I married a champion.

Our first house was 94 East Lancashire Road. It was the middle of winter when we moved in and it was absolutely bitterly cold. The club used to take the players away to train in Buxton. They called it the headquarters and they would train hard and bathe in the spa waters, which were supposed to have healing properties. Ted told me to get the house sorted out and he'd come with me to get the furniture when he got back. He wasn't going to be home until the next week so I decided I would surprise him and get everything done so it would be lovely when he got back.

My sister and brother went with me to get our lovely new furniture. We got a nice carpet, a bedroom suite and a sofa and chairs. He was coming home straight from the match to the house and I was going to have a nice dinner ready for him. I got it all sorted out and ready and I was so proud that I took my sister there so she could see it in all its glory. I turned the key in the lock but, as I opened the door, water was cascading down the stairs. The tank had frozen and burst, so it was filling up constantly and just dashing down the stairs. The bed was soaked and everything was ruined. I cried my eyes out – it was all ruined and he'd never even set eyes on it once. Anyway, they fixed it up for us eventually and we got a few bob back on the insurance, but we were very unlucky that day.

I was six months pregnant with my first baby when Everton made it to the FA Cup final in 1933. I said I couldn't go because I didn't think it would be safe to travel all that way. Dr Davies, the club doctor, told me that I absolutely must go and that he would be there by my side all the time in case I needed him. Ted Jnr was only 6lb when he was born and you could hardly tell I was pregnant because I was sturdily built anyway, so I didn't show much. I wore a nice loose dress and off we went on the train. I'm so glad I went. It was 29 April 1933 and the most exciting day of my life.

There were 93,000 supporters at Wembley that day and it was the first time footballers had numbers on their shirts, so I suppose Ted was the first goalie to ever wear number 1, because Everton were numbered 1–11 and Manchester City were 12–22. Ted made a great save in the first minutes of the game and his confidence rubbed off on the other players.

We won 3–0 that day and King George VI and his wife, Queen Elizabeth, the Queen Mother, presented Dixie Dean with the Cup, but they were only the Duke and Duchess of York in those days. When the train arrived back in Liverpool on the Monday, there were thousands of people waiting at Lime Street station to congratulate them. The team went on a horse-drawn coach from the Town Hall, along Scotland Road, into County Road and all the way to Goodison Park, and there were another 60,000 people inside the ground waiting. We all went into the boardroom and had a drink, then Ted and I got a taxi home. I think the players got a £25 bonus for winning the Cup, which was an absolute fortune back then.

My first baby, Ted Jnr, was born in July 1933 in a private nursing home when we still lived on the East Lancashire Road. Nurse Tyson delivered him; she was very nice and used to come to the house to visit me. Ted would take his big son out in the pram for walks; he was so proud of him. We didn't live there for very long before we moved to Aintree. A lot of the players used to live there and we had quite a nice house in Allendale Avenue. Little Jimmy Dunn lived in the next road; he was a lovely ginger-haired fella who'd come down from Scotland to play for Everton. He was our friend and I liked him a lot. Dixie wasn't far away either; he lived on the top road by us. He was a good man and Ethel, his wife, was nice and very homely. We were all good pals.

I waited another five years before David was born and, to celebrate, Everton won the League again that season. The boys were nearly grown up when I fell pregnant the third time. All we wanted was a daughter but I didn't get pregnant for 12 years after David was born, then Margaret Ruth came along in June 1950. I was so glad we finally got our little girl because Ted wanted a daughter so much and she's so like him. He would wheel her in the pram and he was as proud as punch. We didn't think we were going to have any more children; she was born very late and I was so worried I was going to have another boy.

Football was cancelled for six seasons during the war because all the men were called up to fight. Ted joined the Fifth Divisional Signal Corps stationed out in Syria and he spent some time in India. It was awful. I didn't see much of him and I was so scared he wasn't coming back. Because my boys were at school, I was called up for duty near to where we lived at the silk works in Aintree. My job was to test the silk for the parachutes, so I did my bit for the war effort too. Eventually, Ted came home in one piece and with the unusual honour of having won a Northern Ireland cap to add to his collection. He was approached and signed up while playing for the Signal Corps at Portadown.

When the war was over, everything went back to normal again and the boys wanted to go to matches, so we would all go to Goodison Park together to watch him play. They were big Evertonians and we'd all look forward to the game on a Saturday. We saw some great matches but, whenever the ball was near the net, I was really anxious. Sometimes it was strange to watch him play; it was like he was another person when he was on the pitch. When I was pregnant with Margaret, I asked the doctor if it was wise for me to go to the games, but he said it was OK as long as I sat near him. Not many women went to the match in those days.

When Ted wasn't training he loved to go off and play a round of golf. I stayed at home with the kids and cooked the dinner. I looked after him well but I couldn't make Yorkshire pudding like his mum and he never let me forget it. Because he was a miner, everything they had ran on coal, so she used to make hers in a coal oven and we only had gas.

Coal ovens seemed to get hotter and the Yorkshire pud always had a different taste to it; it was made to a secret recipe they handed down through the family. You couldn't slam any doors in the house at the risk of it sinking in the middle and you had to walk around on tiptoe until it was ready. I spent the rest of my life trying to get it right and I still never succeeded. No matter what I did, it never tasted like his mum's. They would have their Yorkshire pudding with gravy on its own, not on the plate with the rest of the meal. It was like a separate dish that they ate first.

I don't know how much he used to earn but he used to bank it; he was very good like that and he always sent money home to his mum. I didn't begrudge it because she was good to me. She was a widow and still had children to bring up. We were pals and we were always nice to each other. She was so proud of her big son.

People didn't bother us, but if there were boys at our kids' school who wanted an autograph, I would get their autograph books or bits of paper and bring them home for Ted to sign. I felt sorry for the kids and would do it for them. He didn't like people running after him and mythering but I'd get it done for them and give it back to their mothers the next time I saw them. I know what boys are like.

I've had a few kicks in the night when he's been asleep and replaying a game. He used to shout out, too. One night he was terrible and I ended up black and blue, with a great big bruise where he'd launched the ball in his sleep. If Everton lost, he was awful to live with; he sulked and was bad tempered. He was very nervous before a game, too. He kidded on that he wasn't but he was and he went quiet. His heart and soul were in every game; it was just him and the ball that mattered. His job was to get that ball and woe betide anyone who tried to stop him.

Sometimes, during the week, we'd go out to the pictures. He loved Laurel and Hardy and they always seemed to be on. When the boys weren't at school, he would take them with him. On a Saturday night after the game, we'd go out to the Queens Arms on Warbreck Road in Aintree and the Sefton – there were no nightclubs then and we'd just go and have a couple of drinks and go home, but he'd never go out on a Friday night. Nobody would even bother to ask him and, if they did, they'd get refused. He was too dedicated to go drinking before a game. He wasn't a dancer; he couldn't dance to save his life. I loved being a footballer's wife; we were happy, he was a good husband and father and he looked after us all well.

He was a great player and a big tall man, and he was fearless. They wore great big heavy boots in those days but he was never frightened to jump in and claim the ball. He believed the ball was his and nobody was going to take it from him. He was bad tempered, and if you upset him on a match day, you'd had it. The fans loved Ted – they would always tell me to look after him because he played such an important part in Everton's success.

They said he was worth his weight in gold because he had a special gift and could read the way the ball bounced and judge where it was going, even when it was out on the wing. Some of the players were dirty in those days and he would listen to the crowd, who would warn him of what they were doing. They would kick lumps out of each other and were often wounded and bleeding at the end of a game. Dixie Dean was a great player and so were Tommy White and T.G. Jones – they had a good side and they played well together, like a team.

We didn't ever need to move away because he stayed at Everton until he retired in May 1953, then we went into the pub business. He did well, he played right up to the end, and I think it was because I looked after him so well.

Our first pub was called the Chepstow Castle and I think it's still there now. It's really near to Goodison Park and all the lads would come and see him after they'd been to the match. He'd catch beer glasses and say that the first lad who could get one past him would get a pint. They never got one past him because he had those great big hands.

The next pub, called the Blue Anchor, was in Aintree. It had a beautiful bowling green and overlooked the racecourse. Ted really liked it because they thought the world of him there, too. He had no messing around and, when it was time, he'd shoo them all out and home; he wouldn't stand for any nonsense. I liked it too, but it was hard work. I didn't do a lot; I used to make sandwiches and help out a bit and pull the odd pint, but I enjoyed it. We stayed there until we retired, then we moved into a bungalow on Altway, Aintree.

My boys both played a bit of football and, although they had talent, they didn't pursue it. Ted Jnr went to sea – he wanted to be a sailor and off he went. I didn't stop him because he really wanted to go and you have to let them grow up and make their own choices. He lives in London now and he's still a good lad. David lives in New Brighton on the Wirral and Margaret in Pontypridd, South Wales. They both come regularly to see me here in Ormskirk but I miss them all. I think about Liverpool, too. There were some great people there. I think the world has changed now but I miss it the way it was.

Ted died very suddenly and I don't really know what it was but I suspect it was the cigarettes. His only downfall was smoking and he often had a bad chest, but we didn't really know better in those days. We had a good life together. He's been gone nearly 20 years now and I miss him more than ever. His ashes are at Goodison Park, buried at the Gwladys Street End, because that was where he made the best saves.

A few years ago, I went onto the pitch at Goodison to collect a Millennium Award on Ted's behalf. It was during a night match against Leicester. They announced my name and I got the loudest cheer I'd ever heard; it was lovely and I felt so proud. I know Ted would have been thrilled to bits and I'll always remember it.

I've had a great life but I wish he'd lived a few years longer because I'm all on my own again and I've been lonely since I lost him. I never bothered with anybody else; there was only Ted I ever loved and nobody could have taken his place.

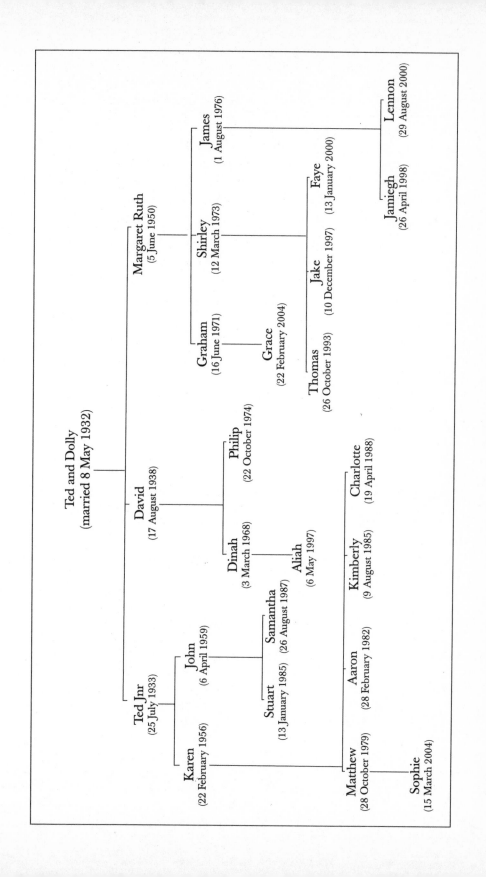